MODELS OF THE FAMILY IN MODERN SOCIETIES

This book reports on two comparative nationally representative surveys of men and women in Britain and Spain, two countries chosen to illustrate the diversity of modern European societies. The British survey was funded within the ESRC Future of Work Research Programme and was carried out by the Office of National Statistics (ONS). Catherine Hakim presents a study of ideal models of the family and family roles, work orientations, patriarchal values, and lifestyle preferences, showing how these impact on women's marital histories, fertility, employment patterns, occupational segregation, and labour mobility, but not on men's labour market participation. Lifestyle preferences and work orientations have a strong impact on women's activities, and especially on married women's employment choices, but patriarchal values (which are most commonly studied by social attitude surveys) have virtually no impact on behaviour. The analyses demonstrate that political and religious values have virtually no connection with orientations to employment and family roles. The book also covers educational homogamy, housing classes and contrasts between ethnic minority groups in core values and labour market participation.

For WRH

Models of the Family in Modern Societies

Ideals and Realities

CATHERINE HAKIM
London School of Economics

ASHGATE

Published by
Ashgate Publishing Limited
Gower House
Croft Road
Aldershot
Hants GU11 3HR
England

Ashgate Publishing Company
Suite 420
101 Cherry Street
Burlington, VT 05401-4405
USA

Ashgate website: http://www.ashgate.com

British Library Cataloguing in Publication Data
Hakim, C. (Catherine)
    Models of the family in modern societies : ideals and
    realities
    1. Family - Great Britain 2. Family - Spain 3. Work and family
    - Great Britain 4. Work and family - Spain 5. Women -
    Employment - Great Britain 6. Women - Employment - Spain
    7. Sex role - Great Britain 8. Sex roles - Spain
    I. Title
    306.8'5'0941'09049

Library of Congress Cataloging-in-Publication Data
Hakim, Catherine.
    Models of the family in modern societies : ideals and realities / Catherine Hakim.
        p. cm.
    Includes bibliographical references.
    ISBN 0-7546-3728-X (alk. paper)
        1. Family. 2. Sex roles. 3. Lifestyles. 4. Households. 5. Work and family. 6. Family life
    surveys--Spain. 7. Family life surveys--Great Britain. I. Title.

    HQ518.H152 2003
    306.85--dc   2002041750

Paperback edition 2004
Reprinted 2004 (hbk)

ISBN 0 7546 3728 X (hbk)
ISBN 0 7546 4406 5 (pbk)

Printed and bound in Great Britain by MPG Books Ltd., Bodmin, Cornwall.

Contents

List of Tables

Foreword

There is no more pressing research and public policy issue in the early years of the twenty-first century than that of the future organization of work and family life. Nevertheless, much contemporary analysis is rooted in established prejudices and divorced from sound empirical data. Dr Hakim's important new study, part of the Economic and Social Research Council's Future of Work Programme, will help advance contemporary analysis and debate and shed light on some of the key policy issues of the moment.

Offering a fresh account of orientations to employment and family roles, her study draws upon nationally representative surveys of men and women in Britain and Spain. It advances a powerful case that lifestyle preferences between paid work and family work are neither homogeneous nor bounded by traditional gender roles. Contemporary changes in the labour market in Western Europe, particularly the rates and forms of women's participation in paid employment, are traced to the choices that women and men make with regard to the balance between paid work and family life. Challenging both established academic positions and the direction of many contemporary public policy initiatives, Dr Hakim's book is essential reading for anyone with a stake in shaping the future of work.

Peter Nolan
Director, ESRC Future of Work Programme

Acknowledgements

The British survey was funded by a grant from the Economic and Social Research Council, as part of the ESRC Future of Work Research Programme 1998–2003. The survey was carried out by the Office of National Statistics in London, and I am indebted to Olwen Rowlands for her help in making it a success. The Spanish survey was generously carried out for me by Análysis Sociológicos Económicos y Políticos (ASEP), and I am indebted to Professor Dr Juan Díez Nicolás for his advice and guidance on making the survey a success.

The following appear in this book by permission:

Table 1.8 reprinted from Hakim, *Social Change and Innovation in the Labour Market*, 1998, Table 1.4, by permission of Oxford University Press.

Table 5.1 reprinted from Hakim, *Work-Lifestyle Choices in the 21st Century*, 2000, Table 4.6, by permission of Oxford University Press.

Table 5.2 reprinted from Hakim, *Work-Lifestyle Choices in the 21st Century*, 2000, Table 3.4, by permission of Oxford University Press.

Table 8.3 reprinted from Murphy and Sullivan, *Housing Tenure and Fertility in Post-War Britain*, 1983, by permission of Professor M. Murphy.

List of Abbreviations

ASEP	Análysis Sociológicos Económicos y Políticos
BHPS	British Household Panel Study
BSAS	British Social Attitudes Survey
CAPI	Computer Aided Personal Interviews
CATI	Computer Aided Telephone Interviews
CIS	Centro de Investigaciónes Sociológicos (Madrid)
ESRC	Economic and Social Research Council (Britain)
EU	European Union
FFS	Family and Fertility Surveys
FTE	Full-Time Equivalent
GHS	General Household Survey (of Britain)
GSS	General Social Survey (of the USA)
HMSO	Her Majesty's Stationary Office (Great Britain)
ILO	International Labour Office (Geneva)
INE	Instituto Nacional de Estadística (Madrid)
ISSP	International Social Survey Programme
LFS	Labour Force Survey
NCDS	National Child Development Study (1958 cohort) of Britain
NLS	National Longitudinal Surveys (of Labour Market Experience in the USA)
OECD	Organisation for Economic Cooperation and Development
ONS	Office for National Statistics (Britain)
OOPEC	Office for Official Publications of the European Communities
SCELI	Social Change and Economic Life Initiative (of the ESRC in Britain)
WVS	World Values Surveys

Abbreviations used in tables

-	empty cell, no cases
..	base number too small
*	less than 0.5%
T	total, all persons

M	men, males
F	women, females
S/E	self-employed
NS	not stated

Chapter 1
Introduction

Affluent modern societies offer people a widening choice of lifestyle. Consumer-oriented industries were among the first to realize this, and initiated a growing stream of research on consumption patterns and related lifestyle choices (BMRB, 1988a, 1988b). By 2000, the average household spent more on leisure goods and services (18%) than on housing (16%), food and non-alcoholic beverages (16%) or motoring (14%).[1] More time was spent on watching TV and other leisure activities than on paid work.[2] Some social scientists believe that personally chosen lifestyle groups are gradually replacing social class and socio-economic group as the most important determinant of consumption behaviour – although this is still disputed (Lamont, 1992; Peterson, 1992; Thompson, 1996; Holt, 1997, 1998; Wilk, 1997). Examples here are the choices between leisure activities focused on sports or on the arts and culture, holidays based on independent travel versus organized tours and cruises, traditional versus modern styles in home decoration and differing tastes in music. There is now a growing literature on consumption cultures (see, for example, Sobel, 1981; Savage *et al.*, 1992: 99–131; Lury, 1996; Slater, 1997). However, social scientists have yet to develop any agreed classification of consumption styles and groups to replace the traditional emphasis in sociology on social class and cultural capital as the principal determinants of consumption patterns (Bourdieu, 1984; Holt, 1998).

A second hugely significant lifestyle choice concerns employment, family models and sex-role preferences. The family division of labour, and associated values, are important in their own right, because they shape activities across the lifecycle, especially for women (Hakim, 2000a). They also shape leisure activities and consumption patterns – as illustrated by the choice between the city centre apartment or the suburban family house with a garden, regularly eating out in restaurants versus home cooking for all occasions. Housing tenure also appears to be a third significant lifestyle choice in the sense that privately owned, privately rented and social housing are all associated with substantial social differences – in employment, values and consumption patterns (Saunders, 1990).

This book focuses on the second element of lifestyle choice: ideal family models and associated sex-role preferences and work orientations. This

Table 1.1 The diversity of sex-role preferences in Europe: percentage of adults supporting each of three models of sexual division of labour

	Egalitarian		Compromise		Separate roles		
	1987	1983	1987	1983	1987	1983	Total
Denmark	58	50	29	33	13	17	100
Spain	**50**	..	**20**	..	**30**	..	**100**
United Kingdom	**49**	**39**	**32**	**37**	**19**	**24**	**100**
Portugal	47	..	26	..	27	..	100
Netherlands	46	41	30	27	24	32	100
France	46	42	30	27	24	31	100
Greece	46	53	30	23	24	25	100
Italy	43	42	32	28	26	30	100
Belgium	38	35	33	25	28	40	100
Ireland	37	32	22	26	42	42	100
West Germany	28	29	37	38	35	33	100
Luxembourg	22	27	34	23	44	50	100
Men – all	41	35	31	34	28	31	100
15–24 years	59	49	28	33	13	18	100
25–39	50	40	31	38	19	22	100
40–54	36	28	34	36	30	36	100
55 and over	27	26	30	28	43	46	100
Women – all	44	41	31	31	25	28	100
15–24 years	62	60	26	25	12	15	100
25–39	52	45	29	32	19	23	100
40–54	39	36	33	34	28	30	100
55 and over	28	31	34	29	38	40	100
Total for EC of 12	43	..	31	..	26	..	100
Total for EC of 10	42	38	32	32	26	30	100

Notes: The question asked: People talk about the changing roles of husband and wife in the family. Here are three kinds of family. Which of them corresponds most with your ideas about the family?

 A family where the two partners each have an equally absorbing job and where housework and the care of the children are shared equally between them.

 A family where the wife has a less demanding job than her husband and where she does the larger share of housework and caring for the children.

 A family where only the husband has a job and the wife runs the home.

 None of these three cases.

Percentages have been adjusted to exclude the 3% not responding to the question and the 2% choosing the last response.

Source: Derived from *Eurobarometer*, No. 27, June 1987.

element is often overlooked or ignored. Indeed, the European Commission is determined to exclude it from discussion. The Commission presents a single model of the family as the one all Europeans aspire to and should adopt. The Commission's preferred model of the family is the Swedish one: all healthy adults work throughout life, with childcare delegated to public services (Hakim, 1999a). However, the Commission's own research shows that the Swedish model is not in fact the most popular preference in western Europe, except perhaps in the small Scandinavian countries. On the contrary, throughout Western Europe and across North America, three distinct models of the family attract substantial support (Table 1.1). In some countries, such as West Germany, Luxembourg and Ireland, people prefer some degree of role specialization in the family, usually with the wife taking the main responsibility for domestic work and family work. In Denmark, followed by Spain and Britain, the dominant preference is for an egalitarian division of paid work and family work. There is no north south divide, and the preferred family model is not determined by economic prosperity.

Table 1.2 reinforces the conclusion that the great majority of European women never adopt the primary (co)earner identity that is entailed by genuinely symmetrical family roles. Denmark is the sole exception, with about half of adult women adopting the primary (co)earner role – but still only half. In most countries, a minority of women accept responsibility for contributing earnings to the family budget, ranging from one-fifth to one-third. Britain is close to the EU average on this indicator. Spain has by far the lowest proportion of women who regard themselves as primary (co)earners, only 18%. This reality is in sharp contrast with the idealism displayed by Spaniards in Table 1.1, a contrast that is repeated throughout this book.

The European Commission dropped the question shown in Table 1.1 from its Eurobarometer surveys in the 1990s. Spanish surveys repeated the Eurobarometer question several times in the 1990s, showing no change since the 1980s. More recent (albeit more indirect) evidence is also available from other surveys, which confirm that the overall picture remained unchanged in the 1990s both in the USA and Europe (Hakim, 2000a: 89–94). For example, the ISSP shows that by the mid-1990s, opinion was evenly divided in the USA, Britain, Germany, Ireland and Italy in response to the idea that 'A husband's job is to earn the money, a wife's job is to look after the home and family' – a statement that supports the segregation of family roles. In most countries, including the Netherlands, there was a small trend away from role segregation as the norm, but in the USA and Britain there was no clear trend. Scott, Alwin and Braun conclude that despite rising public support for women's right to participate in the labour market, the overwhelming evidence from the ISSP confirms the continuing strong

Table 1.2 Adoption of the primary earner role in Europe

	% who regard themself as main (co)earner	
	Men	*Women*
Denmark	77	47
Germany	82	40
Netherlands	87	35
France	81	35
Portugal	78	28
Britain	**72**	**32**
Belgium	76	31
Ireland	70	24
Luxembourg	76	24
Greece	74	23
Italy	62	23
Spain	**70**	**18**
EU 12	75	31

Source: *Eurobarometer*, No. 38, December 1992.

conviction in modern societies that women's family responsibilities, particularly those involving young children, must come first (Scott *et al.*, 1996: 478, 490).

This book updates the picture with new survey data for two contrasting European countries: Britain and Spain. However, these two countries are used as broadly representative examples of social processes at work in all modern societies. Rising female employment rates are having an impact on families, with some debate about the new family models that are now emerging (Mason and Jensen, 1995). This book addresses questions that pertain to all modern societies, and Britain and Spain are treated as illustrative case studies in a discussion that has wider application.

Modern Lifestyle Choices

In modern societies, marriage has moved from status to contract. Prior to the contraceptive revolution of the 1960s (Hakim, 2000a: 44–56) a primary function of marriage was to legitimize the children born to cohabiting couples, as well as providing formally for their maintenance and upbringing. The contraceptive revolution permits marriage and cohabitation without having children, and some 20% of women today choose voluntary childlessness.[3] In addition, the equal opportunities revolution and other changes in the labour market allow women to choose employment careers as an alternative to the marriage career (Hakim, 2000a: 56–72). The exact content and nature of the marriage contract now becomes a matter for discussion and individual agreement within couples, and the family division of labour similarly becomes an open question.

Women have been entering the labour force in increasing numbers in recent decades, raising questions about how the work orientations and aspirations of the workforce are changing, whether women's financial independence within families has grown in consequence and changed family relationships, and even whether women are reluctant to marry because of their economic independence (Oppenheimer, 1977, 1988, 1994, 1997; Mason and Jensen, 1995; Oppenheimer and Lew, 1995). There is evidence that the centrality of work in individual life histories is changing, with work commitment falling among men, but rising among women (Hakim, 1996a: 103–5). An analysis by Bryson and McKay (1997) suggested that sex differences are disappearing and being replaced by substantial differences in work commitment between full-time and part-time workers, which approximates very roughly to the distinction between careerists and secondary earners. Work orientations seem to be undergoing qualitative change, due to the presence of large numbers of women in the workforce and the adoption of more egalitarian attitudes. The studies presented here collected and analysed national survey data for Britain and Spain to explore changing work orientations, the centrality of work and their links to changing sex-role ideologies and norms about family roles.

The literature on attitudes to employment has, in the past, focused on males, especially male *manual* workers, who were almost invariably the main breadwinner in their families (Brown, Curran and Cousins, 1983). Women have more diverse attitudes to work. Some women regard themselves as secondary earners, and this affects their work orientations, criteria for choosing jobs and the relative importance of a long-term career orientation (Hakim, 1997, 2000a). For some women, financial dependence on a breadwinner husband, preferably one with high earnings, remains an aspiration, or at least a realistic possible alternative to financial independence through their own lifelong employment. Among men, the taken-for-granted assumption of lifelong employment, and the assumed need to earn a breadwinner wage sufficient to support a wife and children, seem to be changing very slowly in response to women's adoption of more egalitarian sex-roles and greater financial independence. Changing sex-role ideology, and changing norms about the sexual division of labour in families, are linked to changes in the centrality of work in men's and women's life histories and to changing attitudes to employment within the workforce.

There is now an expanding research literature on work orientations, the 'gender contract', sex-role ideology and norms about family roles, and there is growing recognition that these have changed substantially over time and have a significant impact on employment decisions (Brown *et al.*, 1985; Hakim, 1991, 1996a, 2000a; Pfau-Effinger, 1993; Tam, 1997; Haller *et al.*, 1998). Some studies indicate that sex-role ideology has an *increasing* impact in the 1990s, especially among highly educated women, who are also the most affluent (Hakim, 1997: 42, 2000a: 77–80, 94–9). In countries with a large part-time workforce, such as Britain, part-time work has diversified into reduced hours jobs taken on a temporary basis by people who normally work full-time, permanent part-time jobs and (temporary) marginal jobs taken by secondary earners (Blossfeld and Hakim, 1997; Hakim, 1998a: 102–44), so there is no single, clear-cut dividing line between full-time and part-time workers.

Until recently, there were no general theories predicting developments in work orientations and the family division of labour in rich modern societies that had not been quickly faulted on the evidence (Hakim, 1996a: 3–16). Early theories by Parsons and others predicted an entirely functional, permanent and rigid sexual division of labour in the family that was quickly contradicted by events (Parsons and Bales, 1955). A slightly more dynamic and empirically informed theory explaining (and again justifying) the rational family division of labour was later presented by Becker (1981, 1991), and has again been dated by recent developments, such as voluntary childless marriages. Feminist theories attempting to explain women's historical subordination in the family and in the workforce have generally been unable to move beyond backward-looking research evidence to consider possible futures, and again even the most dynamic theories (such as that offered by Walby) have been quickly faulted on the evidence (Walby, 1990; Hakim, 1996a: 9–16, 2000a: 281–3).

The common element in all these theories is the assumption of homogeneity – in the aspirations and preferences of women and men, in models of the ideal family, and in employment histories. An alternative perspective is offered by preference theory, which posits at least three substantially different ideal models of the family, and heterogeneous women's preferences for a life centred on a career in the public sphere, a life centred on home and family life, or some combination of the two (Hakim, 1999a, 1999b, 2000a, 2001a, 2001b, 2002). This diversity of work and family lifestyle preferences is in sharp contrast to the assumption of common collective ideals in all previous social science theorizing. It also contradicts the European Commission's insistence that EU member countries can and should aim for convergence in family models and uniform female employment rates of 70% across the European Union (EU), alongside convergence in economic and trade policies.

Preference theory also posits that five historical changes in society and in the labour market are producing a qualitatively different and new scenario of options and opportunities for women, so that diversity will tend to increase over time rather than fading away. The five changes are:

- the contraceptive revolution which, from about 1965 onwards, gave sexually active women reliable control over their own fertility for the first time in history;
- the equal opportunities revolution, which ensured that for the first time in history women had equal access to all positions, occupations and careers in the labour market. In some countries, legislation prohibiting sex discrimination went further, to give women equal access to housing, financial services, public services and public posts;
- the expansion of white-collar occupations, which are far more attractive to women than most blue-collar occupations;
- the creation of jobs for secondary earners, people who do not want to give priority to paid work at the expense of other life interests; and
- the increasing importance of attitudes, values and personal preferences in the lifestyle choices of affluent modern societies.

These changes generally started from the mid-1960s onwards in prosperous modern societies, and they were completed in only a few countries by the end of the twentieth century – most notably in the USA, Britain and the Netherlands (Hakim, 2000a). It is clear that Spain is one of the many western European countries that had not completed all five changes by the start of the twenty-first century. So this study compares one country that has and one country that has not entered the new scenario of choices and opportunities for women.

Arguably it is mainly *younger* women in Britain who benefit fully from the new scenario of genuine choice and opportunity. Older women have spent their most formative years and most of their adult life without the benefits of reliable modern contraception, equal opportunities in the labour market and jobs that are attractive to women. Most important, older women grew up without the idea that they could make lifestyle choices. It is the contemporary ethos of personal choice, autonomy and self-realization that makes everyone free to express and forced to choose their identity, values, personality and lifestyle (Rose, 1998, 1999). Our analysis divides British women (and men) into two birth cohorts or generations: those born before 1960, aged 40 and over, and those born from 1960 onwards, aged under 40 in 1999. It is only the latter group that benefits fully from the new options open to women. For comparative purposes, Spanish women and men are also divided into two birth cohorts. But in this case, the younger age group is effectively the post-democracy generation which has benefitted from the liberalization and secularization of Spanish society from 1975 onwards, after the peaceful revolution that transformed Franco's dictatorship into a democracy.

The aim of this study is to operationalize, test and develop preference theory through two national surveys in contrasting countries. Since preference theory is empirically based, we already know that it fits the evidence. The key test is whether it is useful – for example, in predicting employment decisions. Following Einstein, theory is not right or wrong. Theory is either useful or not useful in making sense of the world, helping us to understand change processes and to formulate further questions to address. At the extreme, all theories can be shown to be wrong, incomplete, not supported by some piece of evidence, or internally inconsistent or undefined. As Kuhn (1962: 145) pointed out, if every failure to fit were grounds for theory rejection, all theories ought to be rejected at all times. Theories compete on fitting the facts, more or less, better than others. The most useful theories fit more of the evidence more often and help us to look ahead, to predict. Good theory permits development, revision and modification as new data become available.

This study addresses three main questions. First, can the three lifestyle preference groups be identified with national surveys using structured interviews? Gerson's (1985) classic study demonstrates that the three preference groups can easily be identified in studies using depth interviews. Our challenge was to operationalize the classification of three lifestyle preference groups through the simple, fixed-choice questions that are used in large national surveys, and our aim was to identify the three groups as economically as possible, using as few questions as possible. We also wanted to check that the three preference groups are ideologically coherent. Several social scientists have challenged preference theory on the grounds that the three lifestyle preference groups simply do not exist and cannot be identified in their studies (Crompton and Harris, 1998; Procter and Padfield, 1999; McRae, 2002). Chapter 3 demonstrates that the three groups can readily be identified using just three questions. Other, related questions demonstrate that the groups have a reasonable degree of ideological coherence. However, both surveys, but the Spanish survey in particular, revealed that a political correctness bias affects the operationalization of preference theory through national surveys, especially if these appear to be opinion poll type exercises. There are ways of counteracting a political correctness bias, but they involve breaking some conventions in question design.

Second, our study set out to disprove the assumption that education and, to a lesser extent, social class are the main determinants of an interest in a lifelong career. This assumption leads to the criticism that work-centred women are simply those with higher education, and the aspirations that naturally follow from it, and are not a distinctive group of women in terms of their values.

This challenge to preference theory comes from human capital theory, which has now become such an entrenched part of social science thinking that it is almost never questioned. Labour economics assumes that education is always obtained as an investment for future employment and hence, implicitly, it leads one to suppose that full-time homemakers must be the least educated group of all. It is odd that the thesis arose in the USA, where there is a long tradition of equal education for sons and daughters, where high schools and colleges have always functioned as marriage markets as well as training institutions, and where sex differentials in educational attainment have traditionally been small (Blau and Ferber, 1992: 139–87; Jacobsen, 1994: 271; Hakim, 2000a: 202). The thesis actually made more sense in relation to Europe, where daughters were generally far less educated than sons, and wives less educated than husbands. Paradoxically, once education was opened up to women in Europe, women started to use the educational system as an avenue for upward social mobility through marriage as well as through the labour market. In most European countries, the proportion of women marrying up the education ladder, to a better-educated man with greater earnings potential, is now rising (Hakim, 2000a: 203–17). For other women, higher education helps them to guarantee marriage to a man with higher education and the higher earnings that entails.[4] Either way, a young woman's investment in higher education can be one that pays off in the marriage market as well as, or instead of, in the labour market. Thus human capital theory is clearly wrong to treat educational qualifications exclusively as an investment in an employment career. Social scientists are wrong to assume that non-working wives are invariably less educated than working wives, that highly qualified women are always work-centred, and that discrimination is invariably the main reason for highly qualified wives sometimes having lower earnings than highly qualified men.[5] As Bourdieu (1997) points out, cultural capital (specifically, qualifications) can be invested in the marriage market as well as the labour market. Nonetheless, in Chapter 4 we test whether education is the main determinant of work centrality among women, and whether all highly qualified women are work-centred and never home-centred.

One common, but usually unstated objection to preference theory is the assumption that home-centred women are conservative traditionalists, as well as being poorly educated. The Spanish survey allows us to test whether political and religious conservatism, low education and home-centred lifestyle preferences are all linked. Spain provides a better test case for this question than secular Britain, especially as the authoritarian and patriarchal values of the Franco dictatorship are within living memory.

Third, we assess whether preference theory is useful, for several research issues. We test whether it is useful for predicting female employment decisions and work patterns. We test whether lifestyle preferences determine occupational choices, and hence help to explain the pattern of occupational segregation found in all modern societies (Anker, 1998). Finally, in a more exploratory vein, we assess whether preference theory helps to explain the polarizing trend in housing in Britain as well as the polarizing trend in female employment. This last test helps to identify the outer limits of the utility of preference theory, since there is nothing in the theory itself that predicts a link to housing choices. Preference theory only aims to explain and predict women's choices between family work and market work, and that is what most of our analyses focus on.

For the most part, the analysis is person-centred rather than variable-centred (Magnusson and Bergman, 1988; Cairns *et al.*, 1998; Magnusson, 1998). A key feature of this approach is that it reveals how variables may have a hugely different impact, depending on the context (social group or situation) where they occur. Person-centred analysis recognizes the heterogeneity of respondents, denies that people are homogenous in their responses to social and economic influences and experiences, and often focuses on extreme cases, which can amount to 20% at either end of a distribution. Person-centred analysis is especially appropriate here, given that preference theory identifies qualitative differences between home-centred, work-centred and adaptive women, and our aim is to extend as much as to test the theory.

Using Omnibus Surveys

Our study addresses the above issues using nationally representative data from personal interview surveys in Britain and Spain. A streamlined approach was adopted, to identify and focus on the best diagnostic or strategic indicators currently available on the themes we study, an approach that we label the minimalist survey method. First, we identified a handful of survey questions that have been tried and tested in other surveys, have proven useful both for academic and policy research in recent years, that are general enough to be addressed to people inside and outside the labour force, men and women, and that document the key parameters of sex-role ideology and work orientations. The module of seven core questions was then inserted in the best available omnibus surveys in Britain and Spain.

Omnibus surveys are national social surveys that are run on a regular basis, monthly or quarterly, in which researchers can buy space to insert their module of survey questions, on either a one-off or a regular basis. The best omnibus surveys use nationally representative random samples rather than quota samples. All use personal interviews, either face-to-face or on the telephone. Good omnibus surveys collect a wealth of classificatory and other background data which permit substantive analyses of the results from the module. Because the classificatory variables included in national omnibus surveys vary from one research organization to another, precisely comparable cross-national comparisons are usually ruled out, but broad-brush comparisons are still feasible. For example, in both surveys we were able to compare stated preferences regarding employment with actual work choices, to see if they matched or not. In both surveys, a small amount of methodological work was done to test alternative versions of questions identifying the three preference groups. Final sample sizes were 3651 people aged 16 and over for Britain and 1211 people aged 18 and over for Spain.

Further details on the minimalist survey method, and on the surveys carried out in Britain and Spain in 1999 are given in Chapter 2.

Britain and Spain as Contrasting Cases

Britain and Spain have very different labour markets, with sharp contrasts in female employment especially. Compared to the averages for the European Union as a whole, Britain has above-average workrates for men and women, while Spain has the lowest male and female workrates in the EU (Table 1.3). Analyses of women's employment in the EU in the 1980s and 1990s show Spain and Britain at opposite extremes on most measures, even for prime age women (European Commission, 2000: 46; Benoit-Guilbot and Clémencon, 2001). Part-time jobs constitute a very small element in the Spanish labour market, a clear indication that employers are not providing the kinds of job preferred by secondary earners. In contrast, half of all working women in Britain are working part-time hours, sometimes in very

Models of the Family in Modern Societies

Table 1.3 Workrates and part-time working in the European Union, 1999, ranking by FTE employment rate

	Working age population 15–64 (millions)	Total employ- ment (millions)	Employment rates % of working age population			Part-time workers % of all employed		FTE employ- ment rate
			All	Men	Women	Women	Men	Women
Denmark	3.5	2.7	77	81	72	34	10	59
Finland	3.4	2.3	67	70	65	17	8	57
Sweden	5.7	4.0	71	72	69	40	9	56
Portugal	6.8	4.8	67	76	60	17	6	53
Austria	5.3	3.7	68	77	60	33	4	50
UK	**38.1**	**27.4**	**71**	**77**	**64**	**44**	**9**	**45**
France	37.5	22.7	60	68	53	32	6	45
Germany	55.1	36.1	65	72	57	37	5	44
Luxembourg	0.3	0.2	62	75	49	25	2	41
Ireland	2.5	1.6	63	73	51	31	7	40
Belgium	6.7	3.9	59	68	50	36	4	40
Netherlands	10.6	7.6	71	80	61	69	18	38
Greece	6.9	3.9	55	70	40	10	4	37
Italy	38.6	20.6	53	67	38	16	3	33
Spain	**26.1**	**13.8**	**52**	**68**	**37**	**18**	**3**	**32**
EU15	247.3	155.5	62	72	53	33	6	42

Notes: The FTE (full-time equivalent) employment rate assumes that most part-timers work half-time hours, so that two part-time workers are equivalent to one full-time worker.
Part-time work is self-defined in the EU Labour Force Survey, with some variation between countries in the upper limit for what are regarded as part-time hours.
Sources: EU Labour Force Survey data for 1999 and other sources reported in European Commission (2000).

short 'marginal' jobs of less than ten hours a week (Hakim, 1998a: 125). A more meaningful comparison between countries is offered by FTE (full-time equivalent) statistics that treat two part-time jobs as equivalent to one full-time job. Even when adjusted to FTE workrates, Spain still has the lowest female workrate in the EU, at 32% of women of working age, compared to Britain's above-average 45%. Workrates in Britain, Germany and France are very similar, while Spain is most like Italy and Greece (Table 1.3).

Table 1.4 Labour market indicators for Britain and Spain, 1999

	Britain			Spain		
	All	Men	Women	All	Men	Women
Working age population 15–64 ('000s)	38106	19185	18922	26104	12832	13272
Total employment ('000s)	27361	15101	12260	13773	8779	4994
Employment rates						
as % of working age population	71	77	64	52	68	37
FTE employment rates	61	76	45	50	68	32
% of total employment in:						
self-employment	12	16	12	19	22	19
part-time jobs	25	9	44	8	3	18
fixed-term contracts	7	6	7	33	31	35
Unemployment as % of labour force	6	7	5	16	11	23
Youth unemployment						
as % of 15–24 labour force	13	14	11	30	23	37
% of 20–24 year olds						
in education/training (1997)	24	25	24	45	41	49

Source: EU Labour Force Survey data for 1999 and other sources reported in European Commission (2000) and (for unemployment rates) Eurostat/European Commission (2001). The final indicator is taken from *Employment in Europe 1998*, which reports data for 1997.

Paradoxically, Spain and Portugal are very dissimilar, as Portugal has one of the highest female full-time workrates in the EU, a distinction that is routinely overlooked in commentaries that focus on differences between northern and southern European employment patterns (Hakim, 2000a: 58; Pfenning and Bahle, 2000; Benoit-Guilbot and Clémencon, 2001).

Workrates in Spain are low in part because unemployment rates are high. Decades of high unemployment have discouraged many married women from trying to return to paid work after a domestic break. By 1999, unemployment rates had fallen to 7% for men and 5% for women in Britain compared to 11% and 23% for men and women respectively in Spain (Table 1.4). For every three women in employment in Spain, there is a fourth looking for a job. Female unemployment is more than double the level of male unemployment and has been for many years.[6]

Unemployment is heavily concentrated among young people in Spain, especially young people seeking their first job. One-third of 15–24-year-olds in the labour force are unemployed compared to 13% in Britain (Table 1.4). This is one of the reasons for a massive surge in higher education enrolments among young people, who usually continue to live with their parents while attending university. Unlike Britain, the fees at state universities are low enough to be nominal and entry to higher education is non-selective, so there are few or no barriers to enroling in higher education courses for those with the necessary secondary education qualifications. Classes are often huge in Spain, partly because students are allowed to repeat years, more than once if necessary. Twice as many young people are in higher education or training in Spain as in Britain: 45% compared to 24% of all 20–24-year-olds in 1997 (Table 1.4).

There are differences between Britain and Spain in the character of their labour markets, but on many social indicators the two countries are otherwise similar and in some respects even identical (Table 1.5). Spain has been through a period of massive social, political and economic change since 1975 when the Franco dictatorship was replaced by democracy under King Juan Carlos. The changes were so fundamental as to amount to a peaceful social revolution. Within a short space of time Spain became a modern country, similar to other European countries on most social indicators (Table 1.5). In 1986 Spain joined the European Union, just 13 years after Britain joined in 1973.

Britain and Spain are very similar in life expectancy; the size of the average pay gap between men and women; the average age of women at childbirth; the marriage rate; median age of students in higher education; home ownership; ownership of consumer durables; access to modern telecommunications and IT services; and income distribution. Spaniards have a much higher level of trust in the European Union than do British people, but otherwise there are no large differences in trust in public institutions. The two countries differ more in the distribution of educational qualifications, in divorce rates and in the average size of households (Table 1.5).

By 1999, a two-thirds majority of men and women in Spain had less than upper secondary education, whereas the majority of British men and women had upper secondary education. However, in both countries roughly one-quarter of the population of working age have tertiary level education. Because unemployment is higher among women than men in Spain, women are more likely than men to enrol in higher education courses: 122 women per 100 men in Spain compared to 107 women enrolled per 100 men in Britain (Table 1.5). This is a very recent development, as historically Spanish men have been far better educated than Spanish women.

Education has been a major mechanism for modernization, secularization and social change in Spain since 1975. Opening up the educational system to all, and to women in particular, who had previously been excluded, was a major achievement of democracy. It was designed to produce a more open, meritocratic society, with increased social mobility. The fundamental change in educational standards is reflected in the contrasts between the younger and older generations in our 1999 survey (Table 1.6). Among Spaniards aged 40 and over, a two-thirds majority have no more than primary level education. This group includes the 2% of the sample who are illiterate and the 14% of the sample who never completed primary school but are literate. Only 11% of the older generation have any higher education, compared to one-third of the younger generation.[7] With education made compulsory up to age 16, secondary education has become the norm in the younger generation, although not everyone completes their secondary schooling. The massive increase in educational levels between the two generations was accompanied by the elimination of sex differentials in the younger generation. Among Spaniards aged 40 and over, there is a marked sex differential in educational standards. Among Spaniards aged under 40, there are no sex differentials in educational attainment. Given the enormous impact of relative education levels on interpersonal relationships, both within marriage and within the wider society (Hakim, 2000a: 193–222), these recent changes in education are directly relevant to our survey of sex-role ideology and work orientations. We can expect to find substantial differences between the two age cohorts in Spain. However, it is difficult to disentangle age, period and education effects because so many changes occur simultaneously between the two generations. People aged under 40 entered adult life after the end of the Franco regime in 1975, whereas older people lived most of their adult life under his dictatorship. The social, economic, political and education changes in the subsequent 25 years mean that age, period and education effects overlap almost completely in our survey data for Spain.[8] Surveys with larger samples show, however, that it is education that has the most powerful effects on attitudes, in all periods and at all ages (Marí-Klose and Nos Colom, 1999). This is consistent with Davis' (1982) earlier finding for the USA that education had a strong impact on social and political attitudes, but social class did not.

Table 1.5 Social indicators for Britain and Spain, 1999

	Britain	Spain
Life expectancy at birth – men	75	75
– women	80	83
Average earnings of women as % of men's	72	76
Average household size	2.3	3.1
% of population in households with:		
2 adults and dependent/inactive children	34	33
3+ adults and dependent/inactive children	21	8
Average age of leaving parental home – men	23	29
– women	21	28
Total fertility rate	1.70	1.19
Average age of women at childbirth	28	30
Crude marriage rate per 1000 population	5	5
Crude divorce rate per 1000 population	3	1
% of marriages dissolved by divorce, 1981 marriage cohort	42	9
% of adults who do unpaid childcare, 1996 – men	21	11
– women	37	27
% of adults who do unpaid eldercare, 1996 – men	6	2
– women	10	8
% of men 25–64 with each level of education:		
less than upper secondary	17	63
upper secondary	54	15
tertiary education	29	21
% of women 25–64 with each level of education:		
less than upper secondary	24	67
upper secondary	51	14
tertiary education	25	19
Females per 100 males in tertiary education, 1997	107	122
Median age of students in tertiary education, 1997	24	22
% of people aged 18–24 having left education with low qualifications	7	29
% of households owning their accomodation, 1996	67	81
% of households owning selected items, 1996:		
telephone	94	88
car	72	69
colour TV	97	98
video recorder	82	65
microwave oven	74	38
dishwasher	23	19
% of persons living in private households in 2000 with:		
mobile phone	57	57
personal computer	36	34
internet connection at home	40	17
% of adults satisfied with their own financial situation	69	57

Table 1.5 (continued)

Share of income by quintile, 1996

top quintile	42	41
4th quintile	23	23
3rd quintile	16	17
2nd quintile	12	13
bottom quintile	7	7
total	100	100

Median equivalized income of all persons aged 16+ by level of
educational attainment (indexed, total = 100), 1996:

tertiary education	156	170
upper secondary	113	119
less than upper secondary	86	91

Personal net income from work (indexed, total = 100) by age, 1996

men	16–24	45	46
	25–49	145	120
	50–64	130	125
women	16–24	34	30
	25–49	80	86
	50–64	67	73

% of persons 16+ with equivalized income
below 60% of median by main activity, 1996:

employment	6	10
unemployment	51	34
retired	25	11
other inactive	30	21

% of persons expressing trust in various institutions:

European Union	20	55
national government	36	45
large companies	27	36
political parties	16	19
trade unions	37	32
justice/legal system	48	40

% of persons feeling attached to:

their region	82	94
their country	91	90
Europe	37	68

Notes: Average earnings of women as % of men's are given for weekly earnings rather than hourly earnings, thus increasing the pay gap in Britain where large numbers of women work part-time hours. Dependent children include all children up to the age of 15, plus all those aged 16–24 who are not in the labour force, most of whom are in education.

Sources: Eurostat *European Comission* (2001), quoting Eurostat statistics and Eurobarometer results. Figures are for 1999 unless otherwise specified.

Table 1.6 Changes in patterns of education in Spain

Educational level attained	<40 years			40+ years			Total	
	M	F	T	M	F	T	M	F
Up to end of primary	13	11	12	53	67	61	34	44
Some secondary	51	53	52	33	24	28	48	43
Higher education	36	35	36	14	9	11	18	13
N = 100%	270	258	528	312	366	678	582	624

Table 1.7 Changes in patterns of education in Britain

Age of completing full-time education	<40 years			40+ years			Total	
	M	F	T	M	F	T	M	F
up to 16 years	51	46	48	73	72	72	65	62
17–20	26	34	31	14	17	16	18	23
21 +	23	20	21	13	11	12	17	15
N = 100%	588	704	1292	1009	1177	2186	1598	1881

Notes: The British survey does not provide information on educational qualifications. In the twentieth century, education was compulsory up to the age of 14, 15 or 16 years, but there was no guarantee that people leaving school at this age had achieved basic secondary level qualifications. First level university degrees can be achieved from age 21 onwards in Britain, so this is an approximate indicator of people with higher education qualifications. Data for people aged 16 and over who have completed their full-time education.

Britain also experienced a sharp improvement in educational standards between the older and younger generations, but the change is nowhere near as dramatic as in Spain (Table 1.7). The older generation in our survey generally terminated their education at the minimum level of compulsory schooling, which increased gradually through the twentieth century from age 14 to 15, then to 16 years. They left school when compulsory schooling ended, whether or not they had achieved any qualifications by this age. In the younger generation, only half leave school at age 16. One-third continue with secondary education and possibly attempt some higher education as well. One-fifth complete their education at age 21 or older, which would generally mean they had achieved higher education qualifications. Sex differences are non-existent in the older generation. In our survey, they have increased in the younger generation, with 23% of men compared to 20% of women achieving higher education qualifications (Table 1.7), sometimes by returning to education later in adult life. Although the proportions entering higher education doubled between the older and younger generations, the level in Britain still remains well below that in Spain: one-fifth and one-third respectively have some higher education.

The social indicators in Table 1.5 imply substantial differences in educational standards between Spain and Britain, but some of the differences may be illusory. It is notable that the Spanish survey found only 2% of the sample to be illiterate. Despite education being compulsory up to the age of 14, 15 or 16 in Britain during the twentieth century, many young people leave school without even basic educational qualifications. National surveys of literacy and numeracy reveal that one-fifth of the adult population in Britain is functionally illiterate, and one-fifth are unable to use basic arithmetic (OECD and Statistics Canada, 1995, 1997, 2000: Figure 2.2; Eurostat/European Commission, 2001: 40). So educational standards may differ less than appears from official statistics on levels of schooling attained in the two countries.[9]

From the perspective of preference theory, five particular features of modern societies are most important, and differentiate the two countries. These are the five social and economic changes identified above as creating a new scenario for women.

The contraceptive revolution was achieved in the early 1960s in Britain, producing an immediate but finite drop in fertility levels (Coleman, 1996; Hakim, 2000a: 46–7). By 1995, modern forms of contraception (the pill, IUD and sterilization of either partner) were used by two-thirds of married women and over half of all women. Contraception and abortion are provided free by the National Health Service in Britain. The Catholic Church's opposition to contraception and abortion meant that these were formally illegal until quite late in Spain, and they remain sensitive subjects even after legalization. The sale and advertising of contraception, including the pill, was only legalized in 1979 in Spain, although there had been a black market before then, particularly for condoms. A 1980 survey found that 40% of Spanish women said they had never used any type of contraception, and medical authorities often claimed that modern forms of contraception were dangerous (Borreguero *et al.*, 1986), as they do in patriarchal Japan (Hakim, 2000a: 44–5), so as to dissuade potential users.[10] Late marriage, withdrawal (*coitus interruptus*), and abstinence were the most common methods of limiting fertility and widely used.[11] Sterilization was only legalized in 1983, prompting a huge increase in couples choosing this form of contraception. Abortion was only legalized, under very restrictive conditions, in 1985. However, many Spanish doctors remain conscientious objectors, and refuse to assist women seeking abortions, so that women often travel to London or Amsterdam for speedy and safe abortions, if they can afford it. The Abortion remains the subject of heated debate in Spain (García-Osuna, 1993: 167–84), and is still not available on demand. The 1995 Fertility and Family Survey (FFS) showed that less than half of Spanish women were using modern forms of contraception (Delgado and Castro Martín, 1998). The majority of couples continue to rely on the condom, regarded as the modern replacement for withdrawal, and the use of condoms has been encouraged by concern about Aids. In addition, there are differences in knowledge of and access to modern contraception between urban and rural areas, between social classes and between economically developed regions and other regions (Díez Nicolás and de Miguel, 1981; Borreguero *et al.*, 1986). Because contraception is paid for privately, there are financial as well as other barriers to the widespread use of modern forms of contraception in Spain. In sum, the contraceptive revolution had not yet been fully delivered in Spain by the time of our survey in 1999. The long-term decline in fertility rates, to a level well below Britain's 1.70 (Table 1.5), is explained by social and economic factors: young people's difficulties in achieving economic independence from their parents due to high unemployment; the lack of compatibility between paid employment and women's family work; the fact that Spanish men continue not to contribute to domestic work and childcare; and the lack of social institutions supporting families and the working mother (Delgado and Castro Martín, 1998: 114; Alba, 2000). The positive desire for children is reflected in the long-term decline in childlessness at age 40, from 23% for women born in 1917–21 to 10% among women born in 1947–51 (Marí-Klose and Nos Colom, 1999: 18).

The equal opportunities revolution took place in the 1970s in Britain, with new laws prohibiting sex discrimination in all public spheres of life. These laws are backed up by active policies promoting equal opportunities, by the Equal Opportunities Commission (EOC), which acts as a change agent and public watchdog to police implementation of the laws, and by a national network of employment tribunals with relatively informal procedures which judge complaints against, or from, employers and other bodies, and dictate remedies or fines. As a member of the European Union, Spain also has comprehensive laws prohibiting sex discrimination. However, the Instituto de la Mujer (discussed below) has no legal powers and only limited responsibilities as a change agent. There are no other organizations to support or promote changes of policy and practice, no employment tribunals, and nothing else that ensures that equal opportunities laws are implemented. There are almost no studies assessing the impact of legislation giving women equal rights,[12] and good evidence that the impact has been minimal. A survey of Spanish men showed that men accept the principle of equal pay for women, but they believe that men should have priority in access to jobs and promotion. Women's employment is seen as voluntary and optional, whereas paid work is obligatory for men, so they expect to have priority in the labour market (Inner, 1988). The signs are that they get it. For example, female unemployment rates are double the male rates, the sex differential is highest among the highly qualified, and it seems to be increasing over time (Alcobendo Tirado, 1983: 134; Peinado López, 1988: 75; Prior Ruiz, 1997: 189; Delgado and Castro Martín, 1998: 119). Few young women in Spain feel they have equal opportunities in the labour market.[13]

The expansion of white-collar occupations is a universal phenomenon in modern societies, as jobs in agriculture and manufacturing decline in importance in relation to the newer service industries. Although Britain and Spain have somewhat different industrial structures, both countries have large and growing workforces in white-collar occupations that are attractive to women.

One of the distinctive features of the relatively unregulated British economy is that it has allowed all types of job, all work hours and all employment arrangements to be introduced, if employers and workers find them mutually acceptable. Membership of the EU forced Britain to impose some limitations on long work hours, and to specify minimum terms and conditions for workers, such as annual holiday entitlements. But these recent regulations have not generally inhibited the huge scope for innovation and experimentation in employment contracts – including annual hours contracts, term-time working, flexible work hours and on-call work, in addition to the well-established forms of agency sub-contractors, temporary and fixed-term contracts, and part-time work. Of these 'non-standard' types of job, part-time work is by far the most important and most popular, especially among married women and students. In Britain, half of all working women hold part-time jobs, compared to one-fifth of Spanish women (Tables 1.3 and 1.4). Part-time jobs are particularly attractive to secondary earners, who are earning a supplementary income rather than earning a living. As yet, Spain has few jobs that are attractive to secondary earners, whereas Britain has very large numbers of such jobs. In Spain, one-third of the workforce is employed on fixed-term contracts (Table 1.4). However, these jobs are generally taken by people who are seeking permanent full-time work, and they are less attractive to secondary earners.

Finally, Britain has a culture where people believe they can choose the lifestyle they prefer, both in the broad and in detail. The transition from dictatorship to democracy in Spain undoubtedly caused a massive change in attitudes and values, and gave people a sense of freedom that was previously lacking. In some respects, the two countries have identical values. For example, there is no difference between them in the proportion of the population embracing postmaterialist values: one-fifth overall in the 1990s (Inglehart *et al.*, 1998: 468). However, we would argue that Spaniards generally do not yet enjoy the level of prosperity that prompts a qualitative change in culture, creating a situation where people believe they can freely decide and implement their choice of activities and lifestyle. Just one indicator here is the fact that social conventions surrounding marriage and childbirth are observed far more universally in Spain than in Britain. Cohabitation without marriage is rare, and children born outside marriage are very rare indeed in Spain, unlike Britain. As late as the 1981 marriage cohort, only 9% of marriages ended in divorce in Spain compared to 42% in Britain (Table 1.5).[14] In addition, it appears that social and economic constraints remain more important determinants of behaviour in Spain than in Britain. For example, the 1995 FFS showed that almost all Spaniards want to have children, typically at least two (Delgado and Castro Martín, 1998). Yet social and economic factors have pushed fertility rates well below this level, as noted above. The argument is not only that there are differences in culture and values between the two countries, but that personal preferences and values are now important determinants of behaviour in Britain, but not in Spain, where social and economic factors are dominant and social conventions are still important.

In sum, the five crucial social and economic changes have been fully implemented in Britain, but not in Spain, creating a new scenario for women in Britain, but not yet in Spain. This conclusion does not deny the magnitude and speed of social change achieved in Spain in the relatively short period between Franco's death and our 1999 survey.

Under Franco, the legal rights of married women, the vast majority of women, were severely restricted. Married women were treated as minors in law, owed obedience to their husband and needed his permission to take a job, open a bank account, even to inherit. The 1936–9 Spanish Civil War had destroyed large parts of the economy, and men had priority for the few jobs available. The large numbers of deaths in the Civil War led to a desire to repopulate and to pro-natalist policies that emphasized women's role as mothers. Education was segregated, and domestic skills were emphasized in girls' schools. The Catholic Church's teachings dominated education, and provided the basis for much law (as illustrated by the unavailability of divorce, contraception and abortion), and for gender ideology (Morcillo, 1999; Morcillo-Gómez, 1999).

In the 1930s, one-third of Spaniards were illiterate. Under Franco, few people got beyond primary education, but boys were better educated than girls. Population censuses showed that female economic activity rates remained very low: 9% in 1930, 8% in 1940, 12% in 1950, 15% in 1960 and 13% in 1970 (Prior Ruiz, 1997: 38). Most women worked in agriculture, domestic service, textiles and clothing manufacture, or else worked as family workers in a husband's or a relative's business. The census seems to undercount women's employment, with higher rates reported by employment surveys: 24% in 1970, 32% by 1980 and 43% by 1990 (Delgado and Castro Martín, 1998: 119).

Lack of access to education was an effective means of keeping women at home, and socially subordinate. Female workrates have always varied strongly by educational level in Spain, with workrates of 50%+ among the rare women university graduates. Poor education also encouraged a belief that women were intellectually less able and less competent than men, and thus less suited for employment or positions of responsibility (Prior Ruiz, 1997: 19–79; Morcillo 1999; Morcillo-Gómez 1999). Essentialist stereotypes of men's and women's personalities and abilities persisted until well into the 1990s in Spain (Inner, 1988; Prior Ruiz, 1997: 69–71), yet the research evidence points to few or no sex differences in attitudes and values, remarkably small sex differences in job values, and tiny differences in attitudes between full-time working women and full-time homemakers (Prior Ruiz, 1997). These results could be explained by the political correctness bias discussed in Chapter 3, but are still notable. Finally, direct sex discrimination in pay was widespread under the Franco regime, and labour policies affecting women tended to encourage substantially lower pay for women.

In most countries, legislation on women's rights has come after public opinion has already changed. In Spain, the politicians who formulated the 1978 Constitution, and the new laws introduced in the period 1975–80, were forward-looking, using them to point the way forward to goals and objectives that were well ahead of public opinion at the time. As a result, Spain's legislation affecting women was already fully compliant with European Union equal opportunities legislation even before Spain joined in 1986 (Alcobendas Tirado, 1983).

Some important legislation affecting women was passed immediately after Franco's death, such as the 1975 law abolishing wives' legal subordination to their husbands, and the 1978 Labour Relations Law which outlawed the marriage bar for women in the workforce. However, the key change is in the 1978 Constitution, which prohibits discrimination on the basis of sex, age, marital status, race, religion, (political) opinion and any other personal or social characteristic. The 1978 Constitution declared for the first time men and women's complete equality in law, with equal rights and duties. In the field of employment, these rights were set out more precisely in the 1980 Worker's Statute, with further details spelt out later in various regulations and orders. Although an earlier 1961 law declared the principle of equal pay, only the 1980 Worker's Statute positively prohibited sex discrimination in pay and rendered invalid collective and individual agreements to the contrary. Spaniards make a distinction between declaring that a principle *should* apply, and prohibiting its obverse (Alcobendas Tirado, 1983: 45).[15] So until 1980 the widely accepted general principle of equal pay for women was not seen as prohibiting lower pay for female workers in practice in most occupations. The 1980 Worker's Statute, among other things, requires promotion procedures to be the same for men and women within an occupation; requires equal pay for equal work (not only for similar work) both as regards basic pay and supplements; gives women 14 weeks' unpaid maternity leave with job rights maintained; allows up to three years' unpaid parental leave for each child born with a preferential right to return to the employer; and specifies the right for parents and carers to reduce their hours of work to between half to two-thirds of normal work hours. The government's commitment to equal opportunities was underlined by further legislation in the 1980s: the Discrimination Law of 8/1988 established sanctions for employers found to discriminate, and the Labour Procedure Law of 7/1989 placed the onus of proof on the employer, where a woman had made a complaint.

It is clear that the Spanish laws of 1975–89 concerning employment and flexibility were far ahead of contemporary social and economic realities. Spaniards acquired rights that women felt they could not use immediately, given unemployment levels among the very highest in the EU,[16] but which will easily come into play as the economy expands and as social attitudes change. It appears that most of the legislation had little or no real impact, and few people expected it to. The main function of the new laws was to specify goals and objectives, and the main function of the Instituto de la Mujer is moral exhortation to move towards them.

The Instituto de la Mujer (Women's Institute) was created within the Ministry of Social Affairs in 1983, at the same time as the Spanish Parliament ratified Spain's adhesion to the UN 1980 Convention on equality for women. The Institute's function, *interalia,* is to promote conditions that assist women's participation in political, cultural, economic and social life, to promote equality between the sexes, to carry out relevant research, to advise the government and to channel women's complaints. It has no legal role at all in enforcing equality of opportunity in the labour market in the same way as has the EOC in Britain and the EEOC in the USA. For example, it cannot take employers or the government to court, and it cannot mount investigations of employers believed to be flouting the law. It cannot support or advise women who bring strategic cases or test cases to the courts. Its principal public activities are to commission and publish a series of substantial research reports on all aspects of women's lives and work (for example Inner, 1988; Ramos Torres, 1990; Romero Lopez, 1990; Carrasco,

1991; Garrido, 1992), and a series of equal opportunity plans. A Spanish woman who wants to protest against employment practices she regards as discriminatory has to take her employer to ordinary civil courts herself. In practice, the only case where this happens is when trade unions organize legal action on behalf of groups of female workers. These are often successful, albeit rare events. The principal function of the Instituto de la Mujer is moral exhortation, a profoundly influential mechanism in societies where collectivistic ideologies are important (Hakim, 1996a: 187). Compliance with the law is essentially voluntary in Spain.

There is almost no reference, in the Spanish social science literature, to the existence and impact of legislation enforcing equal pay and prohibiting sex discrimination in the labour market (for example Marí-Klose and Nos Colom, 1999). Social scientists do not consider it worth mentioning the date of such legislation, in order to situate their historical data as being 'before' or 'after' the change in laws. There appears to be a taken-for-granted assumption, in academic and government publications, among men and women, only rarely stated explicitly (Prior Ruiz, 1997: 72), that equality legislation is not important in practice. It would be unusual for a British study of women's position in the labour market and progress on equal opportunities not to mention the 1971 Equal Pay Act and the 1975 Sex Discrimination Act within the two decades following the legislation, and to omit any mention of their contribution to change, even if there was no discussion of updating legislation and the contribution of the employment tribunals to enforcing the law. In Europe, legislation prohibiting sex discrimination and promoting equal treatment of men and women in the labour force is the main tool of social engineering and the principal mechanism used by the European Commission. As such, it is often given special emphasis in research reports (Van Doorne-Huiskes *et al.*, 1995; Hakim, 1996a: 187–201). In contrast, Spanish research reports are silent on the question of relevant legislation. Perhaps the best example is an empirical study of sex discrimination in the Spanish labour market by Peinado López (1988) that was commissioned and published by the Spanish Ministry of Labour and Social Security. Her analysis of women's employment covers the period 1977 to 1984 and looks at entry to first jobs, employment rates, unemployment rates, occupational segregation and the pay gap, but she never once mentions any relevant legislation. This silence on the impact of relevant legislation is strengthened by the Spanish belief that to forbid something in law is to abolish it. As noted in Chapter 3, this also contributes to the political correctness bias in attitude survey results.

The pay gap between men and women in Spain does not, in practice, appear to be much larger than in other European countries at the end of the twentieth century.[17] Immediately after the transition to democracy, in the late 1970s, the pay gap was 28% and this level persisted until well into the 1990s (Prior Ruiz, 1997: 203). Another report quotes a pay gap of 23% in 1987, which varied by occupation, being lowest (5%) in unskilled work and highest (42%) in management (Inner, 1988). Another report quotes a pay gap of 25% in 1995 (Castaño and Palacios, 1996: 119), all of it due to indirect discrimination and differences in the employment patterns of men and women. Most recently, Alba (2000: 110, 114) quotes a pay gap of 26% in 1989 remaining constant to 27% in 1996, then falling to 22% by 1998. The pay gap is substantially smaller, at 16–17%, in the public sector and among people with permanent employment contracts. There appear to be no official reports on the subject, apart from the two case studies of large employers conducted independently by Peinado López (1988: 143–86). Using payroll data for 1981 and 1982, she found that initial pay gaps of 25–27% were reduced to about 10% when education, tenure with the employer, tenure in the job/occupation and age were controlled. In sum, the pay gap in Spain is similar to that in other EU countries and equal pay legislation appears to have had little or no impact in reducing it. In Britain, the only major change in the pay gap occurred in the 1970s, when equal pay laws were introduced. The pay gap has hovered around 20% since 1995 (Hakim, 1996a: Table 6.8), the same as in Spain.

Similarly, occupational segregation in Spain in the 1990s appears to be broadly the same as in other EU countries (Rubery and Fagan, 1993; Hakim, 1998a: Table 1.4). Women are concentrated in lower grade white-collar, personal service and manual occupations. The dramatic improvement in women's educational qualifications following the opening up of the educational system is producing a steady increase in the proportion of women in professional and technical occupations, particularly nursing and teaching. The polarization of female employment in Spain led to a small increase in occupational segregation indices in the 1990s (Prior Ruiz, 1997: 193–6; Alba, 2000: 96–108, 157). On some measures, Spain has a less segregated workforce than Britain, partly due to the scarcity of part-time jobs which are generally the most segregated of all (Hakim, 1998a). Table 1.8 shows that almost half (43%) of Spanish women work in jobs where there is a fairly even mix of men and women and so do one-fifth of men. In contrast, the British workforce is heavily segregated into typically female occupations and typically male occupations, with few people working in mixed occupations.

Table 1.8 Occupational segregation in Britain and Spain

	Britain		Spain	
	M	F	M	F
Male occupations	74	18	78	27
Mixed occupations	6	6	19	43
Female occupations	20	76	3	31
Total	100	100	100	100

Note: Male occupations have up to 40% female workers, mixed occupations have 41–59% and female occupations have 60%+ female workers.
Source: Hakim (1998a: Table 1.4).

   Following the European Commission's lead, Spanish researchers use the sex differential in employment rates as an indicator of sex discrimination. The European Commission regularly relies on the sex differential in employment rates as an indicator of 'the inequalities and injustices that women face as part of their everyday lives', and presents graphs showing that Greece, Spain and Italy have the highest sex differentials while Sweden and Finland have the lowest differentials in employment rates (European Commission, 2001: 30–31). The Commission's interpretation does not seem appropriate. The decision to do paid work or not is personal, and as preference theory points out, there are several family models that European couples can choose from, as illustrated in Table 1.1. In any case, the main reason for lower female employment rates in Spain is the fact that employers have not yet created a large part-time workforce, with the type of jobs that are so popular with married women in other EU countries. If and when they do so, it is likely that the Spanish unemployment problem would be solved overnight, as it was in the Netherlands (Visser and Hemerijck, 1997). Countries with female employment rates above the EU average of around 50% generally have substantial part-time workforces, as illustrated by the Netherlands, Britain, Sweden, Denmark, Germany and, increasingly, France as well. Portugal and Finland are the only exceptions to this rule, with high female full-time employment rates and few part-time jobs, for reasons no one has adequately explained (Table 1.3). When part-time jobs are created in sufficient numbers, many married women working full-time hours switch to part-time work instead (Hakim, 1996a: 61–5), thus vacating full-time jobs for younger labour market entrants.

In conclusion, from the perspective of women's employment, the first important difference between the Spanish and British labour markets is that Spanish employers have not yet created substantial numbers of permanent part-time jobs of the sort that are attractive to women. Female full-time workrates are similar in the two countries: 38% in Britain and 31% in Spain in 1999. Second, female unemployment is more than double male unemployment in Spain, suggesting serious sex discrimination in access to jobs. On most other indicators, the two workforces are roughly similar. The main difference between our two cases is a social one: by 1999 Britain had achieved the new scenario for women while Spain had not yet done so.

Outline of the Book

This and the following chapter set out the focus of the study, how the data were collected, some differences between the two datasets and the two methodological experiments included in the surveys.

Chapters 3 and 4 provide a detailed analysis of the three questions that together identify lifestyle preferences, and the four related questions on sex-role ideology. The original purpose of the four extra questions was, first, to provide an appropriate context for the three classificatory questions in our survey module and, second, to allow some minimal testing of ideological coherence and consistency in the three preference groups. The extra questions led us to conclude that there is a strong political correctness bias (or social desirability bias) in the Spanish results, which then led us to assume that a similar, albeit less visible, bias probably affects survey results for Britain as well. The Spanish results also led us to combine two questions into an index of patriarchal values, which prove to be separate from, but related to lifestyle preferences to varying degrees. The patriarchy index also proved useful in later chapters, because it served to demonstrate that some attitudes and values have little or no impact on women's employment decisions, whereas personal lifestyle preferences are major determinants of employment patterns.

Chapter 3 demonstrates that it is feasible to identify women's lifestyle preference groups with just three fixed-response survey questions. Chapter 4 considers whether education, social class and income are important determinants of lifestyle preferences, and concludes that they are not, in either country. Other correlates of attitudes and values are also examined, including age, marital status and urban/rural residence.

Preference theory claims that there will be much weaker links, if any, between lifestyle preferences and employment patterns in countries that have not achieved the new scenario for women – such as Spain. We also expect results for Spain to show less ideological consistency than in Britain, because personal preferences and values do not yet have the same weight and importance as in new scenario countries – such as Britain.

Chapters 5, 6 and 8 all test for the impact of lifestyle preferences on choices and behaviour. Chapter 5 looks at the impact of attitudes and values on employment patterns in Britain and Spain. Following our earlier review of the literature and recent longitudinal studies (Hakim, 2000a), we feel confident that attitudes and values do have a causal impact on behaviour (rather than being *post hoc* rationalizations), at least in the new scenario, and hence in Britain in particular. As predicted by preference theory, there is a closer fit between women's lifestyle preferences and employment patterns in Britain than in Spain. Furthermore, attitudes predict behaviour, but behaviour does not predict attitudes. Among men, there is no link between sex-role ideology and behaviour. In addition, we assess the relative importance of lifestyle preferences and contextual factors (such as childcare responsibilities) as determinants of behaviour, and show that lifestyle preferences determine *which* contextual factors impact on women's behaviour.

The British dataset was large enough for occupations to be coded to the most detailed three-digit level of the ONS occupational classification, that is, to 371 occupational groups. This allowed us to code occupations to the three-fold typology developed for studies of occupational segregation: mainly male, mainly female and mixed-sex occupations (Hakim, 1998a). Chapter 6 looks at the relationship between lifestyle preferences and occupational choice. In particular, it looks at the thesis developed by human capital theorists (most notably Polachek, 1975, 1979, 1981; Goldin and Polachek, 1987) that women choose occupations that are a good fit with their expected work history over the lifecycle. The evidence from our survey is that there is no link at all between occupational choice and lifestyle preferences at the start of the twenty-first century in Britain. It appears that equal opportunities policies have now eliminated any link that previously existed. On the other hand, lifestyle preferences do determine the type of job taken, and labour turnover.

As noted above and in Chapter 5, housing tenure appears to be a third determinant (or correlate) of lifestyle patterns and women's employment. The British dataset provided information on housing tenure, and was also large enough to explore any association with lifestyle preferences and models of the family. Chapter 8 first sets out the recent evidence for treating housing tenure as a semi-permanent lifestyle choice, and then looks at the relationship with sex-role ideology. We find virtually no link at the start of the twenty-first century, possibly due to changes in housing patterns in the 1990s.

Chapter 7 addresses the *causes* of lifestyle preferences rather than the behavioural consequences. The Spanish dataset included information on political, religious and other ideological influences, including parental characteristics. We explore these data to assess whether they are important determinants of lifestyle preferences and related values. In the event, they have surprisingly little impact.

Chapter 9 summarizes our main findings and draws conclusions about the utility of preference theory for explaining differences between modern societies in women's employment patterns.

The emphasis in this book is on the 1999 survey results. We do not provide an extensive review of the relevant literature here. This has been done in two previous books (Hakim, 1996a, 2000a) to which reference is made where appropriate.

Notes

1   Data are from the 2000/1 Family Expenditure Survey for Britain. Excluding taxes, savings and purchase of capital goods, average household spending was £390 a week. Average weekly expenditure on leisure goods and services was £70, compared to £64 spent on housing, £62 on food and non-alcoholic drink, and £55 on motoring. In the richest 10% of households, spending on leisure goods and services averaged £200 a week, compared to £20 in the poorest 10% of households. Expenditure on alcohol and tobacco would further increase the total spent on leisure goods.

2   Data are from the first national time budget survey carried out in 2000 in Britain. Watching TV and social life accounted for 21% and 13% respectively of total waking hours, compared to 14% spent on paid work.

3   Once children cease to be the primary feature of marriage, the door is opened to same-sex couples also claiming the legal and fiscal advantages of formal partnerships.

4   In Britain, for example, only 6% of all wives were married to a university graduate husband in 1996. The higher a woman's own qualifications, the greater the likelihood of her marrying a university graduate man. Attending university herself almost guarantees a graduate husband: in 1996 almost two-thirds of university graduate women had married a man with equal or better qualifications. However, the exact opposite is found among men (Hakim, 2000a: 216), implying that men do not use the educational system as a marriage market as much as women do.

5   It is well established that the propensity to be in employment, and in full-time jobs, increases as women's education increases. However, this does not mean that all non-working wives have low education while all working wives are highly educated. In our 1999 British survey, the difference in qualifications between working and non-working wives aged 20–59 years is small: 19% and 12% respectively have some higher education, 53% and 64% respectively left school by age 17. Wives with part-time jobs are very similar to non-working wives in terms of education levels. So the main contrast is between the minority of wives in full-time work and all other wives.

6   According to Torns (2000: 223) high levels of female unemployment are not seen as a problem in Spain because women's right to employment is viewed as a social right not a civil right, and only heads of households are regarded as full-fledged citizens.

7   The proportion of respondents with any higher education in our survey is inflated by the decision to classify people completing the Curso de Orientación Universitaria (COU) with people who had some higher education. The COU is a secondary level course, taken after the Bachillerato is completed, and required only for persons intending to proceed to higher education. Given the small survey sample size for Spain, and the tiny number of people with any higher education, classifying COU graduates in the tertiary education group rather than the secondary education group helped the balance of numbers for detailed analyses.

8   Garrido (1992) draws the same conclusion: that the two generations of women in Spain are so different as to have almost nothing in common.

9   The International Adult Literacy Surveys were conducted in 1994, 1996 and 1998 in 20 countries, including Britain, but not Spain. So comparisons between our two countries are not available. The surveys test for prose literacy, document literacy and numerical literacy at five levels of skill, the lowest being functional illiteracy.

10 Del Campo (1991: 103) cites a 1973 survey report by Díez Nicolás that showed that three-quarters of Spanish women had heard of the pill, but almost half believed it to be dangerous and only one-third knew it was more reliable than non-modern methods of contraception

11 There has been a long-term decline in the fertility rate in Spain since the beginning of the twentieth century, despite the lack of easy access to contraception.

12 One reason is the belief that to make something unlawful is to abolish it, and the tendency to conflate fact and value. A recent Spanish report on women's situation stated: 'Legally, we cannot say that sex discrimination exists, however things move very slowly' (Castaño and Palacios, 1996: 112).

13 A 1979 survey found that the majority of all women, working or not, believed that there was discrimination against women in the labour market, particularly in pay and promotion (Alcobendas Tirado, 1983: 205). There seem to be no more recent surveys asking this question, but it is unlikely anything has changed.

14 Divorce was only legalized in 1981 in Spain, in a law that laid down reasons, procedures, arrangements for childcare and the division of family wealth and income, including future pensions.

15 The distinction is also found in other countries. For example, in Japan equal opportunities laws only said that companies should make an effort to promote equality. In 1999, the law was changed to actively prohibit sex discrimination, resulting in ground-breaking court cases.

16 National unemployment rates were close to or above 20% from 1982 to 1999.

17 The pay gap shown in Table 1.5 is for weekly earnings rather than hourly earnings, and thus shows a larger pay gap for Britain (28%) than for Spain (24%) due to the large number of women working part-time in Britain. In addition, the data refer only to people working in manufacturing industry and services, excluding the public sector.

Chapter 2

The Minimalist Survey

Two aspects of the surveys for this study are innovative, or at least unusual. First, the research design adopted a 'minimalist' approach. Second, the surveys were carried out by using a quality omnibus in each country. The arguments for these two methods are set out before presenting details on the two surveys.

The Minimalist Approach

Almost any survey methods textbook written by a social statistician offering advice on how to collect data on attitudes and values tells researchers to use numerous attitude items and questions, usually followed by information on how to use multivariate analysis to reduce the multitude of data items to a more manageable shortlist of synoptic variables or scales. Just one example is a popular textbook by Oppenheim (1992: 147, 187–259). This insistence on a multitude of items being essential is one of the reasons why attitude questions are often excluded from surveys: they become too voluminous and expensive in time and space when compared with questions about behaviour.

We rejected this shotgun approach in favour of a carefully aimed rifle. The idea was to select the questions that worked best as strategic or diagnostic indicators, to identify 'core' items on the topics of interest.

The minimalist approach relies on substantive expertise and a clear theoretical framework to identify the best measures of attitudes and values, in preference to the undiscriminating and uninformed inclusion of multiple, repetitive and often divergent attitude questions, and then using mathematical procedures to sort them into potentially meaningful variables. In practice, researchers are often unable to make much sense of the results of a cluster analysis or other multivariate analysis of attitudes, although this is rarely admitted. We would argue that the shotgun approach to attitude research is theoretically uninformed, and intellectually lazy. We might as well do our theoretical work *before* data collection rather than at the analysis stage.

However, the shotgun approach remains the norm in attitude research. We are not aware of any studies adopting the rifle approach, with a single exception. Kahle (1983) edited a collection in which a team of researchers analysed data from a single new question on social values added to a larger 1976 survey. The single question asked people to choose their two most important life values from a list of nine, which had been carefully selected and aggregated from much longer lists used in previous studies. Because the single question was added to an existing survey, the analysts had access to all the classificatory variables in the survey. The resulting analyses led to a 300-page book, with little overlap between the contributions from each author.

Our streamlined approach required us to select and focus on the best indicators currently available on sex-role ideology and work orientations. We sought to identify a handful of survey questions that have proven most useful in academic and policy research in recent years, that can be addressed to people inside and outside the labour force, men and women, and that document the linkage between sex-role ideology and employment choices. Literature reviews and analyses of existing datasets (Hakim, 1991, 1996a; Hakim and Jacobs, 1997) helped us to identify seven key questions that differentiate between subgroups and are theoretically meaningful. The seven questions which were found to have the greatest diagnostic and theoretical value in studies covering women as well as men were taken from the ESRC's Social Change and Economic Life Initiative (SCELI) surveys (Vogler, 1994; Tam, 1997), the European Commission's Eurobarometer survey series, and Warr's 1981 survey of non-financial work commitment later updated by the British Social Attitudes Survey (BSAS) at periodic intervals (Jowell *et al.*, 1997). The theoretical interest of the seven selected questions is set out in Chapter 3 when discussing the survey results. All of them are questions that had been used before, rather than new items, thus permitting us to look at trends over time on these topics.

The module of seven questions was inserted in nationally representative surveys in Britain and Spain. Together with the classificatory variables on labour market experience, personal and household characteristics available in each survey, we were able to explore interrelationships between norms about the sexual division of labour in the household, sex-role preferences, financial and non-financial motivations for paid employment, their social correlates and their distribution across the workforce and in the wider adult population.

In our study, the survey module was inserted in two omnibus surveys. It would equally well be feasible to insert the module, or some variant of it, in other large interview surveys, in longitudinal studies, in studies based on depth interviews or in case studies of particular social groups.

Omnibus Surveys

Generally, small surveys tend to be low quality. The costs of organizing a national survey can outweigh the benefits if the research requires only a small number of questions. As a result, people may cut corners and accept a data collection that is less than ideal, in order to keep costs low. The alternative is to insert a module in an existing omnibus survey.

An omnibus is a regular survey in which a small module of questions can be put to meet a small survey requirement economically by sharing fixed costs. Omnibus surveys are popular in the private sector, where they are widely used to collect data on consumer preferences, to assess awareness and use of different brands, and to monitor the impact of advertising campaigns and promotions. Most large commercial survey organizations run at least one omnibus, and some run several: one for telephone surveys, another for face-to-face interview surveys and others covering specialist consumer groups, such as young people. In order to ensure speedy turnaround in the data to clients, most commercial omnibuses use computer assisted interviewing – CATI or CAPI. Some companies have established links with firms in other European countries, or with firms across the globe, to facilitate cross-national comparative studies. Omnibus surveys are used rarely in academic research and relatively infrequently in the public sector more generally, possibly because few countries have a central government survey agency that is large enough to run its own omnibus service. Where the facility is available, as in Britain, it tends to be heavily used by government departments, with occasional use by academics (as illustrated by the current study), charities and other non-profit organizations.

The omnibus offers numerous advantages (Hakim, 2000b: 89–90). One-off surveys can be carried out relatively cheaply and very quickly. The omnibus is the ideal vehicle for testing and piloting new questions that will later go into continuous surveys. Regular survey modules can be modified over time to benefit from improvements in question design, and there is the flexibility to add extra questions when results suggest information gaps that require extra information or different questions. Omnibus surveys are also used as sift surveys: to identify special samples for follow-up surveys that address a particular topic in greater depth. For example, people who have had a recent hospital stay can be identified and interviewed more fully in a separate survey about their experience.

These benefits rely crucially on the overall quality of the omnibus exercise. A good omnibus uses random sampling, achieves high survey response rates and question response rates, offers a full account of the methodology and collects a substantial number of classificatory variables.

Fortunately, Britain and Spain both have excellent omnibus surveys which were used for this study.

A new problem that affects interview surveys in Europe, including omnibus surveys, is the continuing decline in survey response rates across all rich modern societies. This is illustrated most clearly by regular and continuous surveys, where the content and methods change little from year to year, and which nevertheless achieve declining response rates. In Britain, the General Household Survey used to obtain response rates above 80% in the 1970s; by the 1990s, 70% was more usual. The British Social Attitudes Survey achieved a response rate of 70% in 1983 when it first started; by the late 1990s response had fallen to around 60%. Surveys in the Netherlands usually achieve response rates of only 40–50%. Perceptions of what constitutes a good response rate have been reduced in consequence, from 85% in the 1970s to 70% in the 1990s in Britain. However, surveys with response rates below 50% are effectively worthless, as they cannot be representative of the population aimed for (Hakim, 2000b: 93).

The British Survey

The British survey was carried out as one project within an ESRC research programme. In autumn 1997, the ESRC initiated the Future of Work Research Programme, with funding of £4 million over a period of five years, 1998–2003. Initially, over 220 proposals were received. This project was one of the 19 proposals shortlisted and subsequently selected for funding within the first round of the Research Programme. The design, scope and timetable of this project were informed by the objectives of the Future of Work Research Programme. In particular, it contributed to two of the six themes chosen by the ESRC: work trajectories and the centrality of work, and employment restructuring and the household. The competition for projects in the second round of the ESRC's Research Programme led to another eight projects being funded, four of them extensions of first-round projects. Our proposal to extend the successful British survey to a cross-national exercise (again based on omnibus surveys) covering Sweden, Finland, Germany, France, Portugal and Spain was unfortunately not selected for funding in the second round. The Spanish survey was subsequently funded independently of the ESRC.

The British survey was carried out by inserting our seven strategic questions in the Office for National Statistics (ONS) omnibus survey in January and February 1999. One of the other topics included in these two months was a module on kin and contact with kin (Grundy and Murphy, 1999).

Table 2.1 Core questions in the British survey

A. Even when women work, the man should still be the main breadwinner in the family.
B. In times of high unemployment married women should stay at home.

A and B – Responses offered: agree strongly; agree somewhat; have no strong feelings either way; disagree somewhat; disagree strongly.

C. Who *should* have the *ultimate* responsibility for ensuring an adequate income for a family? The male partner? The female partner? Or both equally?

D. Who *should* have the *ultimate* responsibility for ensuring that the housework is done properly in a household? The male partner? The female partner? Or both equally?

E. If *without* having to work you had what you would regard as a reasonable living income, would you still prefer to have a paid job, or wouldn't you bother?

F1. People talk about the changing roles of husband and wife in the family. Here are three kinds of family. Which of them corresponds best with *your* ideas about the family?
- A family where the two partners each have an equally demanding job and where housework and the care of the children are shared equally between them.
- A family where the wife has a less demanding job than her husband and where she does the larger share of housework and caring for the children.
- A family where only the husband has a job and the wife runs the home.
- None of these three cases

F2. For half the sample the order of responses was reversed to:
- A family where only the husband has a job and the wife runs the home.
- A family where the wife has a less demanding job than her husband and where she does the larger share of housework and caring for the children.
- A family where the two partners each have an equally demanding job and where housework and the care of the children are shared equally between them.
- None of these three cases

G. Who is the *main* income-earner in your household? (OPINION question)
Is it yourself?
Your partner/spouse?
Both of you jointly?
Or someone else?

The ONS omnibus was launched in 1990 in response to research user demand. It provides a vehicle for government departments to monitor the effects of government policies and the impact of publicity campaigns. Although designed primarily for public sector use, it is also available to voluntary organizations and academic researchers who are looking for a fast, cost-effective method of conducting small, but nationally representative surveys.[1]

The seven core questions are listed in Table 2.1. In this book, they are identified and referred to by the letters in Table 2.1. They include four questions from the SCELI surveys on whether men and/or women should be the main breadwinner, the main homemaker, co-earners or secondary earners, and related issues (A to D); one question (E) on non-financial work commitment (continuing to do paid work despite having a reasonable income); and two Eurobarometer questions on who is the main breadwinner in a household and preferences regarding roles within the family (F and G). Consultation with ONS staff led to several useful improvements in question-wording, and to a small methodological experiment. Question F was presented in two versions, one with the sequence of responses as given in the original Eurobarometer question (F1), and one with the order of responses reversed (F2). The two sets of responses were offered randomly to respondents, so that half the sample replied to question F1, and half replied to question F2. (This was done quite simply by using the house or apartment number: odd and even numbers were shown F1 and F2 respectively.) The two sets of responses were coded separately. For most analyses, the two versions were merged into a single variable used throughout this report. However, the two sets of responses from F1 and F2 were first analysed separately to check what differences there were. As shown in Chapter 3, reversing the order of responses had a substantial impact on the results, particularly among younger respondents, whose views seem to be less stable, more open to persuasion and influence (see Table 3.3). The results of our methodological experiment show that the original Eurobarometer question, showing only one set of responses (see Table 1.1), is biased in favour of the 'egalitarian' response mentioned first in F1.

The ONS omnibus is a multi-purpose survey providing nationally representative data for adults aged 16 and over in Britain, based on a probability random sample and face-to-face interviews with approximately 1800 individuals in private households in each survey month. If an address contains more than one household, the interviewer uses a standard ONS procedure to randomly select just one household. Within households with more than one adult member, the interviewer selects just one person aged 16+ with the use of random number tables. The interviewers endeavour to interview that person; proxy interviews are not taken. Weighting factors are applied to omnibus data to correct for unequal probability of selection. The proportion of households in which the selected informant is the head of household or spouse has varied between 82% and 95%, and was 81% in our sample.

As with all ONS surveys, a quality check on field work is carried out through recall interviews with a proportion of informants to make sure that the interviews actually took place with those informants and that responses to questions are consistent.

For the January–February 1999 surveys, 6000 addresses were selected to produce 5388 eligible addresses for the omnibus. Refusals accounted for 24% of the sample and non-contacts for another 8%. The response rate is normally in the region of 70% to 75%. In practice, the overall response rate achieved for January and February 1999 was 68%, producing data for a total sample of 3651 persons aged 16 and over.

The final sample of 3651 persons (1691 men and 1960 women) included a substantial proportion (20%) of pensioners aged 65 and over, who have distinctive attitudes. Excluding them reduced the sample for the population of working age to 2900. We were able to identify a subgroup of students in full-time education with current or previous jobs (N = 103) and, following exploratory analysis, we decided to exclude all students in full-time education (N = 170) from analyses for the working age population. Students in full-time education were found to be a very distinctive group, with extreme views on the sexual division of labour. They differ markedly even from people aged 16–24 years who have work experience, and were analysed separately, along with pensioners. The final useable sample was thus 2660 for people of working age excluding full-time students and people who have never had a job. Within this group, 1970 persons were in work (1000 men and 970 women), and 690 persons reported information on their last job (460 women and 230 men). The group contained 2345 married or cohabiting couples. These results demonstrate that we were justified in running the work attitudes module across two consecutive months in order to achieve adequate base numbers for detailed analysis.

The Spanish Survey

The Spanish survey was carried out by Análisis Sociológicos, Económicos y Políticos (ASEP), a privately owned social research and consultancy company based in Madrid, under the supervision of Dr Juan Díez Nicolás, a USA-trained social scientist who is Professor of Sociology at the University of Madrid.[2] Professor Dr Díez Nicolás was previously co-founder and last Director General of the Instituto de la Opinión Pública, and the first Director

General of the Centro de Investigaciónes Sociológicas (CIS) in Madrid, both central government bodies. Under the direction of Professor Díez Nicolás, ASEP has carried out numerous attitude surveys on related subjects, such as women's position in society; fertility, contraception and population policy; women in the media; family time budgets; work orientations; work and inactivity; as well as surveys on attitudes to immigrants; attitudes to the environment; social inequality; education and social mobility; health; drugs; political culture; savings and old age; youth and the elderly. In addition, ASEP periodically carries out the Spanish survey for the World Values Survey project directed by Inglehart (1977, 1990, 1997; Inglehart *et al.*, 1998), the Spanish survey for the International Social Survey Programme (ISSP), jointly with CIS, and the Spanish element of the Comparative Study of Electoral Systems.

The seven core questions were translated from English into Spanish by a native Spanish speaker. Consultation with ASEP led to further improvements in question wording. The final version of the questions is shown in Table 2.2. The order of the questions was changed slightly, to place question G between questions E and F rather than last. An additional question H was added to the module for another methodological experiment.

The work attitudes module was included in the November 1999 ASEP omnibus. The survey was designed to obtain a nationally representative random sample of adults aged 18 or over living in private households in Spain, including the Balearic Islands and the Canary Islands, but excluding Ceuta and Melilla (two enclaves in north Africa). Sampling was based on proportional distribution by region and size of place within each region. Strata were defined by crossing the 17 regions with the size of habitat, the latter divided into seven categories: less than 2000 inhabitants; 2001 to 10000; 10001 to 50000; 50001 to 100000; 100001 to 400000; 400001 to 1000000; and over 1 million inhabitants. The sample was stratified by clusters: primary sampling units (municipalities) were selected in a proportional random manner; secondary sampling units (electoral sections) were selected in a simple random manner; and ultimate units (individuals) were selected according to random routes and Kish tables for members of the household. Personal interviews were conducted with respondents at their homes.[3]

Table 2.2 Core questions in the Spanish survey

Me gustaría hacerle algunas preguntas relativas al trabajo de hombres y mujeres dentro y fuera del hogar, a las relaciones entre hombres y mujeres, y otras cuestiones relacionadas.

1. En primer lugar, en qué medida está Vd. de acuerdo o en desacuerdo con cada una de las dos frases siguientes? ...
   A. Incluso cuando la mujer trabaja, el hombre debe ser el que contribuya mayoritariamente a la economía familiar.
   B. Cuando hay altas tasas de paro las mujeres casadas deberían quedarse en el hogar.
Responses offered: Muy de acuerdo, Mas bien de acuerdo, Mas bien en desacuerdo, Muy en desacuerdo.

C. Quién debería tener mayor responsabilidad a la hora de aportar los ingresos necesarios a la familia?
D. Quién debería tener mayor responsabilidad a la hora de asegurar que se lleven a cabo las tareas del hogar?
Responses coded: El hombre, Ambos a parte iguales, La mujer, Otra persona

E. En el supuesto de que pudiera Vd. vivir razonablemente bien sin necesidad de trabajar, trataría Vd. de tener un trabajo remunerado o no se molestaría en buscarlo?

G. Quién contribuye con mayores ingresos a la economía de su hogar?
   Vd. mismo/a
   Los dos miembros de la pareja a partes iguales
   Su pareja
   Otra persona de la familia
   Otra persona

F. Actualmente se habla muy a menudo acerca del cambio de papeles del hombre y la mujer en la vida familiar. De los tres tipos de familia que le menciono a continuación, cual se parece más a su familia ideal?

H. En un mundo en el que el dinero no fuese un problema, cuál de los sigueientes tipos de familia elegiría Vd. tener?
   Una familia en la que los dos miembros de la pareja tengan un trabajo con similares demandas y en la que ambos se reparten equitativamente las tareas del hogar y el cuidado de los niños
   Una familia en la que la mujer tiene un trabajo con menores exigencias que el de su marido y en la que es ella quien se encarga mayoritariamente de las tareas del hogar y el cuidado de los niños
   Una familia en la que el marido es el único que tiene un trabajo remunerado y en la que la mujer lleva el cuidado del hogar
   Ninguno de estos tipos de familia

The completed sample of 1211 people aged 18 and over included 595 men and 616 women. The Spanish sample is much smaller than the British sample (Table 2.3), with a corresponding reduction in the scope and detail of the analyses for Spain. The Spanish sample included a substantial proportion (27%) of people aged 60 and over (most of them aged 60–74 years). Excluding them reduces the sample for the population aged 20–59 to 837. Students in full-time education were excluded from all analyses, as for Britain. Two-thirds of the sample consisted of married and cohabiting couples, of whom 541 were aged 20–59. Due to much lower workrates in Spain, for men as well as women, only 493 people aged 20–59 had a job of any kind, 320 men and 173 women.

Although the Spanish dataset is much smaller than that for Britain, it includes a wider range of classificatory variables, including nature of area of residence (urban–rural); the education, occupation and industry of the head of household; educational level of mother and father; the spouse/partner's employment status; trade union membership; religious affiliation and actual practice; political ideology; vote cast at last election; nationalistic versus regional identity; place of birth; place of residence between the ages of 5 and 15 years; number of books in the home when an adolescent; family income; and own income. This meant that certain themes could only be explored with the Spanish data – most notably the relationship between political ideology and patriarchal attitudes in Chapter 7.

A small methodological experiment was also included in the Spanish survey. In this case, question F was presented in two versions. Both were in the same format as in the British survey, with responses randomly presented in one sequence or its opposite. The first question (F) repeated the question used in the British survey, and focused on people's personal ideal view of family roles. The second question (H) invited people to make their choice in an ideal world in which money was not a problem. The second version was added to address our critics' argument that women's choices on question F must invariably be constrained preferences that took account of their social and economic circumstances. In practice, there was almost no difference between responses to questions F and H among Spanish respondents. More important, the removal of economic constraints often prompted men and women to switch their choice away from the 'egalitarian' model towards the role segregation model of family roles.[4] The two questions are in effect the same question, and economic constraints do not bias responses. Our original interpretation of question F seems to be confirmed.

Spain is especially appropriate for testing versions F and H of our key question. As yet, Spain is less prosperous than Britain. The proportion of adults who are satisfied with their financial situation is lower in Spain than in Britain (see Table 1.5). With a long period of high unemployment

Table 2.3 Base numbers in the two datasets

	Britain	*Spain*
Total sample	3651	1211
excluding FT students	3478	1122
aged 20–59	2389	778
in employment	1835	493
Married/cohabiting couples		
excluding FT students	2409	755
aged 20–59	1735	540
in employment	1373	318

affecting attitudes, Spaniards would be particularly sensitive to economic constraints and financial pressures. If the two versions of the question produce almost identical results in Spain, we can expect even closer results in other countries.

The similarity of responses to questions F and H is indicated by gamma values of .93 overall, .96 for men and .91 for women, .93 for people aged under 40 and .92 for people aged 40 and over. The least consistent group was younger women, but even here there was a gamma value of .90.

Overall, 86% of respondents gave the same response to both questions with no difference between men and women (Table 2.4). There was some variation between preference groups: 91% of egalitarians were consistent; 89% of the group preferring the role-segregated family model were consistent; and two-thirds of people choosing the compromise model were consistent. Overall, people choosing the compromise model are more sensitive to the precise wording of the question than the two extreme groups. This is consistent with preference theory's premise that the adaptive group of women, who are most likely to choose the compromise model, are most sensitive to social signals, social pressure, external prompts, circumstances they encounter and policy signals. They are less ideologically driven than women whose lives are centred firmly on careers or else on home and family.

Table 2.4 The two questions on ideal family models, Spain

| Education level | % making the same choice on the second question | | | | % changing towards | | Base = 100% |
	Egal.	Comp.	Role seg.	All	Egal.	Role seg.	
All	91	67	89	86	6	8	1065
Men							
Up to primary	86	71	93	84	6	10	187
Secondary	95	63	90	88	6	6	238
Some higher	91	86	100	90	3	7	81
Women							
Up to primary	85	69	91	83	6	11	257
Secondary	90	56	80	82	8	10	225
Some higher	100	100	49	97	3	0	73

Note: Data for all aged 18+, excluding students.

The small group of people who changed their response between question F and H, in particular those changing their choice of the compromise model, were examined more closely. They did not have any distinguishing characteristics, other than a tendency to be older, working class, with lower levels of education (including some illiterates), and the lowest levels of personal or family income. This may have led to less certainty about their views, and to greater sensitivity to economic constraints, especially when these factors were combined. For example, the combination of being older and working class, or older and with no more than primary education, produced the highest incidence of people changing their response, about 20%.

Changes in the ideal family model tend most often to be towards greater role specialization. This suggests that the dual-earner 'egalitarian' family model is often chosen from economic necessity in Spain, rather than as a free choice. This result is the exact opposite of what our critics expected.

Most of the analyses in the following chapters were run twice, with both versions of the Spanish question on ideal family models. Results using question H were generally almost identical to those using question F, but there were slightly stronger associations with all correlates: social class, education, income, political ideology, religiosity, family cultural capital.

Operationalizing Preference Theory

One of our research objectives was to develop a methodology for testing preference theory. Given that the theory is empirically based, resting on an extensive analysis of recent trends in women's lifestyle choices in modern societies (Hakim, 2000a), this should have been straightforward. In fact it was not easy, because many of the best studies of women's lifestyle preferences have been based on depth interviews, qualitative research rather than structured interview surveys, as illustrated by Gerson's excellent USA study (Gerson, 1985; Hakim, 2000a: 149–54).

Our goal was to identify one or two questions that would allow us to identify the lifestyle preferences of women. Ideally, these questions would be sufficiently general in character that they could be presented to all adults – women who are full-time homemakers as well as working women, young and old, and men as well as women – thus avoiding the need for separate questions for each group. Initially, the Eurobarometer question used in Table 1.1 seemed the best starting point, as it had successfully been used in several surveys of adult populations in Europe. In practice, the question was found to suffer from a substantial political correctness bias, which is discussed in Chapter 3. Modified question-wording and the exclusive use of question F2 (rather than a combination of F1 and F2) would remedy this problem to some extent. However, another important problem is that there is no precise correspondence between the three family models in question F and the three lifestyle preference groups identified by preference theory.

Preference theory identifies three distinctive groups of women: two smaller groups whose lives are centred on careers, or on home and family respectively, and a larger group of adaptive women who seek some combination of employment and family work without either taking priority permanently throughout life (Hakim, 2000a: 157–92). There is a fairly close correspondence between the role-segregated model of the family in question F (or H) and the women who prefer to be full-time homemakers. The correspondence between the 'compromise' model of the family in question F (or H) and adaptive women is looser. The correspondence between the 'egalitarian' model of family roles and the career-centred woman is very weak. It seems logical that many career-centred women would prefer the family model with symmetrical roles. But not all: many career-centred women employ housekeepers, nannies, childminders and domestic workers to take over virtually all family work, so that there is little or none left to be shared with a spouse. Also, women who are not career-centred may prefer the egalitarian model of family roles because they do not intend to have children, or because they do not yet have children and are under the illusion that children will make no difference to family relationships. Although voluntary childlessness is concentrated among career women, it is found across all groups of women, and fundamentally alters bargaining over the division of labour in the home. Thus we cannot assume that all, or most women who prefer the egalitarian model of family roles are work-centred as defined in preference theory.

Questions E and G on work orientations identify work-centred people, but they are otherwise not helpful for distinguishing between the three lifestyle preference groups.

In sum, attempts to identify the three lifestyle preference groups through structured interviews or survey questions need to use a combination of question F or H and questions on work orientations such as E and G. The specific question-wording is open to development and improvements. Various suggestions are made in Chapter 3, in the light of survey results.[5]

Tests of statistical significance are not presented in the analysis. Such tests are often misunderstood, and misused by many researchers as a substitute for tests of the substantive importance of findings (Morrison and Henkel, 1970). Tests of statistical significance do no more than tell one whether a sample is large enough for results to be considered reliable in the absence of any other information. Our focus is on substantive results, not the adequacy of sample sizes. We are interested in differences between preference groups that are large enough to be substantively important – which generally means they will automatically be reliable as well in a survey the size of the British survey. Where analyses are purely exploratory, this is indicated in the text.

The Spanish dataset is much smaller than the British dataset, only one-third the size, with a corresponding reduction in the detail of the analyses. For example, most of the analyses of the Spanish dataset use only two ideal family models: the symmetrical roles model (egalitarian) and the differentiated roles model, which combines the compromise model and the role segregation model. In practice, in both datasets, there was little or no difference between the groups choosing these last two family models. On a range of other variables, ideological and behavioural, these two groups were fairly similar, so their aggregation makes sense substantively. The main differences were between the majorities aiming for the egalitarian model and the rest of the two samples choosing some degree of role differentiation in family roles as the ideal. Some analyses were simply not feasible with the Spanish dataset, due to the smaller sample. Overall, the Spanish analyses are reliable, at the somewhat broader level at which they are presented. Their principal value is for the contrasts and comparisons with the British results.

Personal Preferences *versus* Public Opinion

Three of the core survey questions identify the three lifestyle preference groups. The first four questions in the module introduce the subject and set a context of relevant questions. These other four questions are 'public opinion' type questions in that they are typical of the generalized attitude questions found in public opinion surveys such as the BSAS, the ISSP, the World Values Survey, the European Social Survey initiated in 2002 and one-off surveys such as the British 1980 Women and Employment Survey (WES).

The first four questions concern what is good for society in general, what people should do generally, as distinct from what people actually choose or prefer for their own lives. We regard the distinction as fundamentally important (Hakim, 1996a: 85, 2000a: 75–8, 2003a), yet it is regularly overlooked by researchers. The results in the following chapters confirm this judgement: personal lifestyle preferences are linked strongly to behaviour, whereas public opinion style attitudes (such as patriarchal values) have at best only a tenuous link to behaviour.[6]

Hofstede (1980: 21, 1991) was the first to make the distinction between what is desired by the survey respondent for their own life and what is considered desirable in society in general. For example, a woman may think it is generally desirable for women to be employed, but prefer not to be employed herself. Public attitude surveys provide information on a society's collective values, myths and taboos. Social research surveys can provide information on the values, priorities and preferences that inform individuals' own lives. However, it is crucial to use questions that ask about personal choices and preferences, instead of agreement/disagreement with the generalized attitude statements that have become conventional – as illustrated by questions A and B in Tables 2.1 and 2.2.

One of the achievements of this study is to confirm that generalized attitudes do not illuminate or inform individual choices, whereas personal preferences do.

Unless otherwise specified, all tables in this book are from the 1999 surveys of Britain and Spain.

Notes

1   The address of the ONS omnibus team is ONS Omnibus, Social Survey Division, ONS, 1 Drummond Gate, London SW1V 2QQ, Tel: 020–7533–5310, e-mail: <omnibus@ons.gsi.gov.uk>.
2   The address of ASEP is Paseo de la Castellana 173, 5th Izquierda, 28046 Madrid, e-mail <asep@sistelcom.com>.

3   In the absence of any single sampling frame with national coverage, this method is used for all national surveys in Spain. For example CIS surveys use some variant of this sampling design, sometimes with quota sampling of individuals by sex and age instead of random sampling within households, as illustrated by the many CIS surveys analysed in Marí-Klose and Nos Colom (1999: 117–23). If an interview cannot be achieved in a housing unit after 3–5 attempts on different days and at different times of the day, then a substitute is selected, generally within the same building, but always within the same electoral section. Electoral sections are relatively small, with an average population of 2000, and are generally highly homogeneous in socio-economic composition. The November 1999 survey had only 1% explicit refusals and 1% non-contacts, a total of 2% non-response. The routine use of substitutes to replace non-contacts, and the rarity of refusals, mean that response rates are never quoted for Spanish surveys. Instead, the focus is on demonstrating sample representativeness. On all the usual socio-economic criteria, plus many other social variables, the ASEP surveys are fully representative of the Spanish population, as depicted by the population census and other surveys.

4   Similar results are reported from a small British study of mothers of young children on their decision to return to work or stay at home (Newell, 1992). Newell found that, in the context of an ideal world, with no financial or other constraints, a higher proportion would choose to stay at home full-time with their children rather than return to employment.

5   One additional question could usefully be added to the module of seven questions in future studies. The question would come immediately after question F on family models and ask: Do you think you have achieved (are likely to achieve) your preference in your current situation (in the future)? The small variations in question-wording permit the question to be adapted for people who are already married or cohabiting, and for young single people who anticipate living with a partner in the future. In addition to Yes/No responses, there would need to be a third response for people who cannot say, do not know, are not sure. Such a question would add substantially to the value of the module, particularly when interpreting results on the impact of lifestyle preferences on actual behaviour.

6   A tenuous link can still be statistically significant if the sample is large enough. For example, a study based on the 1988 ISSP found a statistically significant association, at the national level, between the general belief that women should work full-time when their children are young and women's current full-time workrates (Albrecht *et al.*, 1995). The study covered eight countries: Austria, West Germany, Britain, Ireland, the Netherlands, Italy, Hungary and the USA.

Chapter 3

Patriarchy, Ideal Family Model and Work Orientations

The focus in this chapter and the next is on the internal logic of attitudes and values, on the relationship between sex-role ideology and work orientations, on how these change over time and across the lifecycle, and how they might change in the future. Two summary measures, of patriarchal values and work centrality, are developed. In this chapter, we show how lifestyle preferences can be identified with just three of our survey questions. The other four questions in our module are used to assess the ideological coherence and consistency of the three lifestyle preference groups. In fact we observe some inconsistency between attitudes, and conclude that the survey results are coloured by a political correctness bias, especially in Spain. In Chapter 4 we test the idea that education is the primary determinant of work-centred attitudes, and that all highly educated people are work-centred.

All the core survey questions have been used in previous studies in Britain. So for Britain we can compare the picture at the start of the twenty-first century on all seven questions with data for earlier decades and, sometimes, for other countries as well. For Spain, only the Eurobarometer questions (F and G in Table 2.1) have previously been used and provide comparative data for the 1980s and 1990s in Spain. In addition, we make direct comparisons between Britain and Spain.

The three lifestyle preference groups are only well defined for women. For men, the classification is not complete. In order to permit comparisons between men and women throughout the analyses in this book, the focus is on the separate questions in our survey module. In practice, we find that ideological differences between men and women are almost non-existent on these issues.

There is a widespread expectation among academic social scientists, policy-makers, politicians and the media that attitudes have changed and developed in recent decades, in line with the slow but steady growth of female workrates, to the point that the majority of women now wish to be and regard themselves as equal co-earners with men rather than secondary earners after marriage. Many believe that rising female workrates necessarily mean that most wives have ceased to be financially dependent on men and contribute an equal half-share of household expenses. Rhetoric has far outrun reality on women's economic position.

The reality is that in most modern societies, including the so-called 'egalitarian' Scandinavian countries, women continue to be heavily dependent on male partners. Since direct sex discrimination in pay rates has been broadly eliminated in most advanced economies, the main reasons for wives' continued economic dependence are women's discontinuous work histories, lack of a career orientation, different work orientations, plus a series of invisible factors that lie outside the labour market and are routinely overlooked, such as women's propensity to marry men who are older and better educated, and thus have a significant advantage in work experience and earnings from the very start of a marriage (Hakim, 1996a, 2000a: 110–17, 193–222).

For example, in West Germany, the Netherlands and Belgium, husbands contribute, on average, three-quarters of household income. In Finland, Sweden, Norway, the USA, Canada and Australia, husbands contribute two-thirds of household income, on average (Hakim, 2000a: 116). On average, husbands contribute two to three times more than wives to household income. Among dual-earner couples, husbands contribute about double the wife's contribution in all the above countries and in Britain as well (Hakim, 2000a: 110–17).

The majority of dual-*earner* couples are not dual-*career* couples. In Britain, for example, a minority of 10–20% of couples are dual-career couples. Among dual-earner couples with both partners in full-time employment, only 10–20% of wives had earnings equal to or greater than their husband's (Hakim, 2000a: 111–15). In Spain, three-quarters of wives are completely financially dependent, because very few women remain in employment after marriage, around 20–25%. Women's earnings account for about 25% of total household earnings, with substantial variation across households (Rubery *et al.*, 1998: 197). In sum, financial dependence on men remained the norm for the vast majority of wives at the start of the twenty-first century. Women's earnings, often from part-time jobs, have made only a small difference, reducing dependency rates below 100%. The new surveys of Britain and Spain tell us whether attitudes and values have also changed faster than reality.

Trends in Britain

Comparisons between the British survey results and earlier studies (Tables 3.1–3.5) show that attitudes have changed dramatically in recent

Table 3.1 Responses to the core questions in Britain and Spain

	Britain			Spain		
	All	Men	Women	All	Men	Women
A. Even when women work, man is still main breadwinner						
% who agree/are indifferent	56	58	54	39	40	38
B. In high unemployment, wives should stay home						
% who agree/are indifferent	34	35	33	32	33	32
C. Ultimate responsibility for income-earning						
man/don't know	27	30	25	25	27	23
both equally	72	69	74	74	72	76
woman	1	1	1	1	1	1
D. Ultimate responsibility for housework						
man	1	2	1	2	3	2
both equally	70	72	68	74	72	76
woman/don't know	29	27	32	24	25	22
E. % who would still work even without economic necessity	60	62	58	50	52	48
F. Ideal family roles						
egalitarian	44	46	42	66	65	67
compromise	39	35	41	20	20	19
role segregation	17	19	17	14	15	14
H. Ideal family roles in absence of economic constraints						
egalitarian				65	64	66
compromise				18	18	18
role segregation				17	18	16
G. Main income-earner in your household						
self	50	69	33	40	65	18
both equally	11	12	10	13	12	13
partner	27	6	46	28	3	50
other person	12	14	11	19	20	19
Base = 100%	3651	1691	1960	1211	595	616

Notes: Tiny numbers of people giving a don't know response are grouped with the most conventional response for questions A–E. The 3% of respondents saying don't know or rejecting all three family models are excluded from all analyses of questions F and H. Question H was not asked in Britain.

Table 3.2 Norms on the sexual division of labour, Britain, mid-1980s

	Women working			Women not working	All women 20–59	All men 20–59
	Full-time	*Part-time*	*All*			
The female partner should be ultimately responsible for housework						
% agreeing	44	74	59	81	67	65
The male partner should be ultimately responsible for breadwinning						
% agreeing	30	61	44	70	54	59
I'm not against women working but the man should still be the main bread-winner in the family						
% agreeing or indifferent	39	70	58	64	60	56
In times of high unemployment married women should stay at home						
% agreeing or indifferent	25	35	30	48	38	46

Sources: Hakim and Jacobs (1997: Table 3) and Tam (1997: Tables 7.4a and 7.4b), reporting analyses of 1986 and 1987 SCELI data for men and women aged 20–59 years.

decades in one respect: most people now reject rigid role segregation in the family and a sex-role ideology that allocates the income-earning role *exclusively* to men and the housekeeping role *exclusively* to women (questions C and D in Table 3.1). By the start of the twenty-first century, this sort of inflexible sexual division of labour was endorsed by minorities of one-third of men and women aged 16 and over. Compared with the mid-1980s, there has been a *massive* change in attitudes towards the sexual division of labour in the family. In 1999, only about one-fifth of adults aged 20–59 accept the idea of ultimate responsibilities for income-earning and for housekeeping being allocated by sex, compared to between one-half and two-thirds of adults interviewed by the SCELI surveys 15 years previously (Table 3.2). This is a major change in sex-role ideology in a very short time.

However, widespread rejection of rigid role segregation has not led people to accept a new model of fully symmetrical sex-roles, with both husband and wife jointly responsible for income-earning and domestic work on a day-to-day basis. Rather, the boundary line between the two roles has become blurred, there is majority acceptance that each partner can and should substitute for the other, *in extremis*, and agreement that the sexual division of labour in the family needs to operate with a large degree of flexibility in the modern world. This is demonstrated by the fact that there has been only a trivially small decline in support for the idea that men *should be* the main breadwinner, normally, and that women are in practice secondary earners (question A). In 1999 over half of all adults accept this idea (54% of women and 58% of men), compared to 60% of women and 56% of men accepting it in the mid-1980s (Tables 3.1 and 3.2) – effectively no change at all.

Other attitudes are consistent with this picture. A three-quarters majority of couples of working age continue to regard the husband as principal income-earner and the wife as secondary earner, if she works at all (question G in Table 3.1). Only 10% of couples, on average, claim they are both jointly responsible for income-earning, a proportion that varies little across social class and age groups in Britain. Role-reversal, with the wife as the main breadwinner, seems to be on the increase, with about 10% of couples of working age reporting it. But it appears often to be a temporary situation rather than a permanent and chosen arrangement, as it is often associated with the male partner's unemployment, redundancy or early retirement (voluntary or involuntary).

Comparisons of 1983 and 1987 Eurobarometer data for Britain (Table 3.3) with the 1999 survey, using an identical question (F1), showed that over the last two decades support for the egalitarian symmetrical roles family model first rose, then fell slightly. Support for the role-segregated family has fallen slowly. It is the compromise model, with a primary earner husband and a secondary earner wife who retains the main responsibility for children and domestic work, *not* the egalitarian model, that attracted growing support in the 1990s, and reversed the small decline in the 1980s. It is notable that support for the egalitarian model grew only within the young and highly idealistic 16–24 years age group of women, but not men. Compared with the 1980s, support for the family with complete role segregation declined in all age groups, with support transferred to the compromise model instead.

However, these results depend on the question about family models being asked in the somewhat biased form of the Eurobarometer, with the egalitarian model always listed first (F1). When the order is reversed, to list the role-segregated family first (F2), there is an even greater decline in support for the egalitarian model in 1999 as compared with 1987, little change in support for the role-segregated model, and a substantial increase in support for the compromise model (Table 3.3). After combining the two sets of responses to question F, there seems to be no change in support for

Table 3.3 Responses to the two versions of question F on family models

			Preferred model of the family			
			Egalitarian	Compromise	Role segregation	Base = 100%
All persons	1983		39	37	24	NS
	1987		49	32	19	NS
	1999	F1	47	39	14	1791
		F2	40	38	22	1727
	Total	F	44	39	18	3518
All men	1999	F1	48	37	15	901
		F2	44	33	23	727
	Total	F	46	35	19	1628
All women	1999	F1	46	41	13	890
		F2	38	42	20	999
	Total	F	42	41	17	1890
Men aged 16–24		F1	58	35	7	108
		F2	62	24	14	100
	Total	F	60	30	10	208
Women aged 16–24		F1	83	14	3	101
		F2	50	29	21	121
	Total	F	65	22	13	222
Men aged 25–39		F1	50	44	6	249
		F2	51	29	20	197
	Total	F	51	37	12	446
Women aged 25–39		F1	51	40	9	241
		F2	40	44	16	299
	Total	F	45	42	13	540
Men aged 40–54		F1	55	35	10	239
		F2	38	39	23	182
	Total	F	48	36	16	421
Women aged 40–54		F1	49	44	7	249
		F2	36	47	17	246
	Total	F	42	46	12	495
Men aged 55 +		F1	36	35	29	305
		F2	35	37	28	248
	Total	F	35	36	29	553
Women aged 55 +		F1	29	48	23	299
		F2	33	40	27	333
	Total	F	31	44	25	633

Notes: Eurobarometer data for Britain in 1983 and 1987 covers people aged 18 and over, whereas British survey data for 1999 covers people aged 16 and over. The Eurobarometer question corresponds to question F1 in the 1999 survey. Percentages exclude people not choosing any of the three family models, 3% in all surveys.

the role-segregated model of the family in Britain; all the change over 1987–99 has been away from the egalitarian model of symmetrical roles towards the compromise model (Table 3.3).

Work commitment has generally been measured through a 'lottery win' style question that asks whether people would still do productive work if the basic economic necessity to earn an income were removed (question E in Table 3.1). The question was first used in the USA in 1953, and has been included in several surveys since then, documenting a slow decline in work commitment since the Second World War (Morse and Weiss, 1955; Vecchio, 1980). A similar question has been used in British surveys since Warr's 1981 survey (Warr, 1982; Gallie and White, 1993; Jowell *et al.*, 1997), with the exact wording varying from one survey to another, as shown in the notes to Table 3.4.

Work commitment is strongly correlated with level of education and occupational grade. Work commitment is always highest in professional and managerial occupations, in specialist jobs that require many years of education and/or on the job training to develop skills. Work commitment is always lowest among female part-time workers and in unskilled occupations (Rose, 1994; Hakim, 1996a: 107–9). As the occupational structure shifts upwards over time, with more higher grade and skilled jobs and fewer unskilled jobs, we could expect work commitment to rise steadily in the long run in modern societies. This is certainly the pattern among women, who recently obtained a dramatically larger share of professional occupations after they gained equal access to the educational system. In contrast, there is a long term, slow but steady decline in work commitment among male full-time workers, in the USA and in Britain (Table 3.4). Since professional and occupational upgrading is common among men as well as women, we must look for an explanation outside the labour market.

Part of the explanation lies in the changing age structure of the workforce. Work commitment is always highest among young people just starting out in formal employment, who have everything to prove (Table 3.5). Work commitment declines steadily over the lifecycle, and is lowest among people close to retirement age. As more young men are kept out of the workforce by an extended period of full-time education, the overall level of work commitment among men is reduced. However, this cannot be the whole story, because Table 3.5 suggests that work commitment has also declined among prime age men, while it is rising among prime age women.

The decline in male work commitment and the rise in female work commitment indicate the process of equalization of lifestyles and values among men and women in modern society. Employment and other activities in the public sphere are increasingly prominent in women's lives, replacing the exclusive focus on home and family forced upon women by

**Table 3.4 Trends in non-financial work commitment, Britain, 1981–
1999: percentage saying they would continue to work in the
absence of financial need**

	1981	*1984–5*	*1989*	*1992*	*1999*
All workers	66	70	74	68	63
Women					
All working	58	66	76	67	67
Full-time	65	71	77	69	68
Part-time	54	56	74	64	66
Men					
All working	69	74	72	68	60
Full-time	69	75	72	69	60
Part-time	55	45	80	58	73

Notes: Question wordings vary between surveys, as follows.
1981: 'Considering both kinds of work, that is not only being employed by someone else but
also being self-employed, if you were to get enough money to live as comfortably as you
would like for the rest of your life, would you continue to work (not necessarily in your
present job) or would you stop working?' For non-working people the end of the question
was modified to ask 'would you want to work somewhere or would you want to remain
without a job?'
1984–85 and 1989: 'If without having to work you had what you would regard as a
reasonable living income, would you still prefer to have a paid job, or wouldn't you bother?'
Data for employees working 10 + hours a week.
1992: 'If you were to get enough money to live as comfortably as you would like for the rest
of your life, would you continue to work, not necessarily in your present job, or would you
stop working?' Data for people aged 20–59 years.
1999: 'If without having to work you had what you would regard as a reasonable living
income, would you still prefer to have a paid job, or wouldn't you bother?' Data for people
aged 20–59 excluding full-time students.
Source: Hakim (1996a: Table 4.7), reporting the results of several independent national
surveys of Britain, updated with the 1999 British survey.

discriminatory practices such as the marriage bar. There is a contrary process
operating among men, who find it has become socially acceptable for them
to have competing life interests outside their employment: family time,
leisure activities, sports and hobbies are becoming more central to men's
lives. Women are learning to work, and men are learning to play. Levels of
work commitment have already been equalized in the workforce, and they
may soon be equalized in the population of working age as a whole.[1]

Table 3.5 Non-financial work commitment within the workforce by age, Britain, 1992 and 1999

	Age in years					
	20–30	*30–40*	*40–50*	*50–60*	*Total*	*Base*
1992						
Men working full-time	75	72	64	55	69	1599
Women working full-time	77	69	65	54	69	873
Women working part-time	78	71	57	46	64	635
Men working part-time	..	..	..	..	58	48
1999						
Men working full-time	66	61	59	48	60	894
Women working full-time	67	73	71	59	68	509
Women working part-time	87	70	51	64	66	395
Men working part-time	82	..	..	70	73	37

Notes: The percentage choosing to continue working, even without financial need, is shown for each cell of the table. The questions asked in 1992 and 1999 differ slightly; see note to Table 3.4.
Source: Hakim (1996a: Table 4.8), reporting results of a 1992 survey in Britain, updated with the 1999 British survey.

These long-term changes in life priorities in modern societies have been documented and theorized by Inglehart using a series of World Values Surveys (WVS) in 1970, 1981, 1990–93 and 2000, supplemented by Eurobarometer data for 1970–94 and other datasets (Inglehart, 1977, 1990, 1997; Abramson and Inglehart, 1995; Inglehart *et al.*, 1998). In brief, Inglehart argues that long-term prosperity and security produce a change of emphasis in value systems, away from security and survival towards individual autonomy, diversity, self-expression and individual choice. This suggests a polarization of work commitment across the occupational system, with work commitment remaining stable, or possibly rising, in occupations that permit some individual autonomy and self-expression, and work commitment declining in routine manual jobs, especially when people have alternative life interests and leisure activities. Another factor is the trend towards dual-earner households, which must reduce the breadwinner pressures on men, and increase them among women.

Responses to the question on work commitment (E) are also susceptible to a social desirability bias: the proportion stating they would always prefer a paid job in the absence of financial need remains steady at two-thirds of all men, even among inactive pensioners, a result that was also reported in 1981 (Warr, 1982; Hakim, 1996a: 103–9). Similarly, women who are not in the labour market often say they would prefer to have a paid job.

By the start of the twenty-first century, work commitment among men and women of working age had equalized – in fact, work commitment was slightly higher among women than among men (Tables 3.4 and 3.5). However, work commitment continued to be shaped by women's sex-role ideology. For example, work commitment declines to minimal levels among inactive women who prefer the role-segregated model of the family and believe the income-earning role falls always to men – that is, women with well-defined alternative life interests.

The impact of equal opportunities policies and the rhetoric of equal opportunities is seen in the substantial decline in support for a weak version of the marriage bar (question B in Table 3.1). The marriage bar was the rule, jointly enforced by employers and trade unions for most of the twentieth century, in North America and Western Europe, that women had to resign from their jobs upon marriage. The marriage bar was most common in white-collar work, especially teaching and government service. It only became unlawful in Britain after the Sex Discrimination Act 1975. Most other European countries that practised the marriage bar (formally or informally) also abolished it as recently as this, or when prompted to do so by European Union Directives. Question B proposes that in times of high unemployment, men should have priority over married women in access to jobs. In the mid-1980s, 38% of women and 46% of men of working age (20–59 years) still accepted this idea (Table 3.2). By 1999, the proportion had fallen to about one-quarter of people aged 20–59. This proportion does not vary between people who see themselves as primary earners or as secondary earners. Women who regard themselves as secondary earners are just as likely as men to feel that men should have priority over wives in access to jobs, because their own well-being depends on the employment of their spouse. However, there are sharp differences between women working full-time and women who are out of the labour market: 16% versus 33% respectively support the idea, with female part-time workers falling between these two extremes, the same pattern as was observed in the mid-1980s.

An apparently new development, that was not observed in the mid-1980s SCELI results, is that differences in attitudes between working and non-working men are almost as big as, and sometimes bigger than differences between working and non-working women. The polarization of women's attitudes seems to be echoed in a similar polarization of men's attitudes at the start of the twenty-first century.

Trends in Spain

Since 1975, Spanish social scientists have been monitoring changing social and political attitudes through a series of national surveys carried out by the Centro de Investigaciónes Sociológicas (CIS) in Madrid. Many of the CIS surveys include questions from other European surveys, including the Eurobarometer series. In 1990 and 1994, CIS surveys on attitudes to the family included the Eurobarometer question used in the 1980s (see Table 1.1), allowing us to track changes over the period 1987–99 (Table 3.6).

It appears that attitudes changed rapidly after 1986, when Spain joined the European Union. Surveys done in 1980 and 1981 show that a 61% majority of adults were opposed to the employment of mothers with small children, and 40% were opposed to married women's employment under any circumstances (Martínez Quintana, 1992: 18–20, quoted by Tobío, 2001). By 1987, Spain ranked second only to Denmark and ahead of Britain and Portugal, in espousing the egalitarian model of family roles. In 1983, Greece ranked first in the EU on this measure (see Table 1.1). This prompted the idea that the modern egalitarian symmetrical family is really a reversion to a pre-industrial model, when dual-earner families were an economic necessity (Hakim, 1996a: 93, 2000a: 87). As several scholars have pointed out, the single-earner family is a modern invention of relatively short duration, and it is characteristic of rich families or societies (Bernard, 1981; Rogers, 1981; Davis, 1984; Seccombe, 1993: 202–9; Janssens, 1998), so the label of 'traditional' family is entirely inappropriate.

The 1990 and 1994 CIS surveys suggest gradual change in views on the ideal family model up to the mid-1990s, with a sudden further change in the late 1990s, away from the role segregation model towards the egalitarian model.[2] Throughout this period, the compromise model attracted an unvarying low level of support, in all age groups, at all levels of education, among housewives as well as working women (Table 3.6). This is because part-time jobs are still so rare in Spain that the compromise family model is not a realistic option to the same extent as in Britain.

In sum, the results of the 1999 survey are in line with trends already established in other surveys in the 1980s and 1990s in Spain. Nonetheless, it is remarkable that Spaniards endorse the egalitarian symmetrical roles model even more than do Britons. Questions F and H refer to equality in the response attracting most respondents, so there appears to be a substantial political correctness bias in responses.

Table 3.6 Ideal family model: trends in Spain 1987–1999

	Ideal model of the family			
	Egalitarian	Compromise	Role segregation	Base = 100%
1987 – all	50	20	30	NS
1990 CIS				
All 18 +	47	24	29	2361
Education:				
some primary	30	24	46	590
primary complete	42	26	32	924
secondary education	64	??	14	609
higher education	71	19	10	235
All women	51	22	27	1223
16–32 years	75	17	8	381
33–49 years	50	25	25	345
50 + years	32	24	44	497
Working women	71	22	7	419
Housewives	35	24	41	673
1994 CIS				
All persons	55	22	23	2391
men 15–24	60	28	10	NS
women 15–24	73	20	5	NS
men 25 +	50	21	22	NS
women 25 +	55	20	25	NS
1999				
All – question F	66	20	14	1172
All – question H	65	18	17	1159

Notes: All percentages have been recalculated to exclude the 3–5% don't knows. In some reports, base numbers are not stated.

Sources: 1990 and 1994 CIS survey data derived or recalculated from Table 15 in Cruz Cantero and Cobo Bedia (1991); Table 29 in Cruz Cantero (1995); Table 4.27 in Andrés Orizo (1996); Table 3.7 in Prior Ruiz (1997); and Table 4.5 in Marí-Klose and Nos Colom (1999).

  This pattern of Spaniards being more enthusiastically modern than Britons, at least in stated values, is repeated in responses to other questions as well. On the face of it, Spaniards have adopted a model of the family that has so far been championed in Scandinavia rather than in the Mediterranean countries.

As in Britain, a three-quarters majority of men and women believe that both partners share responsibility for income-earning and housework *in extremis* (Table 3.1). A minority of men and women agree that even when women have jobs, men still remain the main breadwinner: 39% compared to 56% in Britain. Only one-third agree that in times of high unemployment, married women should stay at home and leave the jobs for men. This weak version of the marriage bar received marginally less support than in Britain. As noted in Chapter 1, Spain has had one of the highest unemployment rates in Western Europe for many years, so opinion on this question should be strongly informed by the reality of men and women competing for scarce jobs. Given that the unemployment rate for women is double the rate among men in Spain (see Table 1.4), there is evidence of informal barriers to the employment of women generally and married women in particular, despite attitudes to the contrary.

Question G on the principal income-earner was presented as an opinion question, and analyses of the results presented below confirm that is what it is. In Spain, unmarried sons and daughters continue to live with their parents in their twenties and even into their thirties, especially if they remain in full-time education. This explains why 20% of survey respondents said some other person was the main earner in their household, twice as many as in Britain, where young people leave home early to set up separate households, alone or with friends. Among married and cohabiting couples aged 18+, four-fifths of husbands and wives said the husband was the main breadwinner – slightly higher proportions than in Britain. However, 15% of couples in both countries said they were both equally responsible for income-earning. This is due in part to the large number of small family businesses in Spain, which rely on the work of both spouses for success. So Spain offers many cases of the traditional dual-earner couple who have now acquired the new ideological label of the 'egalitarian' family.

Work commitment is lower in Spain than in Britain (Table 3.1). This is probably due to the different occupational structure, with a much smaller proportion of people in professional and managerial occupations than in Britain.[3] As noted earlier, work commitment is always lower in unskilled occupations. Another factor may be the impact of decades of high unemployment. However, unemployment usually strengthens work commitment, rather than weakening it. There appears to be no political correctness bias in responses to this question, because the word equality does not feature in it.

These attitudes are voiced equally by men and women in Spain, and sex differences are generally non-existent or small in all the survey results, just as in Britain. Overall, the survey results for Spain indicate a substantial political correctness bias. Spain has one of the lowest female employment rates in the EU, and one of the highest female unemployment rates. Social scientists regularly conclude that domestic work and childcare remain women's principal obligations, even when they have a job, while employment remains an obligation for men, with domestic activities an optional extra (Tobío, 2001). Yet Spaniards proclaim their preference for the symmetrical roles family model even more strongly than in Britain.

Political Correctness Bias

It can be argued that people are illogical and muddled, often hold mutually incompatible or contradictory ideas and live with the contradictions by drawing fine distinctions and compartmentalizing ideas. However, the implausibility of the Spanish results led us to consult several Spanish sociologists with expertise in this field for possible explanations. The immediate and invariable reaction was that Spaniards are *au courant* with modern ideas; they certainly know the response they should give to such questions. Spanish colleagues pointed out that 'equality' is the new, modern, post-democracy ideology which everyone espouses in Spain. Everyone pays lip service to the idea that men and women are equal, that class differences are no longer important, that 'even gypsies' should be treated as equal. The post-democracy rebound in public values was strengthened after Spain joined the European Union in 1986, prompting greater eagerness to embrace European fashions, in ideology and politics as in other spheres. However, all our informants pointed out that egalitarian attitudes and values have little relation to actual behaviour in Spain. It appears that the word 'equal' which is used in several of the core survey questions is no longer a factual descriptive term but has acquired enormous value-laden connotations in Spain.

Methodological research shows a small social desirability bias in responses to factual or behavioural questions. For example, there is a tendency for people to under-report unemployment spells and drink-driving offences, to over-report voting and library use, and to exaggerate the status or grade of one's own occupation or of a husband's occupation (in proxy interviews with wives). But the scope for a social desirability bias is much greater in questions about attitudes and values, where there are no simple objective tests of validity (Turner and Martin, 1984).

Of course, the survey questions themselves can be perceived to suggest the type of answer that is expected. For example, it is difficult to collect information on people's 'fear of crime' without immediately suggesting to them, through survey questions, that fear of crime is a public issue and is sufficiently widespread for there to be national enquiries on the problem.

This difficulty arises mostly with closed questions, which ask people to choose between a number of predetermined responses – as in all our core questions. For example, the British Crime Survey (BCS) finds that one-third of respondents state they have a fear of crime. It is thought that in reality the level is less than half this proportion. The question used in the BCS sensitizes people to the issue and seems to legitimize expressions of worrying about crime. In this case, the problem is labelled an acquiescence problem: people feel they should give the expected answer.

Nonattitudes are another problem in attitude research. Nonattitudes are created when people select an answer from those offered, either at random or in line with what they believe is expected, even though they have little or no interest in the question, are only guessing at the meaning of a question, or lack knowledge about basic facts of a question. Nonattitudes pose real problems for research on politics because many people have no real interest in political issues, but provide responses either as a courtesy to the interviewer or to avoid the appearance of ignorance (Smith, 1984). But this should not be a problem for our research topics, as they are close to everyday life and decisions people have to make about their own lives.

The greatest problem with responses to attitude surveys – such as ours – is the social desirability bias, or what we shall refer to as the political correctness bias. The social desirability bias is a tendency for people to give a favourable picture of themselves, to enhance positive characteristics and minimize characteristics that may be perceived negatively (DeMaio, 1984). Some methodologists treat the problem as a personality trait: some respondents need to conform to social standards and thus give the 'right' answer. These studies attribute the political correctness bias to acquiescence, conformity and need for social approval, in some combination. However, most of the evidence points to the problem being a characteristic of certain questions or attitude items, possibly combined with certain respondent characteristics. The problem is magnified in face-to-face interviews, which were used in our two surveys. Methodological studies indicate that if an activity or behaviour is perceived as socially desirable, people's reports of engaging in that activity are doubled; that women are more susceptible than men to the political correctness bias; that the bias is associated with age; and that there is a weak relationship with education, income and occupational status (DeMaio, 1984). One problem with this literature is that it rarely distinguishes between what is 'desirable to me' versus what is 'desirable to society', and does not tell us which of the two has the larger impact on reported attitudes and behaviour. Another problem is that almost all this research focuses on Anglo-Saxon cultures. There is evidence that some cultures are especially prone to the courtesy bias, which leads respondents to say what they believe the questioner wants to hear, out of politeness, to acquiesce with statements presented to them and to offer socially desirable responses. The courtesy bias is a special problem in Asian cultures (Jones, 1983) and in Hispanic cultures (Marín and Marín, 1991).

There is no standard method for detecting a political correctness bias in survey results. It is usually revealed by results that are puzzling or implausible. One example is the unbelievable results of surveys carried out in East Germany shortly after the Berlin Wall came down. The parallel development of the 'two Germanies' from the Second World War up to 1989 was a natural experiment (Hakim, 2000b: 135–7) that attracted many comparative studies in the 1990s. Surveys carried out in spring 1990 suggested that 40 years of socialism had left no discernible trace in East Germany: there was hardly any difference between East and West Germans in the acceptance of democratic norms and values. As Kuechler (1998: 192–3) points out, several interpretations were possible: access to West German TV from the 1970s onwards had neutralized the effects of political socialization in school and workplace, East Germans had internalized Western political values in just four months, or East Germans were smart enough to give the politically correct answers, as they may have done for decades under socialism. On balance, the last explanation seems the most plausible. This example suggests that people can respond very quickly indeed to perceived changes in socially desirable attitudes and values. Spain experienced a dramatic change from Franco's conservative dictatorship to full democracy under a reinstated monarch, with all that entails in terms of changes in attitudes and values. It appears that new values have been adopted just as quickly as in East Germany. There is therefore good reason to treat the Spanish data as subject to a greater political correctness bias than the British data.

Spaniards themselves are aware of having a 'blind eye', or what one social scientist calls an ostrich mentality: anything that is prohibited simply does not exist ('no existe lo que está prohibido', de Miguel, 1974: 96). One example is that most demographers failed to understand that the decline in birthrates in Spain in the 1960s and 1970s, which occurred despite falling ages at marriage, was due to the adoption of modern, reliable methods of contraception, such as the pill. Contraception was banned by the Catholic church and therefore could not exist. Only a few social scientists insisted that the new, efficacious methods were in fact being eagerly adopted by Spanish women (de Miguel, 1974). Another example is the decision by the National Institute of Statistics to suspend the collection and publication of earnings data by sex from 1977 onwards. As explained in the 1981 report, disaggregation by sex was no longer needed, because the 1980 Workers' Statute made sex discrimination unlawful.[4] Studies of the sex differential in earnings in the 1980s and 1990s had to devise ways of getting round this fundamental gap in national statistics until the problem was remedied in the 1990s (Alcobendas Tirado, 1983: 139–48; Peinado López, 1988: 143–86; Prior Ruiz, 1997: 203; Alba, 2000: 108–115). However, many government studies continue to simply ignore the issue (Marí-Klose and Nos Colom, 1999). Spanish studies of women's position in the labour force and in society often note that there is a gap between stated attitudes and behaviour, which seems almost to be taken for granted.

One illustration of the gap between attitudes and behaviour in Spain comes from a 1996 Eurobarometer survey. Although two-thirds of Spaniards in our survey claimed to prefer symmetrical family roles, the European Commission's survey showed that, in practice, Spain along with Greece ranked lowest in the EU on equality of the actual division of household tasks: only one in ten women and men reported a 50–50 sharing of such tasks. In contrast, the gap is relatively small in Britain, as one-third of women and almost half of men reported an equal sharing of household tasks (European Commission, 1998: 13–14), figures that are much closer to support for the egalitarian ideal in Table 3.1.

The political correctness bias is best illustrated in relation to question F on ideal family models. There are two features of this item which would prompt politically correct responses. First, the most popular response to the question refers to *equality* (in English) and the *equitable* division of labour (in Spanish). In contrast, the two other responses do not include any value-laden terms which invite automatic acquiescence. References to equality and equitableness are likely to provoke automatic support. Second, there is evidence from the British survey that reversing the list of responses has a substantial impact on replies. (Unfortunately the two versions of the response list were not separately coded for Spain.) In line with methodological studies of the political correctness bias, we find that question F2 has the greatest impact on the replies of young women (Table 3.3).

Reversing the list of responses from F1 to F2 has a visible impact on results: the proportion choosing the role-segregated arrangement increases by 7–8% among men and women (Table 3.3), with an equivalent fall in support for the other two models. Among women, the biggest fall is in support for the egalitarian model, from 46% in the Eurobarometer version (F1) to 38% with the reversed list (F2). In general, most of the changes are at the two extremes, because the compromise model does not change its position as the middle response in both F1 and F2.

Women are more sensitive than men to the reversed listing of responses, but age is also important. People aged 55 and over have more fixed and stable views. Responses change substantially in all other age groups, generally by 10 to 17 percentage points. However, the group whose responses are most affected by the reversed response list is young women aged 16–24, where support for the egalitarian model of the family falls by 33 percentage points, with increases of 15 to 18 percentage points in support for the other two models (Table 3.3). Thus it is responses among young women that are most vacillating and irresolute, and it is young women who display the largest political correctness bias, possibly due to the impact of feminism.[5]

The methodological experiment with questions F and H in Spain sheds no light on the political correctness bias, and is discussed in Chapter 2.

There is no standard method for measuring and correcting the political correctness bias. Except for Table 3.3, all results reported in this book relate to merged data for questions F1 and F2 together. However, it seems clear that future surveys should minimize the bias in responses by using version F2 exclusively (see Table 2.1) rather than a combination of F1 and F2. Second, references to equality must be removed from all responses. This could be achieved by rephrasing the egalitarian model as: 'A family where the two partners both have demanding jobs and where each partner does half the housework and half the care of the children.' This reformulation should reduce the problem of biased response, but will not eliminate it.

It seems clear that the survey results include a political correctness bias: a large bias in the Spanish survey and a smaller one in Britain. This must be taken into account in all our interpretations of the findings. In effect, the proportions choosing the egalitarian symmetrical roles model of the family are exaggerated relative to the other two options.

Although it is impossible to eliminate the bias from the main body of our research results, we can estimate its impact on the distribution of preferences in the two countries. People who claim to prefer the egalitarian model of family roles but accept, or are ambivalent in response to question A are effectively negating their professed sex-role ideology by accepting that men should always remain the main breadwinner even when women have a job. People in this category can be subtracted from the group supporting the egalitarian family model and added to the compromise family model instead, as a more realistic statement of their preferences and values. If we make this adjustment separately for men, for women and for all persons, the distributions of preferences are changed as follows.

For all adults aged 16 and over who have completed their full-time education in Britain, the original distribution:

Men	45% – 36% – 19%
Women	41% – 42% – 17%
All	43% – 39% – 18%

is adjusted to:

Men	26% – 55% – 19%
Women	25% – 58% – 17%
All	25% – 57% – 18%

For married and cohabiting couples aged 20–59 who have completed their full-time education, the original distribution:

Husbands	46% – 39% – 15%
Wives	38% – 48% – 13%
All couples	42% – 44% – 14%

is adjusted to:

Husbands	28% – 57% – 15%
Wives	27% – 60% – 13%
All couples	27% – 59% – 14%

After the adjustment, there is a clear-cut majority preference for the compromise model, irrespective of the population base. For Spain, the same method of adjustment produces much smaller changes due to the systematic bias in responses to all the core questions. For adults aged 18 and over in Spain who have completed their full-time education, the original distribution:

Men	63% – 21% – 16%
Women	66% – 20% – 14%
All	65% – 20% – 15%

is adjusted to:

Men	48% – 36% – 16%
Women	49% – 37% – 14%
All	49% – 36% – 15%

For married and cohabiting couples aged 20–59 who have completed their full-time education, the original distribution:

Husbands	70% – 19% – 11%
Wives	73% – 17% – 10%
All couples	72% – 18% – 10%

is adjusted to:

Husbands	55% – 34% – 11%
Wives	59% – 31% – 10%
All couples	57% – 32% – 11%.

Even after the adjustment, the proportion of Spaniards choosing the egalitarian family model is twice as high as in Britain.

Patriarchy Index

Questions A and B were selected from a large number of survey attitude statements on sex-role ideology because they offer separate and independently meaningful indicators. Because they are so highly correlated in the Spanish dataset, we decided to combine them into a single measure which can broadly be described as a patriarchy index.

Patriarchy is a feminist concept that has been given many different meanings (Lerner, 1986: 239; Walby, 1990; Hakim, 1996a: 5–13). We use the term to refer to the institutionalization of male dominance over women in society as a whole as well as in the family (Hakim, 2000a: 281). It is important to note that male dominance remains acceptable to the majority of women in modern society, because the majority of women obtain direct and concrete benefits from it, which presumably outweigh the disbenefits (Hakim, 1996a: 113–18, 2000a: 281–3).

Question A is an indicator of acceptance of patriarchy in the family in that it insists on men's main breadwinner role (and the informal power that often goes with it) even when women have paid employment. It suggests that a wife's earnings should have only a minor impact on male dominance in the family, and underlines women's right to financial dependence.

Question B is an indicator of acceptance of patriarchy in public life – specifically in the labour market and, by implication, other public spheres such as politics. If men have priority for jobs in the labour market, they will always hold dominant positions in the workforce – and hence also in politics and public life more generally.

Admittedly, these two items provide a limited index of patriarchy. There are other aspects of the concept that are not covered. Nonetheless, the index is useful in summarizing two attitudes that provoked relatively strong reactions in both countries. With the five-point scales reduced to two codes (accept/indifferent or reject), gamma values average .90 for Spain (.89 for men and .90 for women) and .80 for Britain (.86 for men and .75 for women). The two indicators are strongly associated.

The patriarchy index reveals remarkable similarities in values in Britain and Spain (Table 3.7), and once again there are virtually no sex differences in either country, in either the younger or older generations. One-quarter (28%) of Spaniards accept patriarchy in private and public life; half (53%) reject patriarchy completely; a bare one-fifth (19%) are ambivalent, usually because they regard men as retaining the main breadwinner role even if

Table 3.7 Patriarchal attitudes in Britain and Spain by age

Attitude to patriarchy	Britain			Spain		
	<40	*40 +*	*All*	*<40*	*40 +*	*All*
Accept patriarchy	17	37	29	15	36	28
Ambivalent:						
only accept private						
patriarchy	25	28	27	11	13	13
only accept public						
patriarchy	3	6	5	5	7	6
Reject patriarchy	55	29	39	69	44	53
Base = 100%	1454	2193	3647	531	680	1211

women work. In Britain, two-fifths (39%) of adults reject patriarchy, one-quarter (29%) fully accept it and one-third are ambivalent, almost always because they accept that men remain the main breadwinner in a family, but no longer accept that this allows men to have priority for jobs. Spaniards are most likely to reject patriarchy. It appears that equal opportunities legislation has had a profound impact on values in both countries. Hardly anyone accepts the weak version of the now-unlawful marriage bar in the labour market, even though the idea of men as main breadwinners is still persuasive for many people.[6]

In both countries there are sharp differences between the older and younger generations (Table 3.7), and acceptance of patriarchy declined by similar amounts across generations. Older people in Britain are more likely to accept patriarchy (37%) than to reject it (29%). The majority of younger people reject patriarchy (55%) and only 17% accept it. Similarly, the great majority of younger people in Spain reject patriarchy (69%) and very few (15%) accept it, with few ambivalents. However, even the older generation in Spain is more likely to reject patriarchy (44%) than to accept it (36%), an attitude which is likely to have been developed recently. If changes between the two age cohorts are taken as a rough indicator of trends over time, there is some polarization of attitudes in that the ambivalent middle group declines between the older and younger generations: by 6 percentage points in Britain and by 4 percentage points in Spain. In both countries, younger people have more definite views.

Ideal Family Model

Question F on ideal models of the family is also an indicator of sex-role preferences, as each model makes a clear statement about the respective roles of spouses and partners. As noted above, responses are coloured by the political correctness bias, especially in Spain, but we still expect some degree of consistency with attitudes to patriarchy, given the way the index is constructed. Consistency will not be perfect, as the two variables measure different things: the patriarchy index focuses on *public* values, what is good for society in general, while the ideal family model question focuses on *personal* preferences, what is desired by the particular individual for themselves. As Hofstede (1980: 21, 1991) and Hakim (2000a: 75) point out, it is necessary to distinguish between *choice* and *approval*, between personal goals and public beliefs, between what is personally desired and what is desirable in society in general. This logical distinction might not be spontaneously articulated by many people, but they can still apply the distinction in their responses and in their thinking.

Overall, there is substantial consistency between the two values in both countries (Table 3.8). In line with preference theory, consistency is greater in the younger generation and, once more, there are no sex differences of any consequence (Table 3.9). The majority of men and women who personally prefer role segregation in the family, especially older people, also accept patriarchal values, although substantial minorities (23% in Britain, 15% in Spain) reject them and many more are ambivalent (Table 3.8). The majority of people who claim to prefer symmetrical family roles reject patriarchal values, and among younger people two-thirds or more reject patriarchy. These patterns are duplicated in the subgroup of married and cohabiting couples, who do not display any greater ideological consistency than the general population.

However, there are minorities whose private preference is at odds with their support for public values. In Britain almost half and in Spain one-third of those who report their personal ideal family model as the egalitarian version positively accept or are ambivalent on patriarchy. In the younger generations, one-third of Britons and one-quarter of Spaniards effectively deny their claimed preference for the symmetrical roles model by also endorsing values that treat men as main breadwinners (who may thus have priority for jobs) and women as secondary earners. Possibly, this conflict is created in part by the political correctness bias, but the size of the contradictory groups is still notable. There is no equivalent contradiction among other people: those who accept that egalitarian values should operate in society at large even though they personally prefer some degree of role specialization in the family.

Table 3.8 Patriarchy and ideal family model in Britain and Spain

	Ideal model of the family			
Attitude to patriarchy	*Egalitarian*	*Compromise*	*Role segregation*	*Total*
Britain				
Accept patriarchy	17	31	52	29
Ambivalent	30	40	25	34
Reject patriarchy	53	29	23	37
Base = 100%	914	1005	413	2333
Spain				
Accept patriarchy	13	45	62	27
Ambivalent	18	19	23	19
Reject patriarchy	69	36	15	54
Base = 100%	702	220	163	1085

Note: Data for people aged 16 and over who have completed their full-time education.

In sum, the group choosing the egalitarian model of the family displays the lowest level of ideological consistency, in line with our conclusion that the size of this group is probably inflated by a political correctness bias. In line with preference theory, the younger generation in both countries displays markedly higher levels of ideological consistency.

The larger British survey permits more detailed analysis. It shows that the men and women choosing the compromise arrangement are the most eclectic and discerning in their views. On the question of men always remaining the main breadwinner, they are very similar to the group choosing role segregation, with two-thirds or more agreeing this is men's role in the family. On the question of men's priority access to jobs, they fall closer to the group choosing the egalitarian family model, as two-thirds or more reject this idea. The group choosing the compromise model is relatively large, at two-fifths of all adults, so their finely judged views have a substantial impact on results for Britain as a whole, both on this topic, and in many other analyses. These results confirm that the group choosing the compromise family model falls ideologically half-way between the two extreme groups.

Table 3.9 Patriarchy and sex-role preferences by age, Britain and Spain

Ideal model of the family	*Attitude to patriarchy*			*Base*
	Accept	*Ambivalent*	*Reject*	*= 100%*
Britain				
Under 40 years				
symmetrical roles	10	21	69	635
differentiated roles	23	37	40	623
total	16	29	55	1258
People aged 40 +				
symmetrical roles	22	35	43	796
differentiated roles	46	34	20	1298
total	37	35	28	2094
Spain				
Under 40 years				
symmetrical roles	11	14	76	341
differentiated roles	31	26	43	91
total	15	16	69	432
People aged 40 +				
symmetrical roles	16	21	63	362
differentiated roles	59	19	22	292
total	35	20	45	653

Note: Data for people aged 16 + /18 + who have completed their full-time education.

Work Commitment

The question on work commitment (E) is often interpreted as a measure of the work ethic. This concept has acquired a variety of ideological connotations, and is sometimes labelled the protestant work ethic, as if it were a peculiarly European trait. The work ethic is usually defined as a *moral* obligation to work in order to prove one's value to society. It is treated as a personal value, usually with positive connotations, rather than as an indicator of irrationality, for example. It is possible that the work commitment question could, fairly, be interpreted this way in the past, at least in relation to men. The substantial body of research now available on work orientations among women as well as men suggests that the 'moral obligation' interpretation is no longer appropriate. We prefer to read this question as an indicator of the social desirability of a paid job (or, more generally, any position in the public sphere), even in the absence of economic necessity. The exact reason for a job being socially desirable will vary from one person to another. For men, their occupation and job is often a central part of their identity and the loss of a job (due to unemployment, retirement or losing an election) may be bitterly regretted and resented. For many married women, a job is valued primarily because it gives them access to a social community outside the home, a place where they can meet people and be sociable, as well as earning some money and exercising their skills. Some people like a job because it helps to structure their time, and they have few or no other interests and hobbies. Others like a job because there is nowhere else to exercise certain specialist skills which they spent years of education and training to acquire. So the non-pecuniary value of employment can vary a good deal between people, and is often complex. We cannot assume that there is a single, universal and homogeneous work ethic value behind all responses that claim people would continue to do paid work even in the absence of economic necessity. However, it does seem fair to read such responses as indicating that a job or other activity in the public sphere forms a crucial part of personal identity and lifestyle, and hence would be pursued irrespective of financial reward.[7]

As noted earlier, work commitment declines gradually with age among men and women in western societies (Tables 3.5 and 3.10).[8] The marked sex differential in work commitment, and smaller differences between women working full-time and women working part-time still in evidence in a 1992 survey (Gallie and White, 1993; Gallie *et al.,* 1998: 189; Hakim, 1996a: 105) have now disappeared (Tables 3.4 and 3.5).[9] The key differences now are between women who have dropped out of the workforce (whether from a full-time or a part-time job) and women who persist with paid jobs (whether full-time, half-time or marginal jobs). The surveys provide clear evidence of women's increasing self-selection into employment according to work commitment. In Britain among women aged 20–59, 72% of the unemployed prefer paid work, 66% of working women, but only 39% of inactive women prefer a job in the absence of financial necessity. In Spain, 63% of working women, 47% of the unemployed and 41% of inactive women express commitment to paid employment. These results are consistent with other research showing the polarization of women's employment patterns over the lifecycle.

Table 3.10a Work commitment and ideal family model, Britain: percentage who prefer a paid job without financial need

		Ideal model of the family			
		Egalitarian	Compromise	Role segregation	All
All men		63	62	59	62
All women		68	56	38	58
Men	16–24	74	84	..	77
	25–44	64	62	65	63
	45–64	61	54	50	57
	65 +	61	69	62	64
Women	16–24	81	84	82	82
	25–44	74	62	44	65
	45–64	67	51	25	53
	65 +	42	47	34	42
Men in employment		62	61	54	61
Men not working		66	65	63	65
Women in employment		75	63	51	67
Women not working		56	48	32	47
Married women					
	20–29	70	65	56	66
	30–39	71	64	50	65
	40–49	73	51	26	55
	50–59	69	51	29	54
	all aged 20–59	71	57	38	60
Married men					
	20–29	56	67	84	63
	30–39	61	66	70	64
	40–49	63	66	50	62
	50–59	61	41	43	50
	all aged 20–59	61	60	56	60

Note: Data for people aged 16 and over who have completed their full-time education in the first part of the table, and married and cohabiting couples aged 20–59 who have completed their full-time education in the second part.

Table 3.10b Work commitment and ideal family model, Spain: percentage who prefer a paid job without financial need

		Symmetrical roles	*Differentiated roles*	*All*
		Ideal model of the family		
All men		50	55	51
All women		58	32	51
Men	18–39	51	56	52
	40 +	47	54	50
Women	18–39	63	36	57
	40 +	52	30	45
Men	in employment	49	57	51
	not working	56	44	52
Women	in employment	67	45	63
	not working	50	27	42

Note: Data for people aged 20–59, excluding students.

We expected sex-role preferences to be a strong determinant of work commitment. Women who prefer to be full-time homemakers supported financially by their spouse are more likely to seek an early marriage and unlikely to work after marriage unless economic necessity gives them little choice, and their employment is likely to consist of short-term jobs rather than long-term careers. Conversely, women who are committed to symmetrical family roles must also be committed to paid employment in the long term (Hakim, 2000a: 157–92). For men, there should be no association, since all three family models involve paid work for the husband. Role reversal marriages are as yet very rare indeed, even among couples where the wife has a higher status and higher paid occupation (McRae, 1986). Table 3.10 shows that these expectations are broadly met in Britain and Spain.

There is no difference between men and women in the proportion who claim they would prefer to have a paid job of some sort even in the absence of economic necessity – around 60% in Britain and 51% in Spain. These percentages are relatively high because people over the retirement age of 65 years, virtually all of whom have left the labour force, continue to say they like the idea of a job for social and other reasons, or perhaps because they think this is the appropriate and expected response (Table 3.10a). The lack of sex differences is replaced by sharp differences between the three ideal family model groups among women, but not among men, who expect to work continuously in all three situations. In Britain, work commitment falls from 68% among 'egalitarian' women to 38% among women who prefer separate roles for husband and wife. In Spain, the fall is less dramatic, from 58% among women who prefer symmetrical roles to 32% among women who prefer differentiated roles.

Very young people who have yet to enter the world of work, or who are still new and enthusiastic workers, have the highest levels of work commitment, around 80% in Britain. Thereafter, levels decline. However, the three ideal family models make little or no difference to the decline among men. Among women, declining levels of work commitment vary strongly between the three family models, with the fastest decline in the group preferring a full-time homemaker role: only 25% maintain any interest in employment by age 45–64 years, compared to 67% among the 'egalitarian' group (Table 3.10a).

As expected, there is an element of self-selection into employment among women. Within each ideal family model, women in employment express markedly higher levels of work commitment than women who are out of the workforce, especially in Britain (Table 3.10a/b). Among men, there is virtually no difference at all. This pattern is magnified further when controls for age are added, but it makes no difference to restrict the analysis to couples only. Among British women who are not in employment, prefer the full-time homemaker role and believe that men should always be the main breadwinner, work commitment falls to the lowest levels: 25% for women aged 25–44 and 10% for women aged 45–64 years.

Consistency in values is greatest among married women, for whom choices become concrete decisions rather than hypothetical options (second half of Table 3.10a). The three sex-role preference groups display notable differences in wives' work commitment, even in the youngest age groups (Table 3.10a). The majority of wives who prefer to be full-time homemakers say they would never work in the absence of financial necessity. The majority of wives who prefer symmetrical family roles say they would always work, irrespective of need, and work commitment does not decline with age in this group. Wives who prefer the compromise arrangement fall between these extremes, as many like to have jobs, so long as these do not interfere with their family work (Table 3.10a).

Overall, ideal family model has a strong impact on women's work commitment, but not on men's, as expected. Differences between the three groups of women are much larger than sex differences. There are also consistent links between work commitment and views on who has ultimate responsibility for income-earning and housekeeping (questions C and D). British women who believe that both partners have joint responsibility for income-earning have higher work commitment than those who see this role as falling to men exclusively: 64% versus 43%. There is a weaker association with beliefs on the housekeeping role.

Primary and Secondary Earners

In all three family models presented in our core question F, men have the income-earning role, either exclusively or sharing it to some degree. Logically, the full range of family models should include two further models, in which roles are reversed, with the husband either a full-time homemaker while the wife works full-time, or carrying the main responsibility for the home and family even if he has a job of some sort. In reality, role reversal families are so rare, even today, that there was no point in including the two additional theoretical options in question F. In practice, only 3% of respondents were unable to choose between the three models presented to them. Among men and women in Britain, 1% gave a don't know reply and 2% said they would choose some other family model. In Spain, 2% gave a don't know reply and 1% rejected all three family models. So these three models cover the full range of currently acceptable arrangements, even in rich modern societies. In all three family models, men are primary earners. Women are primary earners in the egalitarian model, but secondary earners in the compromise model and the role-segregated model. The role-segregated model appears to allocate full-time homemaking to the wife, with no earner role. In practice, wives in role-segregated marriages do work at times, either for short periods, or in part-time jobs, in special circumstances or 'emergencies' (Hakim, 2000a: 153, 159). So wives in role-segregated marriages are also secondary earners, but they expect to work rarely, if at all, whereas women in the compromise model expect more frequent spells of work, or even continuous part-time jobs.

Primary earners are people who may decide to work more or fewer hours, or to vary their work effort in other ways, but for whom the question of whether or not they enter the labour force is not in doubt. Secondary earners are people who may choose to work or not according to a range of considerations, financial and non-financial, and thus have intermittent work histories (Hakim, 1996a: 65–6). Secondary earners are not earning a living, they are financially dependent on another person or the state (for example, parents, social welfare benefits, student scholarships) for the basic necessities of life such as housing, food and fuel. Their earnings are supplementary or secondary to this other, larger and more regular source of income.

There is no standard methodology for identifying secondary earners in surveys. Our question G is just one of many approaches. It has the merit of

Table 3.11　Primary earner role and job centrality among couples, Britain and Spain

	Husbands			Wives		
	In work	Not working	All	In work	Not working	All
Britain						
% regarding themselves as main (co)earner						
20–39 years	94	78	93	27	9	22
40–59 years	92	73	89	36	16	30
All ages	93	74	91	32	13	26
% who are work-centred						
20–39 years	60	59	60	19	6	15
40–59 years	50	51	50	23	8	19
All ages	55	53	55	21	7	17
Spain						
% regarding themselves as main (co)earner						
20–39 years	94	..	91	44	8	24
40–59 years	95	96	95	49	10	21
All ages	94	86	93	46	9	22
% who are work-centred						
20–39 years	47	..	44	28	4	15
40–59 years	44	44	44	29	4	11
All ages	45	36	44	28	4	13

Note: Data for couples aged 20–59 years who have completed their full-time education.

being a Eurobarometer question, although reports present only minimal analyses of the results (see Table 1.2).

The analysis in Tables 3.11 and 3.12 is restricted to couples in order to look at role perceptions within a family context. Table 3.11 confirms that in both countries husbands see themselves as primary earners irrespective of their employment situation: 93–94% of husbands in work and 74–86% of husbands without jobs regard themselves as the main earner or joint earner for the household. The absence of a job slightly weakens, but does not eliminate the male breadwinner role. In contrast, a small minority of wives regard themselves as the main earner or, more usually, the joint main earner in the family. Wives with a job are much more likely to regard themselves as a primary earner than wives with no job: 32% versus 13% in Britain, 46% versus 9% in Spain. However, proportions are generally very low in both generations and in both countries, 22% to 26%. Far fewer women are in employment in Spain, but half of those that do work have adopted the primary earner identity compared to one-third at best in Britain.

The contrast with the results on work commitment in Table 3.10 is remarkable. The majority of women, and wives, claim they like to have a paid job, for a variety of reasons, especially the social value of a job. But this does not mean they regard themselves as primary earners, with a long-term commitment to paid employment and to contributing to family finances. Although half to two-thirds of wives express a commitment to work, only one-quarter of wives at most adopt the identity and responsibilities of a main earner. In contrast, the vast majority of men, and husbands, accept the primary earner role, even though at least one-third of husbands would be only too glad to give up work if there were no financial necessity. Work commitment among men is well below their almost universal acceptance of the primary earner role, and women's work commitment is revealed to be primarily an interest in the social and other aspects of a job.

Ideal family model has almost no impact on wives' propensity to adopt the primary earner identity (Table 3.12). As expected, husbands and wives who choose the compromise model or the role-segregated model regard the husband as the main earner in 73% to 91% of marriages, but so do two-thirds or more of spouses choosing the egalitarian model. Surprisingly, a substantial minority of British wives choosing the role-segregated model regard themselves as joint main earners (12%) or even the main earner (15%), and husbands broadly concur. The reasons for this are explored in Chapters 5 and 8, and illustrate the importance of housing as a lifestyle choice. Economic necessity seems to be a more powerful force in this group of women, frequently overriding lifestyle preferences. The compromise group is generally more affluent and can afford to do as it likes. The British survey provides no information on total household income, so we have to rely on other indicators, such as car ownership and home ownership. People who prefer the compromise model of family roles are most likely to have at least one car, most likely to have three or more cars and most likely to own their homes. Their greater affluence allows them to implement their preferences without hindrance, unlike many people in the role segregation preference group, where husbands are often unemployed. Wives in Spain are less likely to report themselves as the sole main earner, 5% compared with 15% in Britain. However, *joint* responsibility for income-earning is more common among Spanish couples – 17% compared to 12% in Britain – and the pattern is repeated across all family models (Table 3.12).

Table 3.12a Primary earner role by family model, Britain

Person perceived as the main earner	Ideal model of the family							
	Egalitarian		Compromise		Role segregation		All	
	Men	Women	Men	Women	Men	Women	Men	Women
Husband	64	64	91	81	76	73	77	73
Both spouses	22	15	4	9	18	12	14	12
Wife	14	20	5	10	6	15	9	15
Other person	*	*	..	..	..	..	*	*

Note: Data for couples aged 20–59 years who have completed their full-time education.

Table 3.12b Primary earner role by family model, Spain

Person perceived as the main earner	Ideal model of the family					
	Symmetrical roles		Differentiated roles		All	
	Men	Women	Men	Women	Men	Women
Husband	72	71	85	89	76	76
Both spouses	21	21	10	9	18	17
Wife	6	6	2	2	5	5
Other person	1	2	3	0	2	2

Note: Data for couples aged 20–59 years who have completed their full-time education.

However, the really surprising finding is that husbands and wives who claim to prefer the egalitarian family model are unanimous in saying that the husband is the sole main earner in two-thirds or more of all families, with the wife a joint or main breadwinner in only one-third of couples in Britain and one-quarter in Spain (Table 3.12). The ideal of *shared* income-earning and homemaking roles is in fact attained by around 20% of 'egalitarian' couples, at most, in both countries, much the same proportion as among couples choosing the other two family models. Among couples choosing differentiated family roles, small minorities fail to achieve their ideal division of labour in the family; but in the egalitarian group a full two-thirds *majority* of couples fail to achieve their ideal, with the largest discrepancy in Spain.

These patterns are repeated across the two age cohorts (20–39 and 40–59 years) in Britain. But surprisingly it is in the oldest age group, among couples in their fifties, where the egalitarian model is most likely to be achieved, with the wife a primary earner in about half of all couples.

Role reversal couples, who report the wife to be the main earner, were studied in some detail in the larger British dataset. They are a very mixed group, suggesting that there are many and varied routes into this situation. Virtually all the wives were in work, but only two-thirds had full-time jobs. Although there is a preponderance of women in the highest grades of professional and managerial work, one-fifth are in manual occupations. One-third of husbands have no job and no income at all, many of them aged 50 and over, and only half the husbands have a full-time job. Skilled manual occupations predominate among husbands' current and previous jobs. The great majority still had a mortgage on their home and it is no doubt this debt that forces couples to accept some flexibility in the main earner role, in order to ensure that housing payments are met. By the late 1990s, welfare benefit rules for the unemployed in Britain had changed to exclude assistance with mortgage payments, effectively forcing people in owner-occupied housing out of the unemployment benefit system. As noted in Chapter 8, housing tenure is associated with sharp differences in women's employment anyway, and the husband's unemployment, or temporary employment in an unsuitable low-wage job, would magnify these differences, creating temporary role reversal couples.

It is sometimes argued that women fail to adopt the primary earner role because they have lower earnings than men. Putting aside complex arguments about explanations for the relatively small 20% pay gap in Europe (Hakim, 1996a: 145–86), Table 3.13 makes it clear that adoption of the primary earner identity is determined primarily outside the labour market, in particular by marital status. In both countries, about half of all single men and women regard themselves as a primary earner. The proportions are lower in Spain than in Britain, because many young people continue to live with their parents until they marry, that is, well into their twenties and thirties. As soon as they start cohabiting with a man, the proportion falls to 33% for women, then falls again to 27% among married women in Britain and to 20% in Spain. Separation, divorce and widowhood force women to adopt the primary earner role again. The pattern for men is the exact opposite. Cohabitation and marriage impose the main earner role on virtually all men, 90% or more, a massive increase on the level among single men. They do not shake off the primary earner identity even when they become separated or divorced. It is clear that men and women adopt, or shrug off, the primary earner role on the basis of sex-role ideology and personal identity outside the labour force, rather than because of their particular jobs and earnings level.

Table 3.13 Primary earner role and work centrality by marital status, Britain and Spain

	All		Aged <40		Aged 40 +	
	Women	Men	Women	Men	Women	Men
Britain						
% who regard themselves						
as main (co)earner						
Single	59	53	50	44	86	89
Cohabiting	33	91	27	90	57	93
Married	27	91	21	94	30	90
Ex-married	88	93	92	74	88	95
Total	44	84	36	73	49	91
% who are work-centred						
Single	39	30	37	26	47	48
Cohabiting	25	55	18	56	49	54
Married	16	55	15	62	16	53
Ex-married	48	61	67	37	44	66
Total	26	52	26	46	26	55
Spain						
% who regard themselves						
as main (co)earner						
Single	36	47	30	40	63	81
Married	20	94	24	91	18	96
Ex-married	72	81	..	..	71	79
Total	32	81	28	65	34	93
% who are work-centred						
Single	25	28	22	22	..	52
Married	11	45	14	43	9	45
Ex-married	25	44	..	..	23	43
Total	16	40	18	32	14	46

Notes: Data for people aged 16 and over in Britain who have completed their full-time education, people aged 18 and over in Spain who have completed their full-time education. The ex-married group comprises people who are separated, divorced and widowed.

Both surveys provide information on personal income from all sources, which, for most people, consists essentially of earnings or pension (if any). A well-paid occupation or other high income generally makes a man a more attractive mate, but virtually all men in both countries adopt the primary earner role irrespective of income level. The sense of obligation to provide for themselves and their family does not depend on earnings level among men, so there is clearly no necessary, causal relationship between the two variables. There is a weak link between income and adoption of the primary earner identity among women,[10] but this is due primarily to well-established selection effects: women with higher qualifications, higher grade occupations and higher earnings are more likely to be in employment than other women (Hakim, 1996a: Table 3.7). The pattern is repeated in both countries, but is clearer in the larger British survey which has no missing data on the income variable.

Work Centrality

We constructed a summary measure of work orientations by combining the questions on work commitment and primary earner identity into an index of work centrality.[11] Adoption of the primary earner identity provides a different, more stringent test of long-term commitment to employment as a permanent feature of one's life than the conventional lottery win question alone. First, it refers to an everyday situation, rather than a hypothetical situation that some people are unable to envisage as reality. Second, there are none of the debates about interpretation that arise on the work commitment question. Work centrality identifies people who are committed to their work over and beyond purely financial motivation and who regard themselves as jointly (or solely) responsible for income-earning in their household. Logically, it is equally open to men and women to feel work-centred. As already demonstrated, even a part-time worker, or a non-working person, can regard themselves as having responsibility for income earning. In addition, in both countries, three-quarters of women claim that *both partners* are ultimately responsible for income-earning (Table 3.1).

The index of work centrality (Tables 3.11 and 3.13) confirms that jobs are central to identities for 55% of husbands and 17% of wives in Britain, 44% of husbands and 13% of wives in Spain. Four-fifths of women and half of all men have other reasons for doing paid work: some are committed to their work but regard themselves as secondary earners who do not have to work continuously (5% of husbands and 43% of wives in Britain); some are secondary earners with no commitment to work (4% of husbands and 31% of wives); and some regard themselves as primary earners but have no work commitment (36% of husbands and 9% of wives in Britain). Work centrality is constant among men, whether they are in or out of employment and age has almost no impact (Table 3.11). Among women also, age has no impact. In both countries, women with jobs are more likely to be work-centred: 21% compared to 7% in Britain, 28% compared to 4% in Spain, but levels generally remain very low among women (Table 3.11). As with the primary earner identity, work centrality changes with marital status rather than events in the workplace, and displays opposite trends among men and women (Table 3.13).

Among men, ideal family model has no impact on work centrality, as expected. Among wives, ideal family model makes a small difference. For one-third of wives who claim to prefer the egalitarian family model, but for *only* one-third, jobs are central to their identity. Here again, there is another contradiction in the survey results, as we would logically expect wives who are genuinely committed to symmetrical family roles to be committed to the occupations and jobs they expect to be doing throughout life. Among wives who prefer differentiated family roles, a four-fifths majority do not regard jobs as central to their identities, which is logical and consistent. Paid work in the public sphere is far more central to male identities than to female identities. Among men and women, there are many people who are simply instrumental workers, who work if and when they need the money, and would stop if they had other adequate sources of income. Work centrality and ideal family model constitute two separate indicators of sex-role ideology which, in combination, define lifestyle preferences.

National Estimates of Lifestyle Preferences

As noted in Chapter 2, there is only a rough correspondence between the three lifestyle preference groups identified by preference theory and the three family models presented in question F. Work centrality is the second essential indicator of lifestyle preference groups. Work-centred men and women are those whose jobs are central to their identity and their lifestyle. This is their essential defining characteristic. We can assume that work-centred women will also prefer the egalitarian model of family roles, although work-centred men might prefer any family model. We therefore reclassify women who claim to prefer the egalitarian family model but who are not work-centred as adaptives. On this basis, national distributions of work-centred, adaptive and home-centred women are shown in Table 3.14 for Britain and Spain.

Table 3.14 shows remarkable similarities between Britain and Spain. In both countries the adaptive group of women is by far the dominant group, at 69–70% of adult women who have finished their full-time education, rising to 73–77% of married and cohabiting women aged 20–59. Both the home-centred group and the work-centred group are small, small enough to be lost from sight in many studies and to be routinely overlooked as distinctive subgroups in the female population. The stereotype of the working woman is thus the adaptive woman, who seeks an even balance between paid work and

Table 3.14   National distributions of lifestyle preferences among women, Britain and Spain

	Home-centred	Adaptive	Work-centred	Base = 100%
Britain				
All aged 16 +	17	69	14	1807
All aged 16–64	14	71	15	1431
Wives aged 20–59	13	77	10	902
All in employment	11	72	17	953
Full-time workers	14	62	24	522
Part-time workers	8	84	8	473
Spain				
All aged 18 +	17	70	13	564
All aged 18–64	14	71	15	442
Wives aged 20–59	15	73	12	285
All in employment	5	67	28	172
Full-time workers	4	63	33	132
Part-time workers	7	79	14	45

Note: All distributions exclude full-time students.

family work, not the work-centred woman, frequently childfree, whose ambitions and values differ little from those of male colleagues. In both countries, two-thirds of all women working full-time are adaptives; another third or one-quarter are work-centred women. Home-centred women are such a tiny minority in the female workforce as to be virtually invisible in most studies.

Home-centred women are nonetheless an important minority group in the female population as a whole. In both countries, they are a larger minority than work-centred women. This is worth underlining, if only because the emphasis in media reports and policy analyses tends to be on the publicly visible group of high achievers who are work-centred. Only rarely do government reports acknowledge that the vast majority of women, are not career-oriented and that many prefer not to do paid work at all. This was the conclusion of the 1999 Listening to Women research programme mounted by the Cabinet Office's Women's Unit in Britain. A national survey of 1000 women aged 16 and over, a series of 24 focus groups with women and other studies showed that the majority of women see themselves as having jobs, not careers, and are prepared to take any job if it fits in with family and childcare commitments. Women want to have a choice whether to work or not, and when they are not working, they want their role as mother to be valued and respected as a job, albeit unwaged. One-third of women believed that home and children are women's main focus in life, and 28% felt that women should not try to combine a career with raising children. Even in the youngest group of women who had not yet become mothers, 20% believed that women cannot combine a career with having children. In the absence of financial need, one-fifth of mothers preferred to be at home full-time; another three-quarters preferred to have a part-time job; only 5% of mothers preferred to have a full-time job. One-quarter of men and women still believe in completely separate roles for husband and wife (Bryson *et al.*, 1999). In sum, there is corroborating evidence from other surveys that home-centred women remain a substantial minority in the population, and that careerist women are a rarity, even at the start of the twenty-first century.

Table 3.14 disposes of the idea that there are fundamental differences in life goals between women in full-time and part-time jobs. There is a substantial difference between the two groups in Britain: two-thirds of women working full-time are adaptives and one-quarter are work-centred, whereas virtually all part-time workers are adaptives. But this is still a difference of degree, rather than a qualitative difference between full-time and part-time workers. In short, the vast majority of working women are adaptives, even when they are working full-time and, as shown in Chapter 4, even when they work in higher grade professional and managerial occupations (see Tables 4.4 and 4.5).

Because of the asymmetric nature of the sex-roles implied by the three family models, we cannot use exactly the same method of estimation for men. None of the family models in our key question presents the option of role reversal, with a home-centred husband supported by a breadwinner wife. So there are no estimates for this group, although all the indications are that it will be very small. Since all three family models present the husband as the sole earner or co-earner, this question is less useful for differentiating between work-centred men and adaptive men. So we rely on the index of work centrality alone for this. Men who are not work-centred are classified as adaptive – although the label does not mean quite the same thing as for women, given that almost all the men in this group normally work full-time throughout life. A tiny proportion of the adaptive group should strictly be classified as family-centred.

Using this method, the male population is divided roughly half and half between the work-centred and adaptive groups in Britain, whatever population base is used (Table 3.15). This is in itself useful information, in that it underlines the point, so frequently overlooked, that not all men are work-centred. The majority of men are work-centred, but it is a small

Table 3.15   National distributions of lifestyle preferences among men, Britain and Spain

	Home-centred	Adaptive	Work-centred	Base = 100%
Britain				
All aged 16 +	?	<48	52	1538
All aged 16–64	?	<51	49	1204
Husbands aged 20–59	?	<46	54	778
All in employment	?	<50	50	1023
Full-time workers	?	<50	50	966
Part-time workers	?	<66	34	94
Spain				
All aged 18 +	?	<60	40	539
All aged 18–64	?	<60	40	448
Husbands aged 20–59	?	<56	44	249
All in employment	?	<58	42	349
Full-time workers	?	<56	44	325

Note: All distributions exclude full-time students.

majority of just over half. The large size of the adaptive group suggests that there is enormous potential for less work-centred lifestyles among men. At the moment, modern societies still do not allow men the same freedoms and choices that women now enjoy, so most men work full-time lifelong. But there is enormous potential for this to change, if women should ever be willing to become principal earners or joint earners in their household. At present, this is still a rare phenomenon. In Spain, less than half of all men are work-centred and adaptives (including some small proportion of family-centred men) are in the majority. This suggests that the potential for change in the family division of labour is even greater in Spain than in Britain.

Conclusions

We have demonstrated that lifestyle preference groups can be identified with just three fixed-choice questions that are already widely used in national surveys in Europe and North America. The question on ideal family models identifies home-centred (or family-centred) women. The questions on work orientations identify work-centred men and women. Together, the questions allow us to classify women as home-centred, adaptive or work-centred. For men, the classification is as yet incomplete. For this reason, we analysed each question in our survey module separately, to permit systematic comparisons of men and women in Britain and Spain. This makes analyses in this and other chapters somewhat lengthy. But it also throws up some unexpected findings along the way, for example on the index of patriarchal values and (in Chapter 4) on differential divorce rates. Overall, the operationalization of lifestyle preference groups is a success, and we have been able to confirm several predictions from preference theory.

Throughout the analyses in this chapter, sex differences are either small or non-existent in Britain and Spain. These results confirm Inglehart's (1991) prediction that sex differences in sex-role attitudes would disappear by 2000 in the most developed societies. There is now a remarkable degree of unanimity between men and women about the sexual division of labour and sex-role ideology. Within each family model preference group, sex differences in values are generally of negligible importance, apart from the huge sex difference in adoption of the primary earner identity. This is our first and fundamentally important finding. Two conclusions follow from it.

First, the survey offers little support for the idea that women are well ahead of men in adopting an 'egalitarian' sex-role ideology, and that men are more 'traditional', as has been argued repeatedly from opinion poll research. Nor is there any evidence of patriarchal men seeking to restrict women's access to jobs and to restrict their economic self-reliance against fierce resistance from women. On the contrary, there is evidence of men being slightly ahead of women in the adoption of 'egalitarian' attitudes, particularly as regards sharing the income-earning role. The patriarchy index reveals no sex differences at all, in either Britain or Spain. In both countries, generational differences are more important that sex differences.

Second, differences between lifestyle preference groups have already replaced sex differences as the principal dividing factor. On every aspect of sex-role ideology, men and women within each family model preference group hold almost identical views, and it is the sharp differences between the three groups that stand out. These results confirm preference theory's prediction that sex and gender are becoming redundant concepts (Hakim, 2000a: 280). Lifestyle preference groups are not visible entities in the same way as sex and gender, but they are now the more important social constructs.

Sex-role preferences and lifestyle preference groups constitute meaningful ideological groups in Britain and Spain, especially in the younger generation. There is sufficient coherence and consistency in responses to related questions, and preferences have the expected association with other values.

The analysis shows that secondary earners have become, and will remain, a substantial element in the workforce, particularly in the female workforce in countries such as Britain that have achieved the new scenario for women. There is no substantively important difference in the level of work commitment expressed by primary earners and secondary earners, but their interest in work is of a different nature.[12] This implies a permanent diversity in attitudes to employment within the labour force, of a more fundamental nature than the cultural, religious and ethnic differences that are currently treated as the main sources of diversity. This new diversity may be helpful in facilitating the redistribution of work and reducing unemployment. But it may also require more complex social insurance and social welfare arrangements than the present system predicated on the lifelong employment of self-supporting primary earners, which the European Commission believes should be the basis for future policy-making. Our survey results have implications for family policy, fiscal policy and labour market policy in all modern societies.

On balance, most of the evidence from the British survey is in line with preference theory. The principal discordant finding is that there is no marked ideological difference between the older and the younger generations in Britain. Preference theory claims that the new scenario for women already achieved in Britain by the end of the twentieth century creates the climate for a qualitatively different perspective on lifestyle choices among the generation aged under 40 and promotes the polarization of preference groups. The limited range of data obtained in the British survey offers little support for this thesis. Attitudes and values change and develop gradually across age cohorts, and there is no evidence of important break points or watersheds, as there are in Spain. However, there is evidence of the polarization of attitudes on patriarchy, and ideological consistency is greater among the younger generation in Britain. It appears that the new scenario, once achieved, affects women of all ages rather than younger women only.

Notes

1   Contradictory trends among men and women produce an apparently unchanging level of work commitment among all employees. This apparent stability has confused many social scientists, as illustrated by Ladipo (2000).

2   The wording of the 1990 and 1994 CIS questions on ideal family model was as follows: 'Como Vd. sabe, actualmente existen distintos tipos de familias. De las tres posibilidades que le voy a leer a continuación, podría decirme cuál se acerca más a su ideal de familia?

– una familia en la que tanto el hombre como la mujer trabajan fuera de casa y se reparten las tareas del hogar y el cuidado de los hijos; una familia donde la mujer trabaje menos horas fuera de casa y, por tanto, se ocupe en mayor medida de las tareas del hogar y del cuidado de los hijos; una familia donde sólo el hombre trabaje fuera de casa y sea exclusivamente la mujer la que se ocupe de las tareas del hogar y del cuidado de los hijos.' Compared to the wording of our 1999 question, it was easier for people to choose the first option, because it does not specify that both spouses hold equally demanding jobs, nor that they share domestic work and childcare equally. So the jump in popularity of the egalitarian option by the end of the 1990s is all the more remarkable.

3   In the 1990s, only 11% of the Spanish labour force was employed in professional, technical and managerial occupations (Lawlor and Rigby, 1998: 313), compared to over 34% in Britain (Hakim, 1998a: 69).

4   The methodological report on the 1981 salaries survey stated that 'No se obtiene información alguna sobre ganancias desagregadas por sexo, ya que legalmente no existe discriminación por este motivo (art. 28 del Estatuto de los Trabajadores)' (INE, 1982: 41).

5   It is well established that young people are especially susceptible to peer group pressure compared with older people. This is illustrated in the results of the 1991/92 Health and Lifestyle Survey in Britain, which showed that difficulties or arguments with friends or family were far more stressful for people aged 18–38 than for people aged 39 and over. In addition, young women were twice as likely as young men to report such stress, suggesting that young women are twice as vulnerable to social pressure from friends and family (Cox *et al.*, 1993: Table 15.15). It seems likely that feminism of one shade or another would be an important source of ideological debate among younger women.

6   One reason for slightly more extreme views on patriarchy in Spain than in Britain is that the undecided middle response was not offered in Spain, although the number of Don't Know responses increased in consequence. Overall, the results from our surveys echo those of a 1996 Eurobarometer survey which found that one-third of men and women in Britain and Spain (and in the EU generally) agreed that 'when jobs are scarce' men should have priority over women for the available jobs. Across the EU, sex differences in responses were small or non-existent, and seem to be due primarily to sex differences in employment rates in each country. Differences between working and non-working women were relatively tiny: 20% and 35% respectively believed men should have priority for scarce jobs. In contrast, there were enormous variations in responses across the EU: only one in ten people in Scandinavia agreed, compared to over half of the Greeks and Belgians (European Commission, 1998: 26–7).

7   Our interpretation of the meaning of work commitment is different from that in Gallie *et al.* (1998: 22–3, 186–206), who focus on the intrinsic value of work, as compared with the extrinsic value of work.

8   In a country where the social obligation to be employed is very strong, such as China, work commitment shows little variation across age groups and social groups. The results of a survey carried out in 2000 in the four largest cities (Beijing, Shanghai, Guangzou and Chengdu) was reported on 8 March 2001 by the Xin Hua Agency. It found that only 61% of women said they would continue to work in the absence of economic necessity (a figure very close to that found in Britain), 32% would stop working and 7% were undecided. There was little variation in response patterns. Among women with higher education qualifications, 64% would continue to work, compared with 63% of women who completed secondary school and 58% of those completing primary school. Among young women, 73% would continue, compared with 61% of middle aged women and 60% of older women.

9   Similarly, a 1996 Eurobarometer survey found no differences in work commitment between men and women in employment (European Commission, 1998: 20).

10 The correlation coefficient between personal income and adoption of the primary earner identity is .03 for men and .19 for women in Spain, and .23 for men and women in Britain. There is no association at all between family income and primary earner identity in Spain, for men or women.

11 The survey results in this chapter and the next are broadly in line with the findings of an ethnographic study within the Future of Work research programme that looked at work orientations and work commitment in the context of job insecurity (Charles, 2001). The study found that most men still regard themselves as main breadwinners, and most women regard themselves as secondary earners, whatever their work histories. For this reason, job loss is regarded as more damaging to male identity than to female identity. When a husband's job loss forced his wife to become primary earner out of necessity, this was seen as a temporary aberration, not necessarily as role reversal. In this context, paid jobs were assessed on two dimensions: their importance for the household and their importance for the individual. This often produced contradictory assessments on the two dimensions. It appears that work commitment as measured in our 1999 surveys measures the importance of a job for the individual, while the primary/secondary earner distinction covers the importance of a job for the household. Using this framework, the work centrality index combines both measures of the importance of paid work.

12 This is displayed convincingly by a study which purports to challenge preference theory, yet confirms the theory with its own research results. Walsh (1999) questioned the idea that part-time workers have different work orientations. However, her own research results show that paid work had a very low priority in the lives of women with part-time jobs. Four-fifths were working part-time voluntarily, with no interest in full-time jobs; four-fifths of voluntary part-timers and two-thirds of involuntary part-timers regarded themselves as secondary earners, being married women or students; almost half had been out of the labour market before they took their part-time jobs, being full-time homemakers or students; and well over half had no intention of ever returning to full-time employment. Naturally, there is some variation within the part-time workforce. This can be seen even with standard data sources such as the census (Hakim, 1998a: 102–77), and does not require special surveys. Unfortunately, Walsh's study only covers women working part-time, so she is unable to prove that they have the same work orientations as women working full-time.

Chapter 4

Correlates of Sex-Role Ideology
and Work Orientations

This chapter tests the idea that education is the primary determinant of work-centred attitudes, and that all highly educated people are work-centred. At the same time, we assess the impact of other factors – social class, income, age and marital status – to see if social, cultural and economic capital are important determinants or correlates of lifestyle preferences. As noted in Chapter 1, human capital theory has promoted the idea that educational qualifications are obtained primarily as an investment in employment careers, with a view to maximizing earnings. In reality, research shows that women obtain education as cultural capital (Bourdieu, 1997) which enhances quality of life and social status, which are valuable in the marriage market as well as the labour market (Hakim, 2000a: 193–222). Widespread access to higher education contradicts the idea of education being exclusively an investment towards future earnings.

Education

The influence of education on sex-role ideology is weak in Britain, but is strong in Spain, where age cohort, historical period and education effects are strongly intertwined as a result of massive recent social change, as noted in Chapter 1.[1]

The only education indicator available in the British survey is age of leaving full-time education, a variable which also identifies students still in full education. Students are the most idealistic and least realistic group, being mostly unmarried, often living with their parents and virtually always financially dependent on someone else rather than themselves. The incidence of student jobs has been steadily rising throughout Europe, in parallel with the transition from an elite higher education system to the mass higher education system already established in the USA (Hakim, 1998a: 145–77). So many students have some limited work experience, either in part-time jobs or summer jobs. By the age of 24, half of all British students have some work experience (Hakim, 1998a: Table 6.5). In the British survey

93

sample, there were 170 students in full-time education, of whom half currently had a job, usually part-time, and another 14% had previous work experience. But this still falls short of full entry into the adult world of permanent full-time jobs, financial independence from parents, the responsibilities of separate housing and marriage or long-term cohabitation. Two-thirds of students prefer the egalitarian model of the family, 63% of men and 69% of women aged under 40 years, compared with the averages of 54% and 51% for all men and women aged under 40. Interestingly, students are just as positive as other young people about the role-segregated model of the family: 11–13% in all cases. It is the compromise model of the family that they find unattractive.

Putting aside students, the impact of education varies between men and women in Britain. Increasing education has no impact on the ideal family model of men. This demonstrates that education has no necessary, causal impact on ideal family model. The weak association among women can be interpreted as due to self-selection into higher education and the higher grade occupations this leads to. Women who have higher education qualifications are slightly more likely to prefer the egalitarian model of the family, by around 15 percentage points (Table 4.1a). Women who aim for symmetrical family roles, for careers giving them financial self-reliance and who reject patriarchal values are most likely to be determined and systematic in their pursuit of secondary and higher level qualifications and the higher grade occupations they lead to. However, as higher education becomes a mass experience, rather than an elite experience, the impact of education on values melts away.

Within the older British cohort (aged 40 and over), longer education produces an increase in support for the egalitarian model, and a small decline in support for the role-segregated model. Within the younger cohort (aged under 40), increasing education has no effect at all on ideal family model; the cohort averages shown in Table 4.6 vary slightly and erratically across education levels. Thus, over time and across cohorts, the small impact of education level has disappeared completely in Britain. As predicted by preference theory, sex-role preferences cut across education levels within the younger cohort in Britain.

Similarly, education has no impact at all on work orientations among men, and only a small impact on women (Table 4.1a). Women with higher education are more likely to adopt the primary earner identity, due in part to self-selection into higher education. The proportion of women aged 20–59 who regard themselves as a primary (co)earner rises from one-third among women with no more than basic compulsory schooling to half among those with higher education. This in turn produces an 11 percentage point increase in work centrality, an increase small enough to be explained by some degree of self-selection into higher education. Overall, then, we conclude that education has no important impact on work orientations in Britain.

Increasing levels of education do have an impact on other attitudes, notably on patriarchal values (Tables 4.1 and 4.2). Increasing levels of education lead people to abandon their belief in rigid role specialization in the family. Between 10% and 17% of men and women stop insisting that men have ultimate responsibility for income-earning while women have ultimate responsibility for housekeeping. Thus there is a small shrinkage in rigid sex-role stereotyping as people move from a basic education to higher education.

Education has its biggest impact on patriarchal values, especially in the older generation (Table 4.2). Sex differences within each generation are trivial, and are not shown. Among Britons with no more than basic compulsory schooling (up to the age of 16), a three-quarters majority accept patriarchal values in whole or in part; only one-quarter reject patriarchal values. In Spain, one-third of people with no more than primary education reject patriarchy. In both countries, the majority of people with higher education reject patriarchal values. This creates potential conflicts in the group with only basic schooling: they are just as likely to favour the egalitarian family model, yet also endorse patriarchal values which are inimical to such a model. Table 4.2 shows that the key dividing line in Britain is between people with only a basic education and people who stay on in education beyond the age of 16. Higher education as such makes little difference. This suggests that the effects of education are in practice bound up with self-selection into education beyond the compulsory minimum.

Table 4.2 also shows that the impact of education on patriarchal values is declining across generations in Britain. Once again, the impact of education is much stronger in the older generation, especially among women, and relatively weak in the younger generation. This suggests that other sources of information, such as the mass media, now have an equally important role in shaping attitudes and values. Alternatively, there is greater homogeneity of values in the younger generation, as noted below in relation to ideal family model.

Education might influence people in another way, in prompting greater ideological consistency between values. For example, we might expect people with higher education to have greater coherence in their sex-role ideology than people with only compulsory schooling. In reality, there is no evidence of such an effect in the British survey. The two groups with the most internally consistent values are at the two extremes: older people with only a basic education who prefer role specialization in the family, and younger people with higher education who favour the egalitarian model of

Table 4.1a   The impact of education on sex-role ideology, Britain

	Terminal education age		
	to 16	*17–20*	*21 +*
Men			
Ideal family model:			
egalitarian	44	46	48
compromise	36	39	35
role segregation	20	15	17
% who believe that ultimate responsibility for:			
income lies with man	36	22	21
housekeeping lies with women	32	22	19
% reject patriarchy	30	48	55
% work-centred	53	46	52
Women			
Ideal family model:			
egalitarian	36	47	51
compromise	45	39	35
role segregation	19	14	14
% who believe that ultimate responsibility for:			
income lies with man	32	16	13
housekeeping lies with woman	40	22	16
% reject patriarchy	27	56	62
% work-centred	24	26	35

Note: Data for people aged 16 and over who have completed their full-time education.

the family. In between the two groups, there is no clear and systematic effect of education in raising or lowering ideological consistency.

As the effects of education are diluted in the younger generation in Britain, it is family model preferences that become the more important factor structuring sex-role ideology and shaping attitudes and values. There is clear evidence in Britain of the increasing importance of personally-chosen values as determinants of lifestyles, replacing education and socio-economic status as dominant forces.

In Spain, education is strongly associated with sex-role ideology (Table 4.1b), but in this case it is in practice impossible, especially with a small sample, to disentangle the overlapping and inter-connected effects of age cohort, historical period and education *per se*. In contrast to Britain, educational level is strongly linked to ideal family model. However, just as in Britain, there is only a link in the older generation (aged 40 and over). In the

Table 4.1b   The impact of education on sex-role ideology, Spain

| | *Educational level* | | |
	Up to primary	*Secondary*	*Some higher*
Men			
Ideal family model:			
egalitarian	45	72	80
compromise	24	19	17
role segregation	31	9	3
% who believe that ultimate responsibility for:			
income lies with man	50	18	9
housekeeping lies with women	45	17	12
% reject patriarchy	32	62	75
% work-centred	39	38	49
Women			
Ideal family model:			
egalitarian	57	69	87
compromise	22	22	7
role segregation	21	9	6
% who believe that ultimate responsibility for:			
income lies with man	17	16	4
housekeeping lies with woman	40	11	4
% reject patriarchy	36	65	84
% work-centred	9	13	47

Note: Data for people aged 18 and over who have completed their full-time education.

younger generation, educational differences in sex-role preferences shrink to nothing, especially among women. So in both countries, education has no impact on ideal family model in the younger generation. However, education continues to have a strong impact on other attitudes, such as acceptance of patriarchal values and of rigid role stereotyping (Table 4.1b). For patriarchal values, education has just as strong an impact in the younger generation as in the older generation (Table 4.2). This leaves some scope for problems of ideological inconsistency in the younger generation of Spaniards.

Just one illustration comes from a study by Tobío (2001) of young urban working women. They expect their husband to be sole provider for the

Table 4.2 The impact of education on patriarchal values, Britain and Spain

	% who reject patriarchy		
	<40	*40 +*	*All*
Britain: terminal education age:			
Up to 16	46	21	28
17–20	60	44	52
21 + years	64	52	58
Total	54	29	38
Spain: educational level:			
Up to primary	45	33	34
Secondary	70	55	63
Some higher	80	77	79
Total	68	44	53

Notes: Data for people aged 16 and over (Britain) or 18 and over (Spain) who have completed their full-time education. There are negligeable differences between men and women within age cohorts.

family, and treat their own earnings as completely separate private money, to spend as they please. Because their job is treated almost as a personal hobby, wives continue to fulfil all the functions of the full-time homemaker, wife and mother, leading to stress from the double workload (Ramos Torres, 1990; Prior Ruiz, 1997).

Finally, there is a remarkable dissimilarity between the two countries as regards the huge sex differential in the association between education and work centrality (Table 4.3). In both countries, educational level has no impact at all on work centrality among men, so there cannot be any necessary causal link. In Britain, education also has a negligible impact on women's work orientations. In Spain, work centrality remains at a negligibly low level among women unless they have some higher education, in which case the sex differential is eliminated at a stroke in the younger and older generations. The results for Spanish women must be explained by self-selection into higher education and the higher grade jobs to which it gives access.

Table 4.3 The impact of education on work centrality, Britain and Spain

	Men			Women		
% who are work-centred	*<40*	*40 +*	*All*	*<40*	*40 +*	*All*
Britain: terminal education age:						
Up to 16	46	56	53	23	24	24
17–20	45	47	46	26	27	26
21 + years	48	57	52	34	35	35
Total	46	55	52	26	26	26
Spain: educational level:						
Up to primary	37	40	39	10	9	9
Secondary	30	49	38	11	16	13
Some higher	35	65	49	48	45	47
Total	32	46	40	19	14	16

Note: Data for people aged 16 and over (Britain) or aged 18 and over (Spain) who have completed their full-time education.

Social Class and Income

One of the many advantages of the ONS omnibus survey for Britain is that it provides detailed occupational coding and full coding of social class and socio-economic groups (SEG), based on the individual's current or last occupation. The survey took place too early for the new socio-economic classification (Rose and O'Reilly, 1997, 1998; Rose and Pevalin, 2002) to be applied,[2] so we use a condensed version of the SEG classification, which is very close to the new classification (Rose and O'Reilly, 1998: v, 25).

As predicted by preference theory, social class and SEG have virtually no impact on the ideal family models of men, women or age cohorts in Britain in 1999. The role-segregated model of the family is most popular among unskilled male manual workers: 22% prefer this model compared to the 19% average for all men and 16% among professional men. However, professional women also favour the role-segregated marriage most of all: 21% compared to the 17% average for all women and 23% among unskilled manual workers (Table 4.4). There is no clear status gradient in preferences, and indeed relatively little variation around the average, for men, for women and in the younger and older generations.

Table 4.4 Sex-role preferences by socio-economic group

| | Ideal model of the family | | | |
	Egalitarian	Compromise	Role segregation	Base = 100%
Men				
Professionals	40	44	16	130
Employers & managers	38	39	23	337
Intermediate				
non-manual	53	30	17	173
Junior non-manual	51	31	18	118
Skilled manual	44	38	18	510
Semi-skilled manual	57	27	16	229
Unskilled manual	41	37	22	64
Total	46	35	19	1628
Women				
Professionals	42	37	21	38
Employers & managers	50	39	11	215
Intermediate				
non-manual	48	37	15	334
Junior non-manual	38	45	17	574
Skilled manual	36	44	20	123
Semi-skilled manual	41	42	17	396
Unskilled manual	37	40	23	123
Total	42	41	17	1890

Note: Data for current and last occupations of people aged 16 and over, excluding those who have never had a job.

Similarly, socio-economic group produces no systematic variation in responses to the two questions on who has ultimate responsibility for income-earning and housework. Among men, the groups most likely to endorse rigid role specialization are those in higher grade white-collar and blue-collar occupations: employers, managers and skilled manual workers. Among women, it is those in lower grade white-collar and blue-collar jobs who are most enthusiastic about the separation of income-earning and homemaking roles. There is clearly no status gradient in responses to these two questions.

Preferences and ideals regarding the family division of labour cut across social status and economic groups. In contrast, there are marked occupational grade and status variations (as measured by SEG) in other values, such as the acceptance of patriarchy. For example, women's responses to question A, on men always being the main breadwinner, vary strongly by socio-economic group, whereas men's responses are little affected. On average, about half of men and women agree that men remain the main breadwinner even when women have jobs. This proportion varies hardly at all by SEG among men, while among women it falls to one-third in the highest grade occupations and rises to two-thirds among women whose current or last job was in an unskilled manual occupation. Overall, acceptance of patriarchal values increases the lower a person's socio-economic status, especially among women, partly due to the dual impact of lower education on patriarchal values and on occupational grade.

In the Spanish dataset, social class identity is subjectively defined and is not a very useful variable. With the post-democracy emphasis on equality for all, almost all Spaniards (93%) classify themselves as middle class, almost never as higher or lower class. With this in mind, survey questions seek to distinguish between the upper, middle and lower sections of the middle class, with only limited success. A full 60% of all adults insist they are 'middle-middle class', only 4% identify themselves as 'upper-middle' and 28% identify themselves as 'lower-middle' class. Another 7% claim to be lower class, and a bare 0.3% of respondents admitted to being upper class. Not surprisingly, there is no association between social class identity and ideal family model, apart from a slight tendency for lower-class people to prefer complete role segregation more often than the average.

Information on gross personal income is available for all respondents in Britain, for people not in work as well as those in employment, so there are dramatic variations in income within the sample, especially among women. Here too, there is no definite pattern for sex-role preferences to vary by level of income. Men with higher incomes often prefer a secondary earner wife, but then so do men with moderate incomes. Men with low incomes tend also to be younger, hence more idealistic, and they are likely to favour the 'egalitarian' model. However, the role-segregated model of the family is also popular among low income men. Among women, there is more of an association between ideal family model and personal income: high earning women prefer the egalitarian model, while women with low incomes generally prefer to be secondary earners. But even here, the link is weak. Ideally we would like to test for a link between women's ideal family model and their total family income, but this information is not available in the British omnibus.

The Spanish dataset does provide information on family incomes as well as personal income, but the information is missing for 19% and 34% of respondents respectively, partly because some respondents refused to answer the questions and partly because many women had no personal income to report so did not answer the question.[3]

In Spain, there is a moderate association between family income and people's ideal model of the family. Men in low-income families are most likely to favour role specialization and men in high-income families are most likely to favour symmetrical roles for spouses. Among women, the relationship is non-linear. Women in the poorest and richest families are most likely to favour role specialization, with the wife as full-time homemaker. There is also a general tendency for the egalitarian model to increase in popularity as family income rises. Similarly, there is a weak association between personal income and ideal family model, both for men and women. However, these associations are due entirely to the dominant intervening effects of education, which determines income (both personal and family income) in Spain, and is strongly associated with ideal family model. As noted earlier, age and education are strongly intertwined in Spain, with large overlapping effects. Income effects are also attributable to education effects.

There is only a weak link between attitudes to patriarchy and gross personal income among men in Britain. The majority of men on low incomes (under £8000 per year) endorse patriarchal values, whereas men with high incomes are very evenly divided between acceptance and rejection of patriarchy. Among women, the association is stronger. The majority of women with personal incomes below £8000 a year accept patriarchal values, whereas the majority of women with high incomes (over £25000 a year) reject patriarchy. These results are consistent with the results on variation by socio-economic status.

In Spain, there is a moderate link between family income and patriarchal values, but again education is the key intervening variable. There is little or no association between personal income and patriarchal values, for men and women. In sum, there is little or no association between income and ideal family model in Britain and Spain. The impact of income on patriarchal values is also weak.

There is a tendency to assume that careerists invariably have higher grade jobs, and that people in less skilled manual work cannot have a work-centred or careerist attitude to their jobs. Our survey contradicts this assumption, which seems to be based on stereotypes more than on evidence. Among men and women, there is only a very weak association between work centrality and occupational grade, as measured by socio-economic group (Table 4.5). Work-centred people are slightly more likely to achieve higher grade occupations, in professional and managerial work. Work centrality is lowest among people in semi-skilled and unskilled manual work. But in all occupational grades, the well-defined sex differential in work centrality is

Table 4.5 Work centrality by job grade and income, Britain

| Socio-economic groups and annual income | % who are work-centred | | | | | |
| | Men | | | Women | | |
	<40	40 +	All	<40	40 +	All
Employers & managers	52	52	52	40	37	39
Intermediate white-collar	53	60	56	38	33	35
Junior white-collar	50	65	54	18	21	19
Skilled manual	48	50	49	30	35	33
Semi-skilled & unskilled manual	33	51	41	22	31	26
Up to £4000	..	..	..	16	9	12
£4000–£8000	29	..	37	13	21	17
£8000–£12 000	33	55	43	24	35	29
£12 000–£15 000	53	56	54	37	29	33
£15 000–£25 000	57	49	53	39	46	42
£25 000–£40 000	50	53	52	61	48	54
£40 000 +	52	56	54	80	..	71
All	48	53	50	28	30	29

Note: Data for all currently in employment, excluding full-time students.

maintained, although it is much reduced among people in employment (Table 4.5). Only in the younger generation does the weak association become slightly more pronounced, suggesting an increasing degree of self-selection into graduate occupations. There is some evidence here of polarization in the younger generation in Britain, with work-centred people more likely to gravitate to the top of the occupational hierarchy, while others remain concentrated in lower grade occupations. However, this polarizing trend is not exclusive to younger women, it appears among younger men as well (Table 4.5).

There are enormous difficulties in researching work orientations, and the notion of 'career' is particularly slippery (Rose, 1994; Hakim, 1996a: 98–109). Nonetheless, the British survey indicates that work centrality is fairly constant throughout the occupational structure, among both men and women, albeit with a marked sex differential which persists even after the equal opportunities revolution. There is no evidence here to support the widespread assumption that all people in managerial and senior professional grades are focused exclusively on their work, and that such a focus is totally lacking in manual occupations. Among women, only about one-third of those in senior grades are work-centred, compared to one-quarter in the lowest grades, which is not a substantial difference. Among men, the variation is even smaller.

Only in the tiny group of professional people does the sex differential in work centrality fade away. Among professionals, 42% of women and 49% of men are work-centred, a much smaller gap than in the broader SEG of employers, managers and professionals (Table 4.5). This may explain why academics, especially feminists, have been so resistant to the idea of a continuing substantial sex differential in work orientations. Within the professional milieu of academia, sex differences in work centrality are minimal, and roughly half of all workers are work-centred. There is a tendency for academics to extrapolate this picture to the entire workforce. However, professionals constitute a tiny, wholly unrepresentative fraction of the workforce: just 8% nationally, 7% of working women and 9% of working men according to the 1991 Census. Female professionals constitute an impossibly tiny and unrepresentative group, even if all academics belong to it.

Where work centrality does make a difference is in earnings achieved (Table 4.5). The British survey does not provide information on earnings, only on gross personal income, a wider concept. However, it is safe to assume that earnings provide the vast majority of income for people currently in employment. Women generally have lower earnings than men, due to working part-time hours and to working shorter hours even in full-time jobs, while men are most likely to work long hours and overtime hours, even in professional occupations (Hakim, 1998a). Men and women have systematically higher incomes if they are work-centred than if they work for other reasons, but the effect is stronger for women. This is partly because work-centred women are motivated to work full-time hours: three-quarters (72%) of work-centred women in employment work full-time hours in Britain compared to less than half (45%) of women working for other reasons. The association between work centrality and higher incomes is stronger in the younger generation, but this applies to men as well as women, again suggesting increasing self-selection into careers and polarization of the workforce in Britain.

The results for men invalidate the argument that women's work orientations are a response to their lower grade jobs and lower earnings. Men are just as likely to be work-centred whether they have low or high earnings, low or high grade occupations. It is not jobs and earnings that determine work centrality, but sex-role ideology and personal identities outside the labour market. Women have a choice between work-centred and home-centred lives, between financial self-reliance and financial dependence. The minority of work-centred women tend to have higher grade jobs and higher earnings than women working for social and instrumental reasons because work-centred women invest more time and effort in their paid work than other women. But the association is relatively weak, because work-centred people are found throughout the occupational structure. Work centrality is not limited to professional and managerial occupations, as is so often assumed.

Lifestyle preferences predict choices, but they do not predict performance or achievement in a role. This is one reason why work-centred people are found at all levels of achievement in the workforce, among women as well as men.

The analysis in Table 4.5 is limited to Britain because the larger dataset permits this level of detail. Results from the much smaller Spanish survey are broadly in line with those for Britain. There is one additional distinctive feature of the results for Spain. As in Britain, education, job grade and income do not affect work-centredness among men. However, it is only among women with some higher education that the percentage who are work-centred rises above the low 13–17% averages shown in Table 3.11. In this group, the level rises to around half, the same level as among men. The association is found in both older and younger generations, as shown in Table 4.3. Higher education in Spain seems to have special importance in attracting, affirming and reinforcing career-oriented women, to a degree not observed in Britain.

In sum, sex-role attitudes and values can vary by socio-economic group, as illustrated by patriarchal values. However, there are no SEG variations of any consequence on ideal family model and work orientations, and therefore lifestyle preferences also cut across social classes and income groups. This means that working-class people are most likely to have discrepant, inconsistent and even conflicting values, and this is especially true of working-class women.

In conclusion, social, economic and cultural capital are not important correlates or predictors of ideal family model in Britain, particularly in the younger generation (aged under 40) that has had the full benefit of the new scenario for women, even though they have a small impact on other aspects of sex-role ideology, notably patriarchal values. Results for Spain are broadly similar, although there are sharper differences between generations and educational groups.

The Ageing Process

The Eurobarometer data for the 1980s give the impression of a gradual shift over time towards majority support for the egalitarian model of the family (see Table 1.1). The results of the 1999 British survey show that in reality attitudes swung back again in the 1990s, with increasing support for the compromise model instead (see Table 3.3). This conclusion is reinforced by a comparison of the ageing process in Tables 1.1 and 4.6. Admittedly, the comparison is not precise, as Table 1.1 combines Eurobarometer 1987 data for twelve EU countries compared to Britain alone in 1999. However, Britain was fairly close to the EU average in 1987, so the global figures on the ageing process across the EU are probably fairly close to the picture for Britain at that time.

The remarkable result is that the ageing process in 1987 and 1999 is so similar as to be almost identical, although exact percentages differ between the two years. There is a twelve-year gap between the two surveys, so sustained changes within age cohorts should be reflected in the later survey; in fact there are none. In practice, in both surveys, there is a steady drop in support for the egalitarian model across age groups, of roughly the same magnitude in both surveys. Among women, for example, support for the egalitarian model drops by 34 percentage points between the oldest and youngest age groups, with a smaller rise in support for the segregated roles model. We conclude that differences across age groups indicate an ageing effect rather than a cohort effect. People learn from experience, especially after marriage and after children are born, that there is an inevitable conflict between a life centred on career and a major involvement in home and family work, so they then work out a more realistic and informed version of their ideal model of the family. It is notable that the largest single fall in support for the egalitarian model among women happens between the ages of 16–24 and 25–39 in Britain (Table 4.6). This is the time when most women get married and have children, making concrete choices between priorities for the first time. There is no equivalent fall in support for the other two family models at this time. As more and more young women go into higher education, and delay marriage and childbirth, this phase of facing up to reality and implementing lifestyle preferences is progressively delayed until later and later ages in modern societies.

In Spain, the ageing process is similar to that in Britain, but with larger changes between generations. Although base numbers are small, there is also some evidence of a swing back towards the compromise model of the family in the very youngest group (Table 4.6).

Table 4.6 Ideal family model by age, Britain and Spain

		Egalitarian	Compromise	Role segregation	Base = 100%
		Ideal model of the family			
Britain					
Men	16–24	60	30	10	208
	25–39	51	37	12	446
	40–54	48	36	16	421
	55 +	35	36	29	553
Women	16–24	65	22	13	222
	25–39	45	42	13	540
	40–54	42	46	12	495
	55 +	31	44	25	633
Men aged <40		54	35	11	654
Men aged 40 +		41	36	23	974
Women aged <40		51	36	13	762
Women aged 40 +		36	45	19	1128
All men		46	36	18	1628
All women		42	41	17	1890
All persons		44	39	17	3518
Spain					
Men	16–24	73	18	9	56
	25–39	81	14	5	163
	40–54	65	23	12	126
	55 +	43	26	31	174
Women	16–24	71	22	6	50
	25–39	81	13	6	163
	40–54	67	19	14	145
	55 +	52	26	22	209
Men aged <40		79	15	6	220
Men aged 40 +		52	25	23	299
Women aged <40		79	15	6	212
Women aged 40 +		58	23	19	354
All men		63	21	16	519
All women		66	20	14	566
All persons		65	20	15	1085

Note: Britain: the analysis includes students in full-time education, for comparison with Eurobarometer surveys for the 1980s, Spain: people aged 18 and over, excluding full-time students.

There are two common themes in the stories women tell about their lives: that everything changed after they had children, and that they had not foreseen how big the change would be, even the change in their own attitudes and priorities came as a surprise to them. This suggests low levels of self-knowledge. Another possible reason for this surprise is that few young women have any direct knowledge of what is involved in caring for and educating babies and small children, because small family sizes mean that nowadays older siblings are rarely drawn into caring for younger siblings, as always happened in families with four or more children. This lack of basic training in childcare in the family of origin also explains the huge demand for books, magazines and other public information on childcare, knowledge that historically was always passed on from mother to daughter.

Table 4.7a shows that ageing effects in Britain are coterminous with changes over the lifecycle and reflect some degree of self-selection into and out of marriage. As people move from being young and single through cohabitation, marriage, divorce or separation and widowhood, support for the egalitarian model of marriage dwindles and support for some degree of role differentiation increases. What is remarkable is that sex differences within each marital status are small or non-existent, except for the fact that women who stay married are most likely to favour the compromise model of marriage while husbands are most likely to favour the egalitarian model. Men and women who quit marriage to become divorced or separated are again a self-selected group, with half preferring the egalitarian model, while 4% reject all three models of marriage, the largest proportion to do so. The widowed have the largest proportion of people who gave don't know responses to the question on family models (4%), suggesting that by this stage they have ceased to care about the sexual division of labour.

A similar but weaker process of adjustment to marriage is evident in Spain (Table 4.7b), and here too there are no sex differences within each marital status. The divorced and separated group is very small and distinctive in Spain, partly because divorce is still extremely rare, having been legalized only in 1981. Uncertainty about family models is again concentrated among the divorced, who have reason to question marriage, and the widowed as well, more surprisingly.

Marriage and Divorce

In both countries, most respondents live as part of a couple. In Britain, three-quarters of the sample live in couple households.[4] Couples are defined as married (2154 cases) or cohabiting (267 cases) people, with or without

Table 4.7a   Ideal family model by marital status, Britain

	Single	Cohabiting	Married	Divorced & separated	Widowed
Egalitarian	57	56	36	50	32
Compromise	26	32	43	29	36
Role segregation	14	10	18	16	26
None of these	2	2	2	4	2
Do not know	1	*	1	1	4
Base = 100%	697	267	2153	265	259

Table 4.7b   Ideal family model by marital status, Spain

	Single	Married & Cohabiting	Divorced & separated	Widowed
Egalitarian	74	61	73	45
Compromise	16	20	15	22
Role segregation	6	17	6	24
None of these	2	*	3	5
Do not know	2	2	3	4
Base = 100%	235	755	33	96

children living at home.[5] In Britain, half of all couples of working age have children aged 0–15 years living with them, and half do not. A tiny proportion (2%) are living as part of a larger household with other adults without children. Two-thirds of all couples are buying their home with a mortgage; one in ten live in public sector social housing (termed council tenants in Britain); a tiny 6% live in privately rented accommodation. In Spain, two-thirds of the sample is married (726 cases) or cohabiting (33 cases), and most of them have children still living with them, of any age. Some analyses are restricted to people of working age (20–59 years), and as usual full-time students are excluded.

Young people aged under 25 have the least stable sex-role preferences. Their preferences change quickly as they grow older, and they are hugely sensitive to alternative listings of the three family models, as noted in Chapter 3 (see Table 3.3). We might expect married and cohabiting couples to have the most stable preferences, partly because they are older, and partly because they are in the situation where concrete decisions about the family division of labour must be made.

If someone chooses a partner with identical views on the ideal family model, they are most likely to fully implement their preferred allocation of family responsibilities. If, however, someone chooses a spouse with different preferences, as a result of poor communication, lack of self-knowledge in either party or because other factors were of overriding importance, there is likely to be some conflict over the family division of labour, which ends in some sort of compromise or else contributes to a divorce. Unfortunately, the two surveys tell us only about the preferences of individuals: the single respondent in each household who was interviewed. There is no direct information on spouses' preferences and the degree of assortive mating on attitudes within couples. We might assume that most people have the wit to choose a partner with the same, or fairly close, sex-role ideology, but there is only indirect evidence to support this assumption (Kiernan, 1992: 99; Hakim, 1996a: 88–91), and ample anecdotal evidence that couples regularly fail to check out each other's fundamental values before sailing into marriage. In addition, spouses' attitudes may change after marriage. There is also evidence from our surveys that perfect matches cannot be attained by everyone, especially in Britain, given the small but important sex differences in the distribution of preferences among couples (Table 4.8). This analysis is restricted to people of working age, so as to exclude the imbalance in the sex ratio among people over pension age, many of whom are widows or widowers.

Table 4.8 shows that among British wives the main preference is for the compromise model that gives them a secondary earner role, whereas the main preference among men is for the egalitarian model which requires wives to be primary earners alongside the husband. There is a sufficiently large sex difference here to produce substantial numbers of marriages nationally that cross preference boundaries, with scope for conflict and disagreements. For example, given that most women are in full-time work prior to marriage, many husbands may erroneously assume their wife will continue in full-time work after marriage, especially if she professes to prefer an egalitarian arrangement. In reality, only half of all women, and half of all married women, who prefer the egalitarian model continue with full-time work across the lifecycle in Britain, as shown in Chapter 5. In Spain, the discrepancy between husbands' and wives' preferences is probably too small to matter.

Table 4.8 Ideal family model of spouses, Spain and Britain

| | Ideal model of the family | | | |
	Egalitarian	Compromise	Role segregation	Base = 100%
Spain				
Men	70	19	11	373
Women	73	17	10	386
Husbands	67	21	12	244
Wives	70	18	12	289
Britain				
Men	49	36	15	1068
Women	44	42	14	1236
Husbands	46	39	15	778
Wives	38	48	14	904
Average number of children <16 at home:				*Total*
per wife	.84	.94	1.09	.92
per husband	.73	1.01	1.16	.89

Note: Base is people aged 20–59 years, then married and cohabiting people aged 20–59 years, always excluding full-time students.

The second important finding in Table 4.8 is that in Britain the sex-role preferences of couples differ from the distribution in the whole sample (see Table 3.1) or even in the working age population (Table 4.8). The differences are small but important because they confirm that married women in particular (and to a lesser extent cohabiting women) are a self-selected subgroup with a lower level of interest in the egalitarian family model and a stronger preference for some role specialization in the family. By definition, the latter choice requires a breadwinner partner to support homemaking and childrearing activities, so it is not surprising that such women are more likely to marry or cohabit. The association is of course weakened in countries, such as Britain, where social welfare benefits have permitted solo mothers to survive financially while remaining full-time homemakers without a male partner, either as a result of divorce or unmarried pregnancy. In some modern societies, such as Spain, there is effectively no state support for unmarried mothers, and social stigma rules it out anyway. In Spain, there is little difference between the preferences of married couples and all aged 20–59, implying almost no self-selection into marriage.

In line with preference theory, couples who favour role specialization have larger families than couples who prefer symmetrical roles. Table 4.8 shows the average number of children aged under 16 years living at home per spouse in Britain, what demographers call the 'own child' measure of fertility. As expected, people who prefer the egalitarian model have the fewest children; people who favour complete role specialization have the largest families. The variation in fertility between the three groups is larger for men than for women, probably because men can continue to father children until later in life, especially if they marry for a second time to a younger wife.

Both surveys show a high degree of consistency between husbands and wives who favour a particular family model – in their sex-role ideology and in their reports of who is the primary earner in the household. We interpret this as *agreement* between spouses with a particular preference, but strictly speaking we have no data on couples' preferences, only on individual married men and women. It is possible, for example, that spouses who favour the role-segregated model – a minority preference in Britain by 1999 – are least likely to have found a perfect match in sex-role ideology, as well as in all the other factors that matter in marriage markets and mate selection (Hakim, 2000a: 196–222), so they are least likely to fully implement their preferences. This might explain some of the discrepancies between preferences and behaviour in this group in Britain noted in Chapter 5.

In both countries, three-quarters of all couples aged 20–59 say that the husband alone is the primary earner (see Table 3.12). In Spain, 17% say both spouses are joint earners, 5% report the wife as main earner, and 2% are living as part of a larger household, usually with parents. In Britain, 12% say the wife is the primary earner (7% among couples with children and 16% among couples without children); 13% say they are joint earners (18% among couples without children and 7% among couples with children). The great majority (75%) of British couples who say they are joint earners have no dependent children at home. Some of these may be voluntary childfree couples; others are young and have probably not yet had any children, and some are old enough for their children to have already left home.

As noted earlier in relation to Table 3.12, there is no connection between stated sex-role preferences and income-earning roles in couples. The only group that comes close to implementing their ideal family model is the compromise group in Britain, with 81–91% of spouses saying the husband is the main earner, and the group choosing differentiated roles in Spain. Couples choosing the egalitarian model of the family are by far the least likely to be implementing their stated aims. In addition, one-quarter of women in Britain who prefer the role-segregated model find themselves obliged to be joint main earners or even sole main earner (Table 3.12a).

We might expect the majority of couples choosing the egalitarian family model to say they are jointly responsible for income-earning. In reality, only 22% of husbands and 15% of wives report this – a small minority. The proportion rises to a maximum of around one-quarter of couples aged 45–64, among wives who really prefer the role-segregated arrangement as well as among spouses who prefer the egalitarian model. Overall, the idealistic younger cohort is the least likely to report egalitarian income-earning roles which, as noted earlier, are largely a matter of personal identity and responsibility. In Spain, joint income-earning is more common, but there is only a small difference between the egalitarian group and the group preferring differentiated roles, so attitudes have no impact here.

The main dividing line in the British sample is between those aiming (however fruitlessly) for the egalitarian model with symmetrical family roles, and those who accept some sort of division of labour between spouses, whether partial or complete. Both among married and cohabiting couples, and in the non-married group, there are relatively few ideological differences between the groups aiming for the compromise family model and the role-segregation model. For Spain, this aggregation is dictated by small numbers in these two groups. Table 4.9 uses this simplified classification to display responses on all other indicators of sex-role ideology, including the summary indexes of patriarchy and work centrality.

Overall, in both countries, there is greater ideological coherence and consistency in the group choosing differentiated roles in the family. The egalitarian group displays an astonishingly high level of internal inconsistency and conflict in values and attitudes, among women as well as men, both among the married couples and in the smaller non-married group. (The non-married group includes singles not yet married as well as ex-married people.) For example, one-quarter to one-third of egalitarian spouses still believe the husband should be the main breadwinner even if the wife has a job, a view which completely negates the idea of privately chosen symmetrical roles. A minority of around 10% still believe in a totally rigid sexual division of labour, namely that ultimate responsibility for income-earning and housework fall to men and women respectively. About one-fifth accept the weak version of the marriage bar for working women. Overall, one-third of egalitarian couples accept patriarchal values that are inimical to the idea of symmetrical roles in the family. Finally, only one-quarter of professedly egalitarian wives in Britain and 17% in Spain are prepared to accept the joint responsibility for income-earning and work commitment that are necessarily entailed by fully symmetrical roles. Among people preferring role specialization, there is roughly the same level of ideological

Table 4.9 Ideological consistency in Britain and Spain

| | Ideal family model | | | | | |
| | Symmetrical roles | | Differentiated roles | | All 20–59 | |
	M	F	M	F	M	F
Britain						
Ultimate responsibility for income-earning lies with men	12	7	34	28	23	19
Ultimate responsibility for housework lies with women	10	12	32	34	22	24
Even if women work, man is still main breadwinner, % who agree	36	30	63	58	50	45
With high unemployment, wives should stay home, % who agree	17	14	37	33	27	24
% accept/ambivalent on patriarchy	39	35	68	64	54	51
% who would still work even without economic necessity	63	72	60	54	61	62
% who regard themself as primary earner	79	49	87	33	83	40
% who are work-centred	50	36	51	19	50	27
Base = 100%	522	542	546	690	1068	1232
Spain						
Ultimate responsibility for income-earning lies with men	7	7	55	41	21	16
Ultimate responsibility for housework lies with women	9	6	49	34	21	14
Even if women work, man is still main breadwinner, % who agree	24	24	70	60	42	36
With high unemployment, wives should stay home, % who agree	16	20	60	55	34	32
% accept/ambivalent on patriarchy	26	26	70	59	40	35
% who would still work even without economic necessity	50	58	55	32	51	51
% who regard themself as primary earner	76	33	83	16	78	28
% who are work-centred	37	21	46	5	40	17
Base = 100%	262	283	111	103	387	390

Note: Data for people aged 20–59, excluding full-time students.

consistency among the married couples and non-married people. Among people choosing the egalitarian family model, the non-married group displays more ideological consistency and coherence than do married couples. People's claim to prefer the egalitarian family model is flatly contradicted by a deep-rooted sex-role ideology that insists on role segregation in the family in around one-third of husbands and wives, compared to one-quarter (at most) of the non-married group. Ideologically confused spouses are not necessarily married to each other, so the total number of marriages affected could be greater than one-third.

This lack of internal coherence and consistency in the sex-role ideology of the professedly egalitarian group may well be the cause of substantially higher divorce rates in this group, as compared with couples who choose differentiated family roles (Table 4.10). Ideological inconsistency and divorce rates are generally higher among women in the egalitarian group, who typically fail to adopt the primary earner identity.

Table 4.10 shows that in both countries divorce rates and separation rates are systematically higher among people who claim to prefer the egalitarian model of family roles. Divorce is relatively new and rare in Spain, and base numbers are much smaller, so the discussion focuses on Britain. In both age groups, among men and women, people choosing the egalitarian family model have higher divorce and separation rates than people choosing some degree of role specialization in marriage.[6] There are several possible explanations for the higher divorce rates. One is the problem of spouses being mismatched on lifestyle preferences, but this problem is found among other preference groups as well, and they have lower divorce rates. Second, there is the problem of people claiming to prefer symmetrical family roles, while in reality they prefer the idea of differentiated roles, with the husband as main breadwinner. A third possibility is that people may genuinely want to implement a marriage with symmetrical roles but find it more difficult than they expected, with husbands underestimating how much domestic work and childcare they have to do, and wives underestimating just what it means to go out to work full-time continuously throughout life. Many couples also underestimate the extra work involved in having and raising children; it is usually childbirth that prompts wives to reduce their work hours, or give up employment altogether. Finally, it is sometimes argued that women in role-segregated marriages are trapped and cannot leave, even if the relationship is unsatisfactory, because they do not have a job to enable them to support themselves. However, the relatively high full-time workrates among these women (see Table 5.4) undermines this explanation. Whatever the reason, it appears that role-differentiated marriages are more successful, and are less likely to end in divorce. There is supporting evidence for this conclusion from the British NCDS cohort study, which

Models of the Family in Modern Societies

**Table 4.10   Divorce rates by ideal family model, Britian and Spain:
percentage who are currently divorced/separated**

| | | Ideal family model | | |
		Symmetrical roles	Differentiated roles	Total
Britain				
Men	<40	11	4	7
	40 +	5	8	7
	all	9	6	7
Women	<40	19	11	14
	40 +	16	8	11
	all	17	9	12
All	<40	16	8	11
	40 +	12	7	9
	all	13	7	10
Spain				
Men	<40	1	..	2
	40 +	7	2	4
	all	5	2	4
Women	<40	5	3	4
	40 +	4	2	3
	all	4	2	4
All	<40	3	3	4
	40 +	5	2	4
	all	5	2	4

Note: Data for ever-married people aged 16 and over (Britain) or 18 and over (Spain) who
have completed their full-time education.

found that full-time homemakers and wives with part-time jobs were
happier than wives with full-time jobs. Childcare work is a major source of
marital dissatisfaction among wives, and frequently prompts a decline in
marital satisfaction among spouses (Hakim, 2000a: 146–9, 179–84).
However, the relatively high level of ideological inconsistency in the
egalitarian group must also be a contributory factor.

Regional Variations

It seems reasonable to expect some degree of regional variation in sex-role
ideology. Local industrial and economic conditions vary hugely across a

Table 4.11   Regional variations in sex-role ideology, Britain

	1	2	3
The North	46	36	38
Midlands & East	41	38	36
London	43	44	41
South East	35	38	36
South West	46	41	36
Wales	42	36	46
Scotland	47	37	39
Britain	43	38	38

Notes: Data for people aged 16 and over excluding full-time students.
The three indicators are:
1. % who prefer the egalitarian family model
2. % who reject patriarchal values
3. % who are work-centred.

country, and if the social and economic environment affects attitudes and values, then there should be substantial regional variation in our survey results. In practice, there is little or no regional variation in Britain, on any of our core indicators (Table 4.11). Rural–urban variations in Spain are also small, even on patriarchal values (Table 4.12).

In Britain, there are small and non-systematic regional variations across all key indicators of attitudes and values (Table 4.11). Depending on the particular value, different regions emerge as having the highest or lowest scores. For example, the South East region (excluding London) has the lowest proportion (35%) of men and women who prefer the egalitarian model of the family, and Scotland has the highest percentage overall (47%). The North has the highest percentage of people preferring the role segregation model of the family (21%) and Scotland has the lowest (15%). Wales has the largest proportion (77%) of men who are work-centred. Among women, London has the highest proportion of women who are work-centred (but still only 30%), and the South East region has the lowest at 21%. The Northern region has the highest percentage of patriarchal men (65%), while London and the South West region have the lowest (56% and 53% respectively). The largest proportion of women who accept patriarchal values is in Wales (65%) and the lowest is in London again (55%). Overall, Wales and the North score highest on patriarchal values (64% in both regions). Similarly, Wales has the highest percentage of people who continue to believe that the income-earning role falls ultimately to men: 33% overall, 38% among men and 30% among women. London has the lowest proportion endorsing this idea, 23%. Wales has the highest proportion of people who still think that women have ultimate responsibility for housework: 35% overall, among men and among women. Again, London scores lowest at 24%.

Overall, London is the only region to emerge as systematically and consistently distinctive. Londoners are most likely to reject patriarchal values (but still only 44% do so), and they include above-average numbers of work-centred men (55%) and women (30%). In the younger generation, London and Wales emerge as having the highest proportion of work-centred people, 42% and 43%, well above levels in all other regions. As noted already, Londoners are least likely to endorse rigid role segregation in the family, as indicated by ultimate responsibility for income-earning and housework. However, as regards sex-role preferences, Londoners are stereotypically average, while people in the neighbouring South East region have the lowest support for the egalitarian model of marriage with symmetrical roles (35%) and high support for the family with role specialization (18%).

Regional variations are explained in part by differences in the age structure of each region. London is unusual in having a population balanced fairly evenly between the younger and older generations, whereas the South East and Wales have a preponderance of people aged 40 and over, including many people over retirement age. However, the popularity of patriarchal values in the North is not explained by the local age structure; it seems to be a distinctive feature of the northern England culture.

In sum, it is the absence of major regional variations that is most striking in the British survey. This finding further confirms the absence of any important variations in sex-role ideology by social, economic and cultural capital. This means that the analyses presented in this book apply equally to all regions in Britain.

The Spanish dataset includes a measure of the size of locality that neatly identifies the rural–urban divide. The remarkable finding in Table 4.12 is that there is no important and systematic rural–urban variation in ideal family model. All three family models are chosen across the entire country, confirming that there are no important variations by social or economic capital.

Table 4.12   Rural–urban variations in sex-role ideology, Spain

Size of locality	*1*	*2*	*3*	*4*
Madrid-Barcelona	65	59	52	23
Other over 1 million	65	52	51	23
400001–1 million	70	55	25	14
100001–400000	75	48	43	13
50001–100000	60	55	40	10
10001–50000	70	56	35	15
2000–10000	61	52	46	12
Less than 2000	51	45	32	11
Spain	65	53	40	16

Notes: Data for people aged 18 and over excluding full-time students.
The four indicators are:
1. % who prefer the egalitarian family model
2. % who reject patriarchal values
3. % of men who are work-centred
4. % of women who are work-centred.

In contrast, there are moderate urban–rural variations in other values, notably on attitudes towards patriarchy. People in the very smallest rural areas are most likely to accept patriarchal values, while people in Madrid and Barcelona are most likely to reject patriarchal values. Madrid, Barcelona and other cities with over 1 million population also have the highest percentages of work-centred men and women, probably because such people are attracted to big cities and the wider range of job opportunities they offer. Otherwise, there is no systematic urban–rural variation in work-centrality or in patriarchal values in Spain. Overall, rural–urban variations in sex-role ideology are small or non-existent in Spain, contrary to expectation.

Conclusions

The findings in this chapter confirm and extend those in Chapter 3 on the internal logic of sex-role ideology and the relationships between key elements. Chapter 3 showed that men and women adopt or drop primary and secondary earner identities across the lifecycle, as they move in and out of marriage. Here we show that adoption of the identity and responsibilities of primary earner is not determined primarily by occupation and earnings level,

as so often argued by feminists. The pay gap is irrelevant in this particular context, as men with low earnings routinely adopt the primary earner role.
 ' People's perceptions of themselves as the (joint) main earners of their household, as secondary earners or as dependents are shaped by their sex-role ideology more than by their employment status. At the start of the twenty-first century, four-fifths of men still see themselves as a main breadwinner, and this varies little across age cohorts and subgroups. In contrast, three-fifths of women see themselves as secondary earners, if they work at all. There are no contradictions here: among couples of working age there is almost complete agreement that men are usually the main breadwinner, even if a change in attitudes means that they are no longer seen as having this role imposed on them automatically and exclusively. In effect, the majority of wives still regard themselves as secondary earners and this leads them to choose part time jobs rather than full-time jobs, and to earn less than their husbands. Many secondary earners even take marginal jobs, working less than 10 hours a week. Secondary earners are concentrated in lower grade white-collar and blue-collar work, while people who regard themselves as primary earners (or equal joint earners) gravitate to higher grade (and better paid) white-collar and blue-collar work. Results for couples are duplicated in the full sample. We have also shown that social, economic and cultural capital are not important correlates or predictors of lifestyle preferences in modern societies.

Perhaps the most important finding is that human capital theory assumptions about education reflecting long-term workplans and careerist values are simply unfounded. Human capital theory thus contributes little or nothing to explanations of women's and men's employment decisions and career plans. Higher education serves as a superior marriage market as well as a source of training and personal development. The ambitious young woman can use the education system as a ladder for upward social mobility, whether she subsequently uses the marriage market or the labour market to achieve higher socio-economic status. To some extent, women can keep their options open; they do not have to make a firm choice in advance. However, work-centred women will generally choose to study more vocational subjects (such as law, medicine, business studies), whereas home-centred women are more likely to choose non-vocational subjects (such as art, history or literature). Adaptive women may choose from the full range of subjects, and they tend to keep their options open longest. Some subjects, such as sociology, attract people with all lifestyle preferences. We have demonstrated that women who obtain higher education qualifications are not exclusively work-centred, and are not pursuing formal education solely as an investment in lifelong employment careers. Women with higher education qualifications encompass the full range of lifestyle preferences, just as in the female population as a whole. As Chapter 5 will show, it is lifestyle preferences, rather than qualifications, that are the strongest determinant of women's employment patterns. In sum, supply side factors do matter, but not in the way theorized by labour economists. It is essential to collect information on people's lifestyle preferences, rather than making assumptions about them or simply leaving them aside.

Notes

1   Garrido (1992) also divides Spanish women into two age cohorts, those under 40 and those over 40, and he also concludes that the two groups are so radically different that it is pointless trying to identify specific causes of the changes observed.

2   Recommendations for the new National Statistics Socio-Economic Classification (NS-SEC) were only confirmed at the end of 1998. They then had to be updated once the *Standard Occupational Classification 2000* (ONS, 2000) was produced for the 2001 Census. In practice, the new NS SEC was only introduced, in the 2001 Census and in government surveys, from April 2001 onwards.

3   Virtually all the 19% of people who failed to provide information on family income simply refused the question. They are just as likely to be men as women, working and not employed, primary or secondary earners. Missing data is higher on personal income because so many women have no income to report. For people in employment, refusals are at the same level as for family income. Almost three-quarters of people with missing data on personal income are not in employment, most of them women.

4   The British survey identified only four men and two women living in same-sex couples. The six same-sex couples mostly preferred the egalitarian model of marriage, but the tiny numbers mean that the results are not reliable. They are excluded from all analyses of married and cohabiting heterosexual couples. The total of six persons in same-sex cohabitations constitute less than 0.2% of the total sample of people aged 16 and over, and less than 0.3% of the total number of married and cohabiting couples in Britain. Our survey results are consistent with those from other national surveys in Britain. The General Household Survey found that in the late 1990s, same-sex couples constituted less than 0.2% of all persons aged 20–59 years. The 1999 Labour Force Survey estimated that 0.2% of households were headed by a same-sex couple. Surveys in the USA suggest that less than 1% of households have a homosexual head. It appears that the importance of same-sex couples has been vastly exaggerated, in policy analysis, in feminist writing and in speculative theorizing about the future of the family by Giddens and others (Morgan, 2002: 27–8, 35–7).

5   Research in North America and Western Europe shows that married and cohabiting couples form qualitatively different groups in terms of financial arrangements, lifestyle, values and their own perception of the relationship (Morgan, 2000; Smock, 2000; Waite and Gallagher, 2000: 36–46; Cohen, 2002). In their attitudes and values, cohabiting couples in our survey are similar to single people rather than to married people. So there are strong arguments for grouping the cohabiting couples with single people rather than with married couples. However, it has become conventional to group cohabitees with married couples in social research analyses. For example, reports on the General Household Survey in Britain define a family as a married or cohabiting heterosexual couple, with or without children. As cohabitees constitute only 11% of the combined

group of couples, they do not have a major impact on results. Results for married couples alone (excluding cohabitees) are generally more sharply defined, and display larger differences between lifestyle preference groups, but also run into the problem of smaller base numbers, as illustrated by the analyses for married couples only in Hakim (2003b).

6   Divorce rates are understated in Table 4.10 because they only show people who have divorced and not yet remarried. People who have remarried after a divorce cannot be distinguished from other married people.

Chapter 5

Ideological Influences on Employment

We already know that sex-role ideology and personal identity shape women's employment decisions. This has been the unanticipated finding from studies that set out to assess how the lack of childcare services constrained women's ability to return to work after having children. Feminists and the European Commission have constantly emphasized childcare services as the key factor affecting women's work decisions, despite clear evidence to the contrary. For example, Portugal has almost none of the childcare services that are deemed essential for women to have real choices about returning to work after childbirth, yet Portugal has one of the highest levels of female full-time employment in the EU, and the female FTE employment rate in Portugal puts it on the same level as Sweden and Finland (see Table 1.3). Very occasionally, the European Commission has admitted that childcare is not necessarily a crucial factor (Hakim, 1997: 46), but it has not sought to find out what is.

Research on the decision to return to work or not, and attitudes towards childcare show that women's choices are determined *first* by a woman's values, and only *second* by practical issues such as the availability and cost of childcare. Some women would not consider returning to work and leaving their children in someone else's care, irrespective of the cost and convenience of local childcare services. Other women would not consider staying at home to care for their children, irrespective of the quality of available services. For example, an analysis of the BSAS concluded that childcare was far less important than a woman's conception of her role at home and her responsibilities as a mother (Thomson, 1995: 80–83). Numerous other studies have presented consistent findings (Hakim, 1997: 35–44). Two studies in the ESRC Future of Work Research Programme also found that a woman's employment decisions after childbirth are shaped primarily by her sex-role ideology and her identity as a mother first and foremost, or else as a worker and a mother combined.

One study by an economist (Himmelweit, 2001) relied on 34 depth interviews with mothers about their decisions to return to work after childbirth or not, plus secondary analysis of BHPS data. She found that young women were aware of having more choices than their mothers ever had, and were tolerant of other mothers who made decisions different from their own. Mothers' decisions were determined primarily by their own identities, as mothers first and foremost, or as working women who also had a child. Women tended to present these identities as fixed, and a constraint which forced their choice in a particular direction. Financial constraints (such as a partner's earnings and any mortgage debt) were considered less important than the 'constraint' of a woman's own identity. Her conception of the motherhood role was presented as an immovable fact of life, and 'affordable' childcare was defined in relation to the mother's self-identity as a mother.

Another study by a social psychologist (Houston, 2001) surveyed 400 women who worked full-time during pregnancy, all of them first-time mothers, with follow-up surveys at 6 and 12 months after the birth. Even this sample biased towards working mothers was found to be heterogeneous in values. The 20% of young women who planned to stay at home as full-time mothers after the birth had different values from those (26% of the sample) who were determined to return to work full-time after the birth. However, the key finding was that the great majority of new mothers are able to fulfil their intentions, whether to return to work or not, without serious difficulty, and that values generally determine behaviour: 82% of those intending to stay at home full-time did so; 76% of those planning to return to part-time work did so; and 62% of the women intending to return to full-time work went back to a full-time job. However, most women saw any return to work as temporary, and intended to seriously reduce their involvement in paid work after the birth of a second child. Social class, education and partner's income were not significant predictors of young women's workplans after the first birth. Employers' maternity leave policies and benefits also had no impact on women's plans or eventual decisions. The main predictor of employment after a birth was the mother's values and ensuing workplans. Some women placed the baby's interests first. Some women placed their own interests first. Most tried some sort of compromise between the two. Women who stayed at home full-time reported much happier babies.

There is no information on childcare in our two surveys. The focus here is on the impact of sex-role ideology on employment patterns across the lifecycle: the decision to work full-time, part-time or not at all. In Britain, there is a substantial part-time workforce, so women have a real choice between full-time and part-time work. In Spain, part-time jobs are scarce, so women generally work full-time or not at all. Long periods of high unemployment in Spain have forced women to make definite choices to keep their jobs or not work at all after marriage, whereas in Britain women move in and out of the labour force throughout the lifecycle (Hakim, 1996a: 120–44). We have already established that social class, income and education have little impact on people's ideal family model, so there is no reason to control for social class. The effects of education are bound up with differences between age cohorts, so we control for age where possible.

The Long-Term Impact of Values

There is a long-standing reluctance in sociology to accept that values can have a major impact on behaviour. Preference theory accepts that attitudes and values have little scope for influencing behaviour in pre-modern societies and, more particularly, in societies that have yet to fully implement the new scenario for women, because most decisions are still shaped by economic necessity and rigid social conventions in such societies. The impact of values and lifestyle preferences only emerges in prosperous modern societies where what Inglehart terms 'post-materialist' values have emerged (Inglehart, 1990, 1997).

In addition, recent research has shown that early studies of the relationship between attitudes and behaviour were methodologically flawed. Improved methodology demonstrates a causal impact of *personal* values on individual behaviour (Hakim, 2000a: 72–82). One major methodological development has been the longitudinal study which follows people over a long span of time (Hakim, 2000b: 109–26). These were developed earliest in the USA. From the 1960s onwards, the National Longitudinal Surveys (NLS) provided longitudinal data that allowed the long-term influence, or insignificance, of work orientations and work plans to be measured rigorously. Of particular interest is the cohort of young women aged 14–24 in 1968 who were interviewed almost every year up to 1983 when aged 29–39 years. This cohort was asked in 1968, and again at every subsequent interview, what they would like to be doing when they were 35 years old, whether they planned to be working at age 35 or whether they planned to marry, keep house and raise a family at age 35.[1] Compared to the length and complexity of work commitment questions included in some surveys (Bielby and Bielby, 1984) the question is crude, and conflates preferences and plans. But presumably because it asked about women's personal plans, rather than generalized approval/disapproval attitudes, the question turned out to have astonishing analytical and predictive power, and was used again in the second youth cohort study initiated in 1979.

There are a number of independent analyses of the extent to which early work plans were fulfilled by age 35. They all show that women achieved their objectives for the most part, resulting in dramatic 'mark-ups' to career planners in terms of occupational grade and earnings (Mott, 1982; Rexroat and Shehan, 1984; Shaw and Shapiro, 1987). Furthermore, career planners were more likely to choose typically male jobs, had lower job satisfaction than other women and adapted their fertility behaviour to their work plans (Waite and Stolzenberg, 1976; Stolzenberg and Waite, 1977; Spitze and Waite, 1980). Work plans were a significant independent predictor of actual work behaviour. After controlling for other factors affecting labour force participation, a woman who consistently planned to work had a probability of working that was 30 percentage points higher than did a woman who consistently planned not to work. Of the women who held consistently to their work plans, four-fifths were actually working in 1980, at age 35, compared to only half of the women who consistently intended to devote themselves exclusively to homemaker activities. Women who planned to work at age 35 were likely to do so unless they had large families or a pre-school child. Women who had planned a 'marriage career' nevertheless were obliged to work by economic factors in half the cases: their husband's low income, divorce or the opportunity cost of not working led half to be in work despite aiming for a full-time homemaker role.

Planning to work yielded a significant wage advantage. Women who had consistently planned to work had wages 30 per cent higher than those of women who never planned to work. Those women who had planned to work in the occupation they actually held at age 35 had even higher wages than women whose occupational plans were not realized. Women who made realistic plans and acquired necessary skills fared best in the labour market. Those who fared worst were women who planned an exclusive homemaking career but ended up working for economic reasons. However, career planners were a small minority of one-quarter of the young women cohort; the vast majority of the cohort had unplanned careers (Table 5.1), as did women in the older cohort aged 30–44 years at the start of the study in the late 1960s (Mott, 1978, 1982; Shaw, 1983).[2]

As far back as the 1980s, the NLS longitudinal data overturned the results of cross-sectional studies showing that women's work behaviour is heavily determined by the number and ages of any children, rather than the other way round. Those who work only if their family responsibilities permit them to do so are in effect fulfilling a prior choice of emphasis on the homemaker career. Fertility expectations have only a small negative effect on young women's work plans, whereas work plans exert a powerful negative effect on young women's childbearing plans (Waite and Stolzenberg, 1976; Stolzenberg and Waite, 1977; Sproat *et al.*, 1985: 78). Factors which have long been held to determine women's labour force participation, such as other family income, educational qualifications, marital status and age of youngest child were revealed as being most important in relation to women with little or no work commitment, who have so far been in the majority. Women with definite career plans manifested a rather inelastic labour supply, similar to that of men (Shaw and Shapiro, 1987).[3]

Table 5.1 Young women's workplans and outcomes in the USA

	Distribution of sample %	% working at age 35
Homemaker career		
Consistently indicate no plans for work: aim is marriage, family and homemaking activities	28	49
Drifters and unplanned careers	47	64
(a) Highly variable responses over time, no clear pattern in plans for age 35	(35)	
(b) Switch to having future work expectations at some point in their twenties	(12)	
Career planners		
Consistently anticipate working at age 35 throughout their twenties	25	82

Source: Hakim (2000a: Table 4.6).

Overall the NLS results have repeatedly shown the importance of motivations, values and attitudes as key determinants of labour market behaviour, occupational status and even earnings, an influence that is independent of conventional human capital factors, and frequently exceeds the influence of behavioural factors (Parnes, 1975; Andrisani, 1978; Mott, 1982; Sproat *et al.*, 1985). These 'psychological' variables are too often omitted from research, so their importance has been overlooked.[4]

Similar results emerge from other longitudinal studies, on the rare occasions when researchers address the long-term impact of values and life goals. Attitudes have a specially strong impact on women's behaviour, because they have genuine choices to make regarding employment versus homemaking in the new scenario. But attitudes and values have also been shown to have a major impact on men as well. For example, Szekelyi and Tardos analysed 20 years of Panel Study of Income Dynamics (PSID) microdata for 1968–88 to show that people who plan ahead and express confidence and optimism about their plans subsequently earn significantly higher incomes than those who do not, after controlling for initial levels of income, education, age, sex, race, type of area and region. The long-term effects of attitudes were stronger than short-term effects. The impact of optimistic planning on earnings was smaller than the impact of education, sex and initial income in 1967 (if included) but it was larger than the impact of age, race and locational variables. Attitudes affected the earnings of both male heads of households and their wives (Szekelyi and Tardos, 1993).

Similar results are reported by Duncan and Dunifon (1998) from another analysis of 24 years of PSID data, this time covering men only. Motivation (as measured in the early twenties) had a large impact on long-term success (as measured by hourly earnings 16–20 years later), and the effect remained after controlling for other factors. Only a small part of the impact of motivation worked through its effect on greater investment in training and education; a substantial part remained after this control. The study showed that values commonly found among women, such as religiosity (as measured by church attendance) and a preference for affiliation (as measured by a preference for friendly and sociable work settings rather than challenging work settings) both had a negative effect on earnings. Work orientations that emphasized challenge rather than affiliation and a clear sense of personal efficacy boosted earnings in the early forties.

More recently, the British Household Panel Study (BHPS) has also shown that sex-role ideology strongly influences employment decisions among highly qualified women, who can afford to choose between competing lifestyles, given homogamy (Table 5.2). Whatever their level of education, a two-thirds majority of women have an ambivalent or adaptive, sex-role ideology. Contrary to popular belief, higher education has only a small impact on women's sex-role ideology (Table 5.2). As expected, workrates are higher among highly qualified women than among other women: 82% versus 65% or an increase of 17 percentage points. However, the impact of sex-role ideology is greater, especially among highly qualified women, raising workrates by 28 percentage points, from 64% among women with traditional attitudes to 92% among women with modern attitudes.

In sum, there is already solid evidence that attitudes, values and life goals have an important impact on outcomes in adult life, for men as well as women. However, there has been little attempt to integrate this new knowledge into sociological theory (Hakim, 2002). Preference theory builds on these research results to argue that all women's choices, including the decision to have children or not, and how many to have, as well as employment decisions, are guided by their fundamental values and goals. Preferences do not express themselves in a vacuum, but within the context of local social and cultural institutions, and the particular circumstances of each individual's life. So preferences do not predict behaviour precisely or uniquely. In particular, preferences predict lifestyle choices, but they do not predict performance and achievements within each choice. Within each lifestyle preference group, some women will be vastly more successful than others, and some will be total failures. As noted in Chapter 4, educational attainment has little or no impact on lifestyle preferences, so there will be

Table 5.2 The impact of sex-role ideology on women's workrates

	Percentage of each group in employment		Distribution of sample	
Sex-role ideology	Highly qualified women	Other women	Highly qualified women	Other women
Modern	92	76	23	14
Ambivalent	84	66	63	67
Traditional	64	54	15	20
All women aged 20–59	82	65	100	100
Base = 100%	746	2700	746	2700

Notes: Highly qualified women have tertiary level qualifications, beyond A level (that is, above the level of the Baccalaureate or the *Arbitur*). Other women have no qualifications or only secondary school qualifications (up to A level). Sex role ideology was scored on the basis of nine attitude statements, including the ISSP item 'A husband's job is to earn the money, a wife's job is to look after the home and family'. Of the other eight attitude statements, six concerned the role of a mother and two concerned the role of wives and adult women more generally.
Source: Hakim (2000a), Table 3.4, reporting 1991 data from the British Household Panel Study.

some careerist women who go no further than a clerical job, while others will achieve senior professional or managerial occupations. The association between lifestyle preferences and social class is weak.

Employment Patterns in Britain

Table 5.3 shows current employment status and work histories for the full sample aged 16 and over. In the younger generation, 8% of men and 6% of women are still in full-time education, and another 4–5% are unemployed. However, a four-fifths majority of men are in employment, almost always full-time work. One-third of women are in full-time work, one-third are in part-time jobs and one-quarter are full-time homemakers.

In the older generation, one-third of men and women are already retired. Half of older men are in employment, typically full-time work, compared to two-fifths of women. One-fifth of older women are inactive before they reach retirement age. Whereas almost all men work full-time hours, working

Table 5.3 Employment patterns in Britain by age

	Men			Women		
	<40	*40 +*	*All*	*<40*	*40 +*	*All*
Current status						
Full-time work	74	46	57	37	21	28
Part-time work	7	5	6	31	21	25
Unemployed	5	4	4	4	1	2
Student	8	*	4	6	*	4
Retired	–	36	21	–	38	22
Other inactive	6	10	8	23	19	20
Work history						
Current full time work	74	46	5/	3/	21	28
Current part-time work	7	5	5	31	21	25
Previous full-time work	9	48	32	17	35	28
Previous part-time work	1	1	2	8	20	15
Never had a job	9	*	4	7	3	4
Base = 100%	679	1012	1691	777	1183	1960

women are split half and half between full-time and part-time work, in both age groups.

Almost all men and women have some work experience: only 4% have never had a job. Women who are out of work have dropped out of full-time and part-time jobs, whereas men have usually dropped out of previous full-time jobs (Table 5.3). Men who have never had a job are typically young, and most are still in full-time education. Women who have never had a job are spread across all ages and the full lifecycle. It remains true today that a small fraction of women never do any paid work at any time in their life.

Students in full-time education bridge the gap between the economically active and economically inactive populations. About half of male students have never had a job, but almost half had a job, typically part-time, at the time of the survey. Jobs are even more common among female students: over half had a job at the time of the survey, and only one-quarter had never had a job. All students are excluded from analyses of employment patterns in this chapter. This has a small but still noticeable impact on results for Britain, because roughly half of students have jobs, and their work orientations are clearly different from people whose principal activity is paid employment.

This problem does not arise in Spain, where students generally do not have jobs because they live at home and are supported by their parents.

Ideological Influences on Employment in Britain

Ideal family model has no systematic impact on men's employment (Table 5.4). In all groups, men work full-time throughout life, with hardly any part-time jobs until the pre-retirement or early retirement age of 50–59. Among women, ideal family model has only a small impact on overall workrates. In Britain, its effect is seen mainly in the choice between full-time and part-time work (Table 5.4).

Half (53%) the egalitarian women have full-time jobs compared to one-quarter (26%) of the compromise group and, surprisingly, 41% of the group favouring role segregation. Another 21% of the egalitarians have a part-time job, compared to half (46%) of the compromise group and just 16% of the women who prefer a full-time homemaker role. After the 20–29 years age group (when many women have not yet married or had children), these employment patterns are relatively stable across the lifecycle. In essence, egalitarian women mostly work full-time throughout life, whereas women preferring the compromise arrangement mostly work part-time throughout life. Women who favour full-time homemaking are an anomalous group: they have a lower 57% overall workrate, but they typically hold full-time jobs rather than part-time jobs. The reasons for this are explored later, in the section on contrary groups, which shows that, in certain situations, economic necessity overrides lifestyle preferences.

It is well established that women's workrates, especially full-time workrates, rise with their occupational grade, as measured by social class or socio-economic group (Hakim, 1996a: Table 3.7, 2000a: Table 4.4), with a polarizing trend over time. This pattern is repeated in the 1999 British survey, among all women aged 20–59, and among married and cohabiting women aged 20–59. However, the impact of preferences is maintained within each occupational grade and social class. The lowest full-time workrate, 16%, is thus found among wives with manual occupations (skilled, semi-skilled or unskilled) who favour the compromise model of the family. In contrast, full-time workrates rise to over two-thirds of wives with professional occupations who favour the egalitarian model of the family. The impact of preferences on women's full-time workrates cuts across social class and occupational grade.

It is often assumed that women who take the trouble to gain higher education qualifications must be career-oriented, in contrast with women who leave school with only basic qualifications. Yet studies that have

Table 5.4 The impact of ideal family model on workrates by age, Britain

	Egalitarian		Compromise		Role segregation		All	
	M	F	M	F	M	F	M	F
% in employment	83	74	90	72	72	57	84	71
% with a FT job								
20–29	88	54	83	41	74	53	84	50
30–39	86	48	96	25	76	31	89	35
40–49	80	59	87	18	71	55	82	39
50–59	60	52	82	29	58	30	67	38
All 20–59	79	53	88	26	68	41	81	40
% with a PT job								
20–29	3	18	2	27	0	10	3	19
30–39	1	28	*	50	2	12	1	36
40–49	5	21	3	58	0	11	3	37
50–59	9	17	2	38	10	28	7	28
All 20–59	4	21	2	46	4	16	3	31

Note: Base is people aged 20–59, excluding full-time students and people not choosing one of the three family models.

examined the work orientations of university graduate women have found that their lifestyle preferences are just as diverse as those of non-graduate women, with careerists a distinct minority (Hakim, 2000a: 94–9, 149–54). These results are echoed in our findings in Chapter 4. A national survey carried out in 1991 in Britain also found small differences in sex-role ideology between graduate women and non-graduate women: two-thirds of both groups had an ambivalent perspective on women's role in the family and the workplace (Table 5.2). However, as noted earlier, sex-role ideology strongly influenced employment decisions among highly qualified women, who have access to interesting and well-paid jobs if they choose to work, and can afford childcare. Table 5.5 presents an equivalent analysis based on the 1999 survey.

The British survey provides no information on educational qualifications, so we rely on age of leaving full-time education as a proxy indicator. In Britain, first degrees are normally completed by age 21, so we identify university graduates as people who left full-time education at age 21 or later.

Table 5.5 The impact of sex-role ideology on women's full-time workrates by education, Britain

	% working full-time		Distribution	
	Highly qualified	Other women	Highly qualified	Other women
Ideal family model:				
symmetrical roles	67	49	52	42
differentiated roles	44	27	48	58
Work orientations:				
work-centred	78	52	35	25
other reasons for job	44	31	65	75
Attitude to patriarchy:				
reject	61	46	65	45
accept/ambivalent	48	28	35	55
Lifestyle preferences:				
work-centred	82	56	22	14
adaptive	46	32	64	72
home-centred	54	37	14	14
Average FT workrate for				
all aged 20–59	56	36		
Base = 100%	245	1008	245	1008

Notes: Data for people aged 20–59, who have completed their full-time education. In the absence of information on educational qualifications, the highly qualified are defined as those completing their full-time education at age 21 and over, because in Britain first degrees are normally completed by age 21. People completing full-time education at age 20 or earlier are assumed to have qualifications below tertiary education level.

Those leaving at age 20 or earlier are assumed not to have tertiary level qualifications, although there are tiny numbers of people who do complete a first degree before age 21 in Britain.

As expected, higher education does raise women's full-time workrates, by about 20 percentage points, from 36% to 56% (Table 5.5). However, sex-role ideology has an even stronger impact, especially among university graduate women. Among graduate women who prefer differentiated family roles, 44% work full-time compared to 67% among women who seek symmetrical family roles. Work orientations have a similar impact, raising full-time workrates from 45% to 78% among work-centred women. In contrast, attitudes to patriarchy have a small impact among graduate women, but a more substantial effect on non-graduate women. The pattern among non-graduate women is otherwise similar to that for graduate women, but with smaller differences between groups, as was the case in Table 5.2.

The second part of Table 5.5 shows full-time workrates in each of the three lifestyle preference groups. Apart from the anomaly of relatively high workrates among home-centred women, it is clear that lifestyle preferences have a larger impact on highly qualified women than among women with secondary education or less, raising workrates from a low of 52% (or 45%) to 82%.

The results in Table 5.5 also duplicate the earlier 1991 survey finding that qualifications have only a small impact on sex-role ideology and lifestyle preferences. Work-centred and home-centred women are relatively small minorities at both levels of education. The great majority of graduate and non-graduate women are adaptive: 64% and 72% respectively.

Education has its biggest impact on attitudes to patriarchy rather than on personal preferences. Among women who left school at age 16 or earlier, two-thirds endorse patriarchal values. Among women who left school after age 16, including the university graduates, two-thirds reject patriarchal values. Those who extend their education beyond the compulsory minimum already have, or develop, values that reject male dominance in private and public life. However, the change in attitude has only a modest impact on women's full-time workrates, although it may be influential in other areas of life.

Our proxy measure for educational qualifications undoubtedly weakens the results in Table 5.5. Given this weakness, it is remarkable that sex-role ideology and lifestyle preferences emerge as generally more important than qualifications in raising women's full-time workrates, and are especially important among graduate women.[5] The analysis here focuses on full-time workrates because these produce more well-defined results than with overall workrates, including part-time jobs. In Britain, the label 'part-time' is applied to an enormous variety of work hours, ranging from jobs with less than 10 hours a week to jobs with over 37 hours a week (Hakim, 1998a: Table 5.4). Full-time work is a sharper indicator of a serious involvement in paid employment. Using this measure helps to overcome the weakness in the education indicator.

Commentaries on women's rising workrates tend to assume that dual-earner couples espouse egalitarian values and aim for an equal division of domestic and family work in the home, and then express surprise that men in dual-earner couples still do not do their fair share of housework and childcare. Blossfeld and Drobnic (2001) is a classic example. Table 5.6 demonstrates that attempting to deduce the sex-role ideology of husbands and wives from the mere fact of them both having jobs is foolish. On all three indicators of work orientations, ideal family model and attitude to

Table 5.6 Are dual-earner couples egalitarian in Britain?

	Dual-earner couples		Full-time workers		Wives in PT work	Wives not in work
	M	F	M	F		
Ideal family model:						
symmetrical roles	44	41	44	56	26	31
differentiated roles	56	59	56	44	74	69
Work orientations:						
work-centred	55	21	55	33	10	7
other reasons for job	45	79	45	67	90	93
Attitude to patriarchy:						
accept/ambivalent	53	50	53	42	59	63
reject	47	50	47	58	41	37
Base = 100%	699	673	674	334	339	256

Notes: Data for married and cohabiting couples aged 20–59 who have completed their full-time education. Dual-earner couples are those where either spouse reports being in employment; some of the men may not in fact have a working wife.

patriarchy the majority of dual-earner couples are not aiming for equality, even in modern societies. On the contrary, the majority of these couples favour differentiated roles in marriage and accept patriarchy in public and private life, with no differences between spouses. The majority of husbands regard their jobs as central to their identity while wives do not (Table 5.6). Dual-earner couples are not the innovators and trail blazers they are often assumed to be. Part of the reason is that so many of them consist of 1.5 workers: the husband works full-time while the wife works part-time and retains responsibility for domestic and family work – the classic compromise model of the family. The majority of wives in part-time work do not hold egalitarian values. In fact, there is almost no difference in the sex-role ideology of wives with part-time jobs and wives who do no paid work at all (Table 5.6).

If we focus instead on couples where both spouses have full-time jobs, the picture is only marginally different (Table 5.6). In this case, the majority of wives prefer symmetrical roles and reject patriarchy, but they are small majorities of just over half of all wives. The proportion of wives who are work-centred increases from one-fifth to one-third, but this is still a minority. A two-thirds majority of wives with full-time jobs are working purely for the money or for social reasons; they are not careerist in orientation, as are the majority of their husbands (Table 5.6). These results underline the dangers of attempting to deduce values and ideals from short-term behaviour and national data on female workrates. Studies that take a longer-term or lifecycle perspective show that very few women achieve the long-term workforce participation that is characteristic of male work histories (Hakim, 2000a: 105–10).

The percentage of women in full-time work is a better indicator of a serious involvement in paid work than the overall workrate, especially in Britain, where part-time jobs are beginning to outnumber women's full-time jobs. Full-time jobs are a fair indicator of commitment to employment as a central feature of lifestyle and personal identity, and are an indicator of commitment to being a major contributor to family finances, rather than financially dependent. In Table 5.7, we focus on married and cohabiting couples, because it is only after marriage that women have real choices to make about the relative importance of career and family in their lives. In particular, it is only after marriage that women can implement lifestyle preferences that entail dropping out of the labour force to become full-time homemakers.

Among wives of working age, on average one-third (36%) are in full-time jobs. Among wives who prefer differentiated roles in marriage, and who work for social or mainly financial reasons, full-time workrates fall to 21% (Table 5.7). Among wives who seek symmetrical family roles, and who are work-centred, full-time workrates leap to 72%. Overall, sex-role preferences and work orientations have the effect of doubling full-time workrates, with some overlap between the two (Table 5.7). It is unusual in social science research to find two indicators with such a powerful impact on behaviour. Here we have two attitude variables that jointly raise female full-time workrates from 21% to 72%. Attitudes predict behaviour but, as we have already seen in Table 5.6, behaviour does not predict attitudes.

In contrast, ideal family model and work orientations have no impact on male full-time workrates, which vary slightly around 84% (Table 5.7). This is strong evidence that men do not have as much choice about their lifestyle as women do. It seems likely that in the future men will start to demand some of the freedom of choice that women have already achieved. There is a small hint of this already. Men who prefer symmetrical family roles, most of whom will have married women with similar stated values, have slightly lower full-time workrates than men who believe in differentiated family roles: 80% compared to 87% (Table 5.7). It seems that men in egalitarian marriages feel able to ease up on the breadwinner role, just a little bit.

The analysis in Table 5.7 was repeated separately for couples aged 20–39 and 40–59 years. Results were hardly any different in the two generations in Britain. Ideal family model and work orientations seem to have the same

Table 5.7 Impact of ideal family model and work centrality on full-time workrates (%) among couples in Britain

| | *Ideal family model* | | |
	Symmetrical roles	*Differentiated roles*	*All*
All wives aged 20–59	53	26	36
work-centred	72	60	67
other reasons for job	47	21	30
All husbands aged 20–59	80	87	84
work-centred	79	89	84
other reasons for job	81	85	83

Note: Data for married and cohabiting couples aged 20–59 who have completed their full-time education.

impact on the older generation as on the younger 'new scenario' generation. The analysis was also repeated for all men and all women of working age, with much the same results.

In line with preference theory, the percentage of wives who prefer the egalitarian family model and are work-centred is very small, at 10% of all wives aged 20–59 (Table 5.8). The majority of wives are in the opposite corner of the table: 54% compared to 24% of husbands. The distribution of married men and married women across the four categories in Table 5.8 is fundamentally different. It appears that the attitudes and values that male and female workers bring to their jobs are fundamentally different – as employers have long suspected. This may help to explain different patterns of career development and work history, and consequential differences in the average pay gap between men and women (Hakim, 1996a: 120–86, 1996b). There are even greater differences between the attitudes and values that female part-time workers bring to the workforce compared to those of full-time workers (Table 5.6).

Are all these results merely reflecting the impact of childcare responsibilities on women's lives and not on men's lives? Table 5.9 suggests not. The indicator of parental responsibility in Table 5.9 is whether the respondent is the parent of one or more children aged under 16 living at home. On average, almost half of all couples have one or more children under 16, 46% of wives and 44% of husbands. People who prefer differentiated roles are more likely to have children, especially the husbands. This is partly because they tend to be a little older, on average. In

Table 5.8 Distribution of the sample in Britain

	Ideal family model		
	Symmetrical roles	Differentiated roles	All
All wives aged 20–59	38	62	100%
work-centred	10	8	17
other reasons for job	29	54	83
All husbands aged 20–59	46	54	100%
work-centred	24	30	54
other reasons for job	22	24	45

Note: Data for married and cohabiting couples aged 20–59 who have completed their full-time education.

line with preference theory, women who are work-centred are less likely to have children: 31% compared to the average of 46%. To some extent, women choose between a life centred on home and children and a life centred on paid work outside the home. Apart from this, there are only small variations around the average for all married women. Certainly, the variation in parental responsibilities in Table 5.9 is too small to begin to explain the dramatic variation in women's full-time workrates in Table 5.7. Further analysis showed that sex-role ideology is the main factor differentiating women who continue with full-time work and those who quit their jobs, not the presence of children. Women who have dropped out of full-time jobs are more similar in ideology to other non-working women than to women currently working full-time. Women in part-time jobs are ideologically similar to non-working women; the presence or absence of children under 16 at home makes no difference to their attitudes and values. So there is no evidence here to support the argument that values are a *post hoc* rationalization of choices already made.

Table 5.10 summarizes the results for Britain, and shows the relative importance of practical constraints, such as parental responsibilities, versus lifestyle preferences as determinants of female full-time workrates. Our aim in Table 5.10 is to identify the factors that collectively push wives' full-time workrates up to the same level as husbands' full-time workrates, or depress their workrates down to nothing. For illustrative purposes, the exercise is repeated for all men and women aged 20–59. However, this exercise is theoretically less meaningful. Women's attitudes and values predate, and anticipate, marriage and childbearing, but women only make hard choices

Table 5.9 Parental responsibilities among couples in Britain: percentage of people in each category with child(ren) under 16 at home

	Ideal family model		
	Symmetrical roles	*Differentiated roles*	*All*
All wives aged 20–59	42	48	46
work-centred	31	31	31
other reasons for job	45	51	49
All husbands aged 20–59	35	52	44
work-centred	39	59	50
other reasons for job	31	43	38

Note: Data for married and cohabiting couples aged 20–59 who have completed their full-time education.

between a career and a family-centred life if, and when, they actually marry and have children. The analysis is restricted to people who left full-time education before the age of 21, the best indicator we have for identifying non-graduates. We already know that higher education raises women's full-time workrates by a substantial 20 percentage points. However, graduates represent only one-fifth of the women in our sample; the vast majority of women are non-graduates. Given the highly selective character of higher education in Britain, graduates have higher levels of ability and motivation than in the wider population. So their behaviour is somewhat different. The analysis here is person-centred rather than variable-centred (Magnusson and Bergman, 1988; Cairns *et al.*, 1998; Magnusson, 1998). A key feature of this approach is that it reveals how variables may have a hugely different impact, depending on the context (social group or situation) where they occur. Person-centred analysis recognizes the heterogeneity of respondents, denies that people are homogenous in their responses to social and economic influences and experiences, and takes account of extreme cases, which can amount to 20% of cases at either end of a distribution.[6]

Table 5.10 shows that a combination of lifestyle preferences and just two contextual factors can push women's workrates up to 100% or down to 0% among non-graduate wives. Results are a little weaker for all women aged 20–59 (graduates and non-graduates combined). A work-centred lifestyle preference roughly doubles non-graduate wives' full-time workrates as noted earlier. In contrast, patriarchal values have very little impact and

Table 5.10 Ideological influences on full-time workrates (%) among non-graduates

Cumulative impact of 3–4 factors added in ascending/descending order	Wives	Husbands	Women	Men
+ 4 has a mortgage to pay off	100	83	88	87
+ 3 not parent of child(ren) aged <16	72	77	72	80
+ 2 rejects patriarchal values	72	82	62	83
+ 1 work-centred lifestyle preference	64	76	56	76
All aged 20–59	**32**	**84**	**36**	**80**
+ 1 home-centred lifestyle preference	31	74	37	65
+ 2 parent of child(ren) aged <16	9	76	10	71
+ 3 in public rented housing	0	43	7	41

Note: Data for people aged 20–59 who completed their full-time education before the age of 21 and are not currently studying and are almost certainly non-graduates.

childcare responsibilities have no impact at all on workrates among work-centred women. Having a mortgage to pay off has a substantial impact, raising workrates from 72% to 100%. The reasons for this are discussed in Chapter 8, but include selection effects as well as motivational factors. The attractions of home-ownership and the financial burdens of associated mortgages, have had a significant impact in raising wives' employment in recent decades in Britain. Further analysis showed that having a mortgage was not influential except among work-centred wives and, to a lesser extent, work-centred women generally. It appears that lifestyle preferences determine *which* social and economic contextual factors women respond to. There are consistent results also on the factors that depress women's workrates.

Full-time workrates among home-centred women are no lower than average, although they are lower for adaptive women. Children, however, have a large impact, depressing workrates from 31% to 9% among home-centred non-graduate women, with a weaker impact on adaptive women, depressing full-time workrates to 17%. Housing has only a tiny impact: living in public rented housing depresses workrates a little further from 9% to 0% among home-centred women, but it has no impact at all on adaptive women.

These results corroborate the NLS results for the USA reviewed earlier and summarized in Table 5.1. Wives who work only if their childcare responsibilities allow them to do so are in effect fulfilling a prior choice of emphasis on homemaking as life's central activity. Childcare responsibilities have little or no impact on the employment of work-centred women. Similarly, housing can have a major or minor impact depending on which lifestyle preference group is looked at. The heterogeneity of women's lifestyle preferences renders it impossible to produce universally valid statements about which social factors determine female workrates. It is essential to differentiate between the three groups of women.

In sum, a tiny number of factors can collectively push women's workrates up to the maximum or down to the minimum, but lifestyle preferences are the only factor that is important in both cases.

Once again, ideology has no impact on men's full-time workrates. Parental responsibilities also have no effect, because men's role in most families is primarily as income-earner, not as carer. Once again, Table 5.10 confirms the lack of genuine choices in men's lives, as compared with women's lives in Britain in the twenty-first century.

Contrary Groups

The neat pattern of preferences determining women's workrates, especially full-time workrates, is broken by the relatively high 41% full-time workrate among women aged 20–59 who prefer complete role segregation in the family (Table 5.4). This discrepancy is fairly common in Europe. For example, Albrecht *et al.* (1995) showed that in most European countries the percentage of women working full-time when their children were young (pre-school or school age) was substantially higher than the percentage of women who believed mothers should work full-time when their children are young, a result they attribute to economic necessity. Nonetheless, we explored this anomalous finding with some care. The reasons for the anomaly illustrate how economic necessity can sometimes override lifestyle preferences.

Women who seek to be full-time homemakers can only hope to implement this preference after marriage, or when they start cohabiting with a breadwinner partner and they are more dependent than other women on having a partner who is a 'good provider'. A substantial proportion of the women in the anomalous group are still single (not yet married) or ex-married (separated, divorced or widowed). Once they are excluded, the full-time workrate falls to 34% among women living with a husband or partner (see Table 8.9). Further analyses in Chapter 8 reveal that the unusually high workrates in this anomalous group of wives result from a combination of two factors: having a mortgage and a husband who is not in work or is in insecure employment, resulting in periodic spells of unemployment. Mortgage-holders have systematically higher full-time workrates and this applies to men as well as women. Wives who prefer to be full-time homemakers also have husbands with comparatively low employment rates.[7] The combination of a husband who cannot guarantee a steady stream of earnings and a mortgage that requires regular repayments, forces wives who would normally choose to be at home to remain in full-time jobs (see Table 8.9). Wives who prefer role segregation in the family but do not have a mortgage to repay have a much lower workrate of 24%, which is close to the 19% workrate found among wives who prefer the compromise model (see Table 8.9).

As noted in Chapter 4, there is no association of any importance between socio-economic group (or occupational grade) and ideal family model (see Table 4.4). But couples who aim for role specialization seem to experience more financial stress from the husband's failure to be in continuous employment in one-third of couples. One-third of men aged 20–59 who normally prefer to be the sole breadwinner were out of work. One-third were effectively unemployed, but this was variously described as unemployment, sickness or early retirement. Presumably, many had been made redundant or forced to take early retirement. Since they still had a mortgage to pay off, the value of any redundancy payoff cannot have been large, and they would therefore need to continue in employment.

A second factor is that one-fifth of women who prefer the role segregation model of the family were working in male-dominated occupations which, as noted in Chapter 6, almost never offer part-time jobs (see Table 6.3). In effect, these women were forced to choose between working full-time or not at all, thus boosting the full-time workrate in this group of contradictory cases. The male occupations in question were mainly white-collar, including professional and technical occupations. In this case, the absence of part-time work options forced an unnaturally high rate of full-time employment.

The survey also identifies another anomalous group which is larger and arguably more puzzling. Wives who prefer to be full-time homemakers, yet hold full-time jobs, constitute only 4% of all wives aged 20–59. Wives who claim to prefer the egalitarian model of the family, with symmetrical roles, yet have no job at all, constitute 9% of all wives aged 20–59, twice as many. It might be argued that fully symmetrical roles require the wife to be in continuous full-time work, so that those in part-time jobs are also anomalous cases. Using this logic, the size of this second group of anomalous cases rises from 9% to 18% of all wives aged 20–59, four times larger than the other group. This anomaly is harder to explain. It is *not* explained by childcare burdens. Egalitarian women are generally less likely to have dependent children under age 16 at home, compared to women who prefer differentiated roles. If they do have children, they are no more likely to have babies at home. Women who aim for the egalitarian family model yet do not have a job are *less* likely to have dependent children at home than non-working women who prefer differentiated family roles. We take the view that this contrary case must be due in part to the political correctness bias that pervades both the surveys. Following the line presented in Chapter 3, we regard most of these women as belonging to the adaptive preference group, because they are not work-centred and therefore not genuinely committed to symmetrical roles.

Ethnic Minorities

It has long been established that in Britain black women have higher full-time workrates than white women, while women from the Indian subcontinent generally have lower workrates, especially Muslim women. These differential workrates have been confirmed by successive population censuses, special surveys of the ethnic minority population and analyses of the Labour Force Survey (Jones, 1993; Owen, 1994: Table 6.2; Dale and Holdsworth, 1998; Sly *et al.*, 1998, 1999). The census is the only data collection that is sufficiently large to permit detailed analyses of employment patterns in each social-cultural group, or what are usually labelled ethnic minority groups. These large differences in employment patterns within a single country testify to the importance of cultural and ideological factors, and contradict the thesis that social institutions and economic conditions in each country are the primary determinants of women's workrates.

   Black and white British women are subject to the same social structural environment, the same fiscal system and welfare state, and the same labour market with a substantial level of occupational segregation by sex (Hakim, 1998a). Yet the behaviour of black women continues to differ radically from that of white women. White British women often drop out of full-time employment when they acquire a partner and have children. If they remain in a partnership (marriage or cohabitation), they generally work part-time hours, or not at all, for the remainder of their working life, with frequent transfers in and out of the labour market (Dale and Holdsworth, 1998: Figure 4.1). This pattern of employment became the dominant pattern towards the end of the twentieth century (Hakim, 1996a: Table 5.2). The vast majority of white women hope and expect to be supported by a husband who remains the primary breadwinner while they specialize in homemaking and family work. Paid work is regarded as a complement to their family role, not an alternative to it.

In contrast, black British women (most of them of Caribbean descent) are usually in employment throughout the lifecycle, even when they are married or cohabiting, even when they have children at home, and they typically hold full-time jobs. Whether or not they have a partner, black women regard themselves as primary earners, plan their worklife on the assumption of continuous full-time lifelong employment, and expect to support their children financially as well as socially and emotionally.

In general, the likelihood of choosing a part-time job in preference to a full-time job is twice as high among white women as among ethnic minority women in Britain, after controlling for lifecycle stage and level of qualifications (Dale and Holdsworth, 1998: 84). Higher full-time workrates among black women are achieved in spite of the usual childcare problems, not through preferential access to childcare, and despite the fact that fewer black women achieve high grade professional-managerial positions and the higher earnings these jobs offer. Higher full-time workrates are observed across all occupations, not only in the professional-managerial occupations where women are more likely to remain in full-time work (Dale and Holdsworth, 1998). These results are observed by everyone who studies black–white contrasts in Britain, and even among women working in the same industry (Siltanen, 1994; Hakim, 1996a: 72). They contradict the thesis that institutional and societal factors are dominant in shaping women's employment patterns.

The British survey sample is large enough to contain just over 200 people who declare themselves to be members of ethnic minority groups, just 6% of the sample, the same as in the national population. Although the ethnic minority subgroup is small, it is large enough for us to explore the impact of sex-role ideology and work orientations on women's workrates, and to assess whether the higher full-time workrates of black British women are due to distinctively different attitudes.

The ethnic minority subgroup is too small to affect overall results for Britain. This means that all results reported for Britain in this book apply equally to the white British population alone, and to the complete British population. The question identifying ethnic minorities invited people to classify themselves into one of the following categories: white, black Caribbean, black African, other black, Indian, Pakistani, Bangladeshi, Chinese or none of these groups.[8] There are important cultural differences between these groups. For example most Indians are Hindu, while most Pakistanis and Bangladeshis are Muslim. However, small numbers force some aggregation of the groups. In order to obtain sufficient numbers for separate analysis, we grouped all three black groups (N = 62), the three groups from the Indian subcontinent (N = 99, 56 Indians and 43 others) and all others (N = 50). In each group, roughly half of respondents are male and half female. However, non-response reduces the numbers of black men, of women from the Indian sub-continent and, surprisingly, Chinese/other men. A low proportion of the black respondents were married, whereas the majority of people from the Indian subcontinent were married.

Overall, ethnic minority groups have attitudes that distinguish them from the white majority and are generally more extreme, in both directions. In brief, ethnic minorities have a stronger work ethic and stronger attachment to paid work. Some are more egalitarian than whites and reject patriarchy; others prefer role segregation in the family and warmly endorse patriarchal values.

The work ethic is markedly stronger among ethnic minorities, men and women, than among whites. Even in the absence of economic necessity, three-quarters of ethnic minorities prefer to have a paid job compared to under 60% of whites. There are three reasons for this strong commitment to paid jobs. First, all ethnic minorities suffer discrimination in the labour market, and more widely, as compared with the white majority. Just one example is the fact that unemployment rates among ethnic minority groups still remain two to four times higher than among whites (Sly *et al.*, 1998, 1999). This is likely to make them even more tenacious of their jobs. Second, there is a large element of self-selection among people who migrate from one country to another; immigrants are generally those with high aspirations and strong motivation to succeed, plus a tendency to self-reliance. These attitudes are likely to be transmitted to their children and succeeding generations, so that even second and third generation immigrants would have distinctive work orientations as compared with the white majority who never had to make the same hard choices or deal with the same level of adversity in a new country. Third, there are differences in age structure. Immigrant communities tend to be younger than the white community, and work commitment is stronger among younger people.

Among black women only, work commitment is complemented by a strong tendency to regard oneself as a primary earner: 62% compared to 44% of white women. In contrast, most women in the other groups regard themselves as secondary earners or complete dependents: 69% compared to 56% of white women. Overall, black women are distinctive in being just as work-centred as white men (51% in both cases), while paid work is even more central to the identities of ethnic minority men (60% compared to 51% among white men). In contrast, the work orientations of other ethnic minority women do not differ at all from the white majority.

As expected, the work orientations of black British women are closer to those of men than of white women. Although base numbers are small, these results are found consistently across subgroups and are reliable. They are also consistent with preferences regarding the family division of labour and attitudes to patriarchy among ethnic minorities.

As noted in Chapter 3, sex differences in attitudes are generally small or non-existent in our surveys. This applies primarily to the white population. Among ethnic minorities, there are marked sex differences in sex-role ideology (Table 5.11). Most notable of all are the values of West Indian women: the majority reject patriarchal values, the only group to do so, and a two-thirds majority prefer egalitarian family roles. In contrast, one-third of West Indian men prefer role segregation in the family and most accept patriarchy. Numbers are too small for these results to be completely reliable, but they are indicative of serious conflicts in values within this cultural group. More generally, men in all ethnic minority groups are twice as likely as women to prefer the role-segregated model of marriage. Among people with origins in the Indian subcontinent, especially the Muslim subgroup, support for the egalitarian family falls to its lowest level – one-fifth of men and one-third of women – and acceptance of patriarchal values rises to its highest level – 98% of men and 88% of women (Table 5.11). Generally, ethnic minority groups express greater support for patriarchal values. There is high consistency in the three groups from the Indian subcontinent, despite their religious differences, and broad consistency between the three black groups, despite the distinctive views of West Indian women.

Do these attitudes impact on full-time workrates? Unfortunately the survey sub-samples are too small to draw conclusions separately for each ethnic group. Analyses must be restricted to people aged 20–59 and this further reduces base numbers. Overall, the impact of values on full-time workrates is broadly the same among the ethnic minority groups (taken together) as among whites. In other words, the analyses shown in Tables 5.7 and 5.10 apply equally to whites and to all other ethnic groups. This means that the reason black women have higher full-time workrates than white women, while women with origins in the Indian subcontinent have lower workrates, is not because attitudes and values have a stronger impact on their behaviour, but simply because they have different attitudes and values. Black women are markedly more likely to espouse egalitarian family roles and job centrality is twice as high among them as among all other women in Britain. In consequence, the full-time workrate among black women is 20 percentage points higher than among white women (Owen, 1994: 84). Similarly, workrates are lower among Indian, Pakistani and Bangladeshi women because they endorse patriarchal values almost unanimously, generally prefer differentiated family roles and have work orientations

Table 5.11 Sex-role ideology among ethnic minority groups

	White		*Black*		*Indian*		*Other*	
	M	F	M	F	M	F	M	F
Ideal family model:								
egalitarian	46	40	40	64	21	33	43	47
compromise	36	43	30	21	36	45	33	43
role segregation	18	17	30	15	43	22	24	10
% work-centred	51	26	63	51	58	21	62	26
% accept patriarchy	61	61	72	64	98	88	62	54
Base = 100%	1459	1718	21	32	48	31	11	32

Note: Data for people aged 16 and over who have completed their full-time education.

similar to those of white women, with low levels of job centrality. Differences between ethnic groups are explained by ideological and cultural differences, which persist despite the fact that they all live in the same society, work in the same labour market and experience the same welfare state and social structure. Analyses of the LFS and the census tend to focus on the visible correlates of ethnic minority employment rates, such as qualifications, giving the impression these are causes rather than the consequences of divergent sex-role ideologies and work orientations. For example, black Caribbean women, and black women more generally, are just as likely as white women to obtain tertiary level qualifications: one-fifth in all cases, in marked contrast to the low level of qualifications among Pakistani/Bangladeshi women; in consequence, they also have a relatively high proportion, one-third, in the professional, managerial and technical occupations (Sly *et al.*, 1998: 603–5). These are outcomes of their expectation of lifelong full-time work as primary earners rather than purely accidental characteristics that are independent of high full-time workrates. The original source of these outcomes is the particular array of attitudes and values that make West Indian women behave more like men than other women in Britain.

In sum, results for ethnic minorities in Britain show that the impact of ideology and values can override social and economic constraints, including racial and sex discrimination. This is the exact opposite of the previous example of an anomalous group among whom the financial pressures of a mortgage overrode lifestyle preferences.

Employment Patterns in Spain

The employment data in the Spanish survey differs from that in Britain: it is fuller in some areas, more restricted in others. However, the smaller sample size is the main constraint on analyses.

Entry to the labour market is more protracted in Spain than in Britain. It is not until age 24 that over 50% of men and women in our sample are in employment.[9] The majority of people aged 18–24 are not in work, but are full-time or part-time students, unemployed or otherwise out of the labour market. Full-time students and the unemployed constitute a substantial proportion of the under 40 age group (Table 5.12). Exit from the labour market also comes early in Spain, because pensions can be drawn from age 50 onwards. From age 55 onwards, over 50% of men in our sample are not in employment. Among women, over half are out of the labour force from age 45 onwards. Hence workrates are generally lower in Spain, for men as well as women (Table 5.12).

People work long hours in Spain and part-time jobs are rare, partly due to high levels of labour market regulation (Ruivo *et al.*, 1998). Even part-time employees work relatively long hours. People working less than 15 hours a week are classified separately as marginal workers, but there are so few of them that they amount to less than 1% of the sample. We have grouped together employees working part-time or marginal hours with people working in a family business, all of whom work less than 30 hours a week. Thus grouped together, part-time jobs are held by only 4% of men and 7% of women in the Spanish sample (Table 5.12). Full-time work is the norm in Spain, forcing women to choose between a job with long hours or being a full-time homemaker. The majority of women do no paid work.

For married and cohabiting couples, information is also provided on the partner's employment status (Table 5.13). The majority of married women have a husband in full-time work. In contrast, only one-fifth of all wives are in employment, rising to 31% for wives aged 20–59. It is notable that unemployment falls away to trivial levels among married people; it is mostly a feature of the young and single.

There are dramatic differences between generations. Half of the younger wives have a job compared to a bare 16% among the older generation aged 40 and over (Table 5.13). Among wives aged 20–59, these proportions rise to 50% and 27% in employment in the younger and older generations respectively. In effect, there has been a sea change in recent decades as regards wives' employment in Spain.

Table 5.12   Employment patterns among respondents in Spain

	Men			Women		
	<40	*40 +*	*All*	*<40*	*40 +*	*All*
Full-time work (employees & all S/E)	65	48	56	34	13	22
Part-time job	7	1	4	12	4	7
Unemployed	11	6	9	10	2	5
Student	16	0	7	18	0	7
Retired	1	44	24	2	21	13
Other inactive	*	*	*	24	61	46
Base = 100%	271	313	584	260	367	627

Notes: Part-time jobs include people in marginal jobs of less than 15 hours a week and family workers, all of whom work part-time hours. Almost all Other inactives are full-time homemakers.

Table 5.13   Employment patterns among partners in Spain

	Wives of men			Husbands of women		
	<40	*40 +*	*All*	*<40*	*40 +*	*All*
Full-time work (employees & all S/E)	45	12	22	94	52	66
Part-time job	4	4	4	0	1	1
Unemployed	6	2	3	4	2	3
Student	2	0	*	0	0	0
Retired	4	7	6	2	43	29
Other inactive	39	75	65	0	2	1
Base = 100%	109	259	368	130	251	381

Note: Base is married and cohabiting couples. See also notes to Table 5.12.

Ideological Influences on Employment in Spain

Sex-role ideology has little or no impact on male workrates in Spain, in the sample as a whole and in the two age cohorts: under 40 and 40+ years (Table 5.14). Attitudes to patriarchy, work orientations and ideal family model are not related to employment patterns among men. The slightly reduced workrate among men who prefer complete role segregation in the family is due to their being older than the other groups.

Sex-role preferences have a moderate impact on female (full-time) workrates, especially in the older generation of Spanish women. Among women who favour the role-segregated model of marriage, full-time workrates fall to a trivial 10% (15% in the younger generation and 8% in the older generation). Among women who favour the egalitarian model of marriage, full-time workrates are trebled, to 36% (Table 5.14). The compromise group falls between the two extremes, closer to the egalitarians in the younger generation, closer to the group preferring role segregation in the older group. Part-time work is relatively uncommon in Spain and is found proportionately in all groups. Access to part-time jobs seems to be determined by local circumstances in Spain, rather than by lifestyle preferences, as in Britain. The overall result is that workrates among women who aim for the egalitarian model of marriage are three times higher than workrates among women who prefer to be full time homemakers. 46% versus 13% (Table 5.14), but the pattern is strongest in the older generation of women.

Work orientations have an even stronger impact on women's workrates, especially in the older generation. Two-thirds of women who are work-centred have full-time jobs, double the average for women and beginning to approach levels found among men. Women who work for social or instrumental reasons have the low workrates typical of Spanish women: one-quarter are in full-time jobs and another 11% have part-time jobs (Table 5.14).

In contrast, attitudes to patriarchy are only loosely linked to employment patterns among women (Table 5.14). The link is only found in the older generation, where workrates increase from 14% among women who accept patriarchal values to 42% among women who reject patriarchy. In the younger generation, patriarchal values cease to have any impact on employment patterns.

Overall, however, the results for Spain reveal a massive discrepancy between stated sex-role preferences and actual behaviour. A three-quarters majority of women aged 20–59 prefer the egalitarian family model, a far higher proportion than in Britain, where it is less than half (see Table 4.8). Yet unlike Britain (see Table 5.4), the majority of egalitarian women in Spain have no job at all and only one-third are in full-time work. Even in the younger generation, only 52% are in employment and 40% are working full-time. The tiny group of women who prefer complete role specialization in the family are the only group in Spain to fully implement their preferences, in both generations. Admittedly, most work-centred Spanish women do achieve their preference for a work-centred lifestyle, However, this is a tiny group, less than one-fifth of Spanish women even in the younger generation (see Table 3.13). For the majority of Spanish women there is a huge gulf

Table 5.14   The impact of sex-role ideology on workrates in Spain

	Men			Women		
	% FT	*% PT*	*All*	*% FT*	*% PT*	*All*
All aged 20–59	79	4	83	34	10	45
Ideal family model:						
egalitarian	75	3	78	36	9	46
compromise	73	10	82	24	15	39
role segregation	61	0	61	10	3	13
Work orientations:						
work-centred	84	3	88	68	9	77
other reasons for job	74	5	79	27	11	38
Attitude to patriarchy:						
accept/ambivalent	76	3	79	24	7	31
reject	80	5	85	40	12	52
People aged 20–39	79	7	87	43	15	58
Ideal family model:						
symmetrical roles	71	5	76	40	12	52
differentiated roles	63	14	76	28	15	43
Work orientations:						
work-centred	92	6	98	74	10	84
other reasons for job	73	8	81	35	16	51
Attitude to patriarchy:						
accept/ambivalent	82	7	89	41	12	53
reject	78	8	86	44	16	60
People aged 40–59	77	1	78	25	6	30
Ideal family model:						
symmetrical roles	80	1	81	31	5	36
differentiated roles	73	0	73	12	7	18
Work orientations:						
work-centred	78	1	79	59	7	67
other reasons for job	77	0	77	19	5	24
Attitude to patriarchy:						
accept/ambivalent	71	0	71	10	4	14
reject	83	1	84	35	7	42

Note: Data for people aged 20–59 years who have completed their full-time education.

between their stated preferences and actual behaviour. The gulf is probably exaggerated by the political correctness bias, but it is still large.

Table 5.15   The impact of sex-role ideology on women's full-time workrates by education, Spain

	% working full-time			*Distribution*	
	Highly qualified	*Other women*	*All*	*Highly qualified*	*Other women*
Ideal family model:					
symmetrical roles	62	34	40	89	70
differentiated roles	..	18	20	11	30
Work orientations:					
work-centred	82	57	68	45	12
other reasons for job	40	26	27	55	88
Attitude to patriarchy:					
reject	58	35	40	86	60
accept/ambivalent	..	20	24	14	40
Lifestyle preferences:					
work-centred	82	63	72	44	10
adaptive	41	29	30	53	75
home-centred	..	11	13	3	15
Average all aged 20–59	59	29	34		
Base = 100%	65	323	388	65	323

Notes: Data for people aged 20–59 who have completed their full-time education. The highly qualified are defined as those with some higher education, including university degrees. Other women are those with qualifications at primary and secondary level, up to Bachiller Superior, BUP.

Education has an even stronger impact on female workrates in Spain than in Britain. Table 5.15 presents an equivalent analysis to that in Table 5.5 for Britain, comparing the relative impact of higher education and lifestyle preferences. Highly qualified women in Spain are just as likely to work full-time as highly qualified women in Britain: 59% and 56% respectively. Higher education produces a bigger jump in Spanish workrates: +30 percentage points compared to +20 in Britain. However, lifestyle preferences produce an even larger increase in workrates: +50 percentage points among women with no more than secondary education and at least +40 percentage points among women with higher education (Table 5.15). It is remarkable that after controlling for education and lifestyle preferences, women's full-time workrates in the two countries are very close. As usual, attitudes and values make no difference to male workrates in Spain, which vary slightly by education level.

Where Britain and Spain do differ is in the distribution of lifestyle preferences among women with higher education. Almost half of the Spanish graduates emerge as work-centred, twice as many as in Britain (Tables 5.5 and 5.15). However, there is virtually no difference between the lifestyle preferences of women without any higher education in the two countries.

In sum, education has a more powerful effect on Spanish women than on British women, probably because the opening up of the educational system was a more dramatic change in Spain and was accompanied by a host of other social, political and economic changes. Even so, lifestyle preferences remain an important determinant of female workrates, whereas other values, such as attitudes to patriarchy, have little effect.

Table 5.16 presents an equivalent analysis to that in Table 5.6 for Britain. The difference between them is that we have better data for couples in Spain. Married and cohabiting persons report the employment status of their partners and spouses, so we can identify dual-earner couples and single-earner couples more precisely in Spain.

Compared to Britain (Table 5.6), there is virtually no link between couples' employment profile and their sex-role ideology in Spain (Table 5.16). Whether they are in a dual-earner couple or a single-earner couple, the majority of spouses claim to prefer the symmetrical roles model of the family. Men and women in dual-earner couples are more likely to reject patriarchal values than those in single-earner couples, but the difference is relatively small. One-quarter of wives in dual-earner couples are work-centred, a sharp increase on 3% of wives in single-earner couples, but still a small minority of wives. We concluded earlier that behaviour does not predict values in Britain and this conclusion is even more valid for Spain. Differences in sex-role ideology between dual-earner and single-earner couples are trivial in Spain. Once again, spouses are virtually unanimous within each type of marriage, suggesting almost complete assortive mating on sex-role ideology within couples. There are no differences of any substance between the older and younger generations in this analysis.

The link between attitudes and behaviour is tested the opposite way round in Table 5.17, which considers whether couples implement their ideal family model. This can only be tested properly in Spain, where we have the advantage of the Spanish survey providing information on both spouses' employment status. Once again, spouses within each preference group give almost identical accounts of their employment activities. Table 5.17 shows even more clearly than Table 5.16 the weak impact of ideal family model on actual behaviour. Among couples who believe in role specialization in the family, two-thirds rely on the husband as sole breadwinner, but so do half of

Table 5.16   Are dual-earner couples egalitarian in Spain?

	Dual-earner couples		Single-earner couples	
	Men	*Women*	*Men*	*Women*
Ideal family model:				
symmetrical roles	84	80	56	64
compromise	12	15	29	19
role segregation	4	5	15	17
% work-centred	45	25	43	3
% reject patriarchal values	67	75	55	54
% regard man as ultimately responsible for income	13	11	30	22
% regard woman as ultimately responsible for housework	15	7	27	21
Base = 100%	100	107	135	146

Notes: Data for married and cohabiting couples aged 20–59. Dual-earner couples are those where both partners are in the labour market (either in employment or looking for a job). Single-earner couples are those where only the husband is reported as being in the labour market. For each type of couple, there are two accounts available: the wife's and the husband's.

the couples preferring 'egalitarian' symmetrical roles. This 20 percentage point difference in wives' workrates is nowhere near as large as might be expected from the contrasting ideal family models. On the other hand, dual-earner couples in Spain are closer to being dual-career couples, in the sense that wives with jobs are generally working full-time and long hours.

The analysis was also repeated separately for the two generations. In this case, there is a clear difference between them (Table 5.17). Younger couples (aged 20–39) achieve a fair match between their ideals and outcomes. Depending on whether you use the wife's or the husband's account, half to two-thirds of couples choosing symmetrical roles have both partners in the labour market; single-earner couples fall into a minority. Figures are the exact opposite for couples choosing role specialization models of the family: the majority have a full-time homemaker wife. Among older couples (aged 40–59), the majority rely on the husband as sole breadwinner, irrespective of the ideal model of the family. The proportion of single-earner families is a little higher among couples choosing differentiated family roles (two-thirds to three-quarters) than among the egalitarian couples (just over half). It is fair to say that it is only the group choosing role specialization that achieve their goals in the older generation, whereas both preference groups achieve

Table 5.17 The impact of ideal family model on spouses' employment pattern, Spain

| | Ideal family model | | | | | |
| | Symmetrical roles | | Differentiated roles | | All | |
Activities of spouses	M	F	M	F	M	F
All aged 20–59						
Both work full-time	36	32	11	17	28	27
Both in employment	43	39	15	20	34	33
Both in labour market	49	45	20	25	40	39
Husband in labour market,						
wife not	45	49	69	63	53	53
Both out of labour market	6	6	11	12	7	8
Base = 100%	164	191	81	85	253	279
People aged 20–39						
Both work full-time	44	37	28	28	40	34
Both in employment	52	45	28	34	46	42
Both in labour market	62	54	36	44	55	51
Husband in labour market,						
wife not	36	44	64	56	43	47
Both out of labour market	2	2	0	0	2	2
Base = 100%	78	94	25	32	108	127
People aged 40–59						
Both work full-time	28	27	4	10	18	21
Both in employment	35	33	9	12	24	25
Both in labour market	38	36	12	14	28	28
Husband in labour market,						
wife not	53	53	72	67	60	57
Both out of labour market	9	11	16	19	12	15
Base = 100%	85	97	56	53	145	152

Note: Data for couples aged 20–59 who have completed their full-time education.

their goals, in broad terms, in the younger generation of Spaniards, that is, the post-democracy generation.

In sum, there is a link between sex-role preferences and wives' employment in Spain, but it is weak and emerges mainly in the younger generation. Ideal family model is not a primary determinant of women's

Table 5.18   Impact of ideal family model and work centrality on full-time workrates (%) among couples in Spain

	Ideal family model		
	Symmetrical roles	Differentiated roles	All
All wives aged 20–59	34	18	29
work-centred	79	..	78
other reasons for job	24	17	22
All husbands aged 20–59	86	77	83
work-centred	84	85	85
other reasons for job	88	68	82

Note: Data for married and cohabiting couples aged 20–59.

employment in Spain, as it is in Britain. In contrast, work-centrality is a major determinant of women's employment behaviour.

Table 5.18 shows the joint impact of our two indicators of lifestyle preferences. In Spain, ideal family model has a small impact on women's full-time workrates, whereas work centrality raises workrates by a massive 50 percentage points. As usual, these values have no impact on male workrates.

It is notable that after controlling for ideal family model and work centrality, female workrates in Spain shoot up to the same level as in Britain (compare Tables 5.18 and 5.7). In both countries, three-quarters of women who are work-centred and prefer symmetrical family roles are in full-time work, despite the large differences between the two countries in female employment generally. There are important differences in the distribution of the sample in each country, but in both cases only a tiny minority of wives of working age, about one in ten, combine work-centrality with a preference for symmetrical family roles, the two components of the work-centred lifestyle preference (Table 5.19). In this rare group of women, full-time workrates come close to those of men.

The falling birthrate in Spain attracts much attention, and some anxiety (Garrido, 1992; Cruz Cantero, 1995: 31–47; Delgado and Castro Martín, 1998; Alba 2000). It is largely a result of the recent legalization of contraception and the introduction of modern, reliable, coitus-independent forms of contraception that give women independent control of their fertility, with or without the knowledge and cooperation of male partners (Hakim, 2000a: 44–50). Young women are now choosing to have fewer children than under the pro-natalist Francoist policies that were in force up to 1975.

Table 5.19   Distribution of the sample in Spain

	Ideal family model		
	Symmetrical roles	*Differentiated roles*	*All*
All wives aged 20–59	70	30	100%
work-centred	12	1	13
other reasons for working	58	29	87
All husbands aged 20–59	67	33	100%
work-centred	28	16	44
other reasons for working	39	17	56

Note: Data for married and cohabiting couples aged 20–59.

Nonetheless, the vast majority of currently married women have children and in most cases children continue to live with their parents well into adult life (Table 5.20). The indicator of parental responsibility in the Spanish survey is simply the presence of offspring in the same household as adults. For married couples, it is fair to assume that any children would be their own children. On this basis, four-fifths of all wives have children still living with them. The percentage is much higher than in Britain (46%) because in the Spanish dataset children can be of any age. This is helpful, because children live with their parents until they marry, particularly if they are in full-time education. In practice, this means that many children live at home until well into their late twenties, and even into their thirties in Spain, so that parental responsibility for them lasts much longer than in Britain.[10] However, the important finding in Table 5.20 is not the high incidence of parental responsibilities, but the fact that there is little or no variation between the groups identified. Thus, parental responsibilities are not likely to be a major determinant of the large variation in workrates between the groups.

Unfortunately, we do not have more precise information on parental responsibilities (such as the age and number of children), and no information at all on other practical constraints on people, such as housing loans. We cannot compare the relative importance of social and economic factors and of lifestyle preferences as determinants of women's employment in Spain. In any event, the Spanish sample is too small, with less than 300 married women aged 20–59, for further analyses to produce reliable results for all three lifestyle preference groups separately.

Table 5.21 summarizes our results for Spain, showing the sharp contrast between the impact of lifestyle preferences on women's full-time workrates

Table 5.20   Parental responsibilities among couples in Spain: percentage of spouses in each category living with child(ren) at home

	Ideal family model		
	Symmetrical roles	Differentiated roles	All
All wives aged 20–59	81	79	80
work-centred	71	67	70
other reasons for job	83	79	82
All husbands aged 20–59	75	71	73
work centred	76	70	73
other reasons for job	74	71	74

Note: Data for married and cohabiting couples aged 20–59 who have completed their full-time education.

in both generations and the weak link between patriarchal values and behaviour. The Spanish sample is too small for the results to be completely reliable, but the pattern is striking. The difference between the two values is large enough for us to classify them as causal and non-causal values respectively. As noted in Chapter 2, we must distinguish between personal preferences and public opinion: the former have causal powers but the latter do not. Some attitudes and values have a profound impact on behaviour, while others are of little or no consequence.

In both Britain and Spain, women's lifestyle preferences predict behaviour. However, behaviour does not predict values in Britain and even less so in Spain. Overall, the link between attitudes and values and behaviour is weaker in Spain than in Britain. However, there are indications that things are changing in the younger generation of Spaniards. In this group, there are signs that they are able to turn their preferences into reality, in broad terms, unlike their parents' generation.

Causal Processes

In line with preference theory, we have interpreted our results as showing the impact of attitudes and values on behaviour, not vice versa. Correlations and associations at a single point in time do not of course prove causality in either direction. There has been some debate over whether sex-role ideology

Table 5.21 Causal and non-causal values by age, Spain: percentage of women working full-time in each group

	<40	*40 +*	*All*
Lifestyle preferences:			
work-centred	73	70	72
adaptive	38	22	30
home-centred	..	4	13
Patriarchal values:			
accept/ambivalent	41	10	24
reject	44	35	40
All women 20–59	43	26	34

shapes and determines employment decisions, or whether attitudes are a *post hoc* rationalization of decisions determined by economic and social factors. Preference theory accepts that both processes occur, to different degrees, at different times, but posits that the emphasis has changed, and will continue to change, in modern societies. Our analysis has shown that in two modern societies certain attitudes determine behaviour, but behaviour does not determine attitudes. So lifestyle preferences are not simply a *post hoc* rationalization of prior decisions, but a motivational force with causal powers. Lifestyle preferences are not the sole determinant of women's employment, but they are the only factor that shapes the lives of all women. The particular social and economic factors that are also influential vary greatly between the three lifestyle preference groups.

In Britain, the new scenario for women occurred early enough for the younger generation of women in our survey (aged under 40 years) to benefit fully from the new opportunities and freedom to choose their own lifestyle. In this group in particular, we interpret sex-role ideology as the principal determinant of employment decisions. Values alone can never be the sole determinant of the shape of anyone's life. As the saying goes, 'life is what happens while we are making other plans'. Unforeseen circumstances, opportunities and difficulties impact on everyone's life. This unpredictable circus of events reduces the impact of values and lifestyle preferences on behaviour, but does not deny it. In sum, the younger generation of women in Britain provide a fair test of preference theory; the results are broadly as predicted and are interpreted in line with the theory.

Somewhat surprisingly, the results for the younger generation of Spanish women also lend themselves to a preference theory interpretation, even though the new scenario is clearly not fully achieved in Spain. Part-time jobs and other employment arrangements that suit secondary earners are still rare in Spain. Modern forms of contraception are not freely and cheaply available in all parts of the country. The labour market operates with what appears to be a substantial level of sex discrimination as regards access to jobs, although the pay gap seems to be much the same as in other European countries. Spain is clearly a modern society and will achieve the new scenario for women in the near future. But Spanish women are behaving as if it were a reality already. For many Spaniards, the rhetoric is the reality.

Results for the older generation in Britain and Spain relate to an economic and social situation prior to the new scenario for women. For these two groups, there is less certainty that employment decisions are primarily the outcome of intentions, plans, preferences, attitudes and values. However, there is no sharp dividing line between the two generations of women in Britain. There is a sharp dividing line in Spain, due to recent political, economic and social changes, but the impact of lifestyle preferences is just as strong in the older generation of Spanish women. So it seems fair to interpret all results in terms of the impact of sex-role ideology on women's behaviour.

Conclusions

Sex-role ideology and ideal model of the family have a substantial impact on employment behaviour in modern societies where women have gained real choices as to how they live their lives. Our results for Britain and Spain show that female heterogeneity is an important correlate and determinant of behaviour both prior to and after the new scenario for women is achieved. Sex-role ideology and lifestyle preferences can no longer be ignored in research on female employment.

British reports on LFS results routinely show how childcare responsibilities structure women's work patterns. These findings are themselves structured by the fact that the LFS collects information on the numbers and ages of children in a household, but not on women's attitudes and values. The results of our survey show that it is sex-role ideology and work orientations or lifestyle preferences, that are the driving forces in women's employment decisions today. Children are not, of themselves, of any great importance, because preferences also simultaneously determine whether or not a woman has children, the number of children and their importance relative to her employment activities. Admittedly, it is more straightforward to collect data on co-resident children than on attitudes and values. But it is intellectually lazy to pretend that variables that happen to be available are genuine causal factors rather than loose proxies for unmeasured but important and relevant determinants of behaviour.

It was the NLS analyses in the USA that first identified the long-term effects of women's lifestyle preferences on workrates, occupational choice and earnings. These studies showed that even women who aimed to be full-time homemakers found themselves working in adult life – half did so compared to four-fifths of the women who were career planners (Table 5.1). There are similar findings in our British survey, with surprisingly high workrates among home-centred women, whom we expected to be out of the workforce. The lowest full-time workrates are found among adaptive women who favour the compromise family model, not among women who aim for a full-time homemaking role. A variety of factors can override sex-role ideology and personal lifestyle preferences: a husband's unemployment or forcible early retirement, financial pressures arising from children going into higher education, the 'pull' factor of finding oneself in a job one likes and is successful at, and the unrelenting financial pressure of having a mortgage on one's home. But overall, the remarkable feature of the results of our two surveys is that social and economic circumstances play a relatively small part in shaping women's workrates, or full-time workrates, in the younger generation. Lifestyle preferences are the dominant factor in modern societies.

Notes

1   Two versions of the question have been used in the NLS. In the initial 1968 survey respondents were asked 'Now I would like to talk to you about your future plans. What would you like to be doing when you are 35 years old?' From 1969 onwards the question was modified to read 'Now I would like to talk to you about your future job plans. What kind of work would you like to be doing when you are 35 years old?' In both versions, keeping house or raising a family was a possible response.

2   The large new youth cohort initiated in 1979 showed that the new cohort of young women entering the labour market in the 1980s had stronger work expectations and work commitment than did previous cohorts. In 1979, young women were only half as likely as young women in 1968 to say they expected to be housewives not in the paid labour force at age 35, with only one-quarter planning to be housewives (Sproat *et al.,* 1985: 76–8, 318, 335–6).

3   An even bigger USA study, the National Longitudinal Study of the High School Class of 1972 (NLS72) has produced results that corroborate those of the NLS. It showed, for example, that young women who subsequently became mothers before the age of 25 differed significantly from those who remained childless: they were less work-oriented, more likely to plan to be homemakers at age 30, less likely to plan a professional career and held more traditional sex role attitudes and aspirations *before* they gave birth. Parenthood strengthens pre-existing traditional attitudes in both young white men and women (Waite *et al.,* 1986; Morgan and Waite, 1987). None of these results are

acknowledged or reflected in recent analyses of NLS72, which compare men's and women's occupational aspirations while ignoring sex-role attitudes, to the point that women hoping to be full-time homemakers at age 30 are simply excluded from analyses (Rindfuss *et al.*, 1999).

4   Some studies have shown work commitment to have a much bigger impact among married women than social structural factors, especially when the husband's attitudes are also taken into account. Geerken and Gove show these two factors produce a 50–70 percentage point increase in economic activity rates of wives in the USA (Geerken and Gove, 1983: 66). A study of Canadian working wives also found strong associations between work commitment, higher status jobs and the husband's support for his wife's employment (Chappell, 1980).

5   As usual, the analysis was repeated for men, but sex-role ideology has almost no impact on men's workrates, even when education is controlled.

6   Some will argue that this analysis should be based on regression analysis instead, with lots of controls. There is a tendency to perceive multivariate analysis as better for causal analysis but, as Esser (1996), Hedström and Swedberg (1996) and Lieberson (1985: 155) all point out, it does not go beyond description and is in fact less illuminating on causal processes. The excessive use of controls can be counter-productive. The initial zero-order association found in cross-tabulation and correlation is often a closer approximation to the true association (Lieberson, 1985: 42, 120–51, 185–211).

7   The British survey does not provide information on the characteristics of spouses. We assume that wives and husbands have consistent preferences as regards ideal family model, so the information on husbands in Table 8.9 is indirect.

8   The question is peculiar, combining racial, cultural and nationality-based categories. It has been adopted as the standard classificatory question for population censuses and official surveys in Britain because it corresponds to the way people identify themselves in Britain, so it actually works well in the field. The classification is based on the idea that ethnic group is what people categorize themselves as belonging to in answering the question. In Britain, people perceive four principal groups: 'white', 'black', 'Asian' and 'other', which includes mixed-race people (Owen, 1994: 6–11).

9   In principle, Spaniards who extend their education beyond the compulsory stage (up to age 16) can graduate with a Bachillerato by age 18, a first university cycle Diploma by age 21 and a second university cycle Licenciatura (equivalent to a BA) by age 23 (Lawlor and Rigby, 1998: 210). In practice, the high incidence of repeaters (up to 20% of students in any school year) means that students often take far longer to complete a course of study. People can remain students into their late twenties and even early thirties. The student wastage rate is one of the highest in Europe: less than 50% of students finish their university degrees compared to 90% in Britain (Lawlor and Rigby, 1998: 214).

10   The pattern in Mediterranean countries is for children to live in the parental home while they are in full-time education and often well beyond that up to marriage. Youth unemployment is thus subsidized by parents (Gallard *et al.*, 2000).

Chapter 6

Ideological Influences on Occupational Choice

Differences between the British and Spanish omnibus surveys mean that some questions can only be addressed with one of the two surveys. This chapter looks at the impact of sex-role ideology and work orientations on occupational choice. The focus is on occupational segregation, which is sometimes loosely called job segregation, although the central issue is people's choice of sex-typed occupations rather than the particular jobs created by employers. Only the British dataset, with a sample of over 3600 people, is large enough to permit analyses of the sex segregation of occupations. Also, only the British omnibus survey codes occupations at a sufficiently detailed level for worthwhile comparative analysis of the attitudes of people working in male and female occupations.

Polachek's Thesis

In all societies, there is a tendency for women to specialize in certain types of work, while men specialize in other types of work. For example, men are carpenters while women are cooks; men are train drivers while women are nursery nurses. Initial attempts to explain the sexual differentiation of occupations often relied on some idea of men's and women's talents being naturally differentiated. However, research quickly showed that there was a large random element in which occupations were designated as 'male' or 'female' in any particular society. For example, dentists are typically female in Finland, but mostly male in the USA; doctors are usually female in Russia, but typically male in the USA and some other European countries. In southern Europe, restaurants and cafes are usually staffed by waiters, whereas waitresses are more common in northern Europe (Hakim, 1996a: 145–86). Natural talents may be relevant to occupational choice, but they are nowhere near a complete or sufficient explanation.

A second approach to explaining the sex segregation of occupations relies on the different work orientations and work histories of primary and secondary earners. The essential thesis is that married women (who mostly

163

regard themselves as secondary earners) choose occupations that are compatible with family work, such as occupations that can be done on a part-time basis or that can be done intermittently. The thesis builds on the observation that certain occupations, such as schoolteaching and secretarial work, employ women almost exclusively, not only in Europe, but across the whole world (Anker, 1998: 252–64). Teaching is an ideal family-friendly occupation because it allows mothers to be at home with their children during school holidays, including the long summer holiday. Secretarial work has the advantage of offering plenty of part-time and temporary jobs, with few or no penalties from taking a career break.

This thesis, well grounded in empirical observation, was converted into a somewhat different form when it was operationalized and tested by Polachek (1975, 1979, 1981, 1995; Goldin and Polachek, 1987) and other social scientists (England, 1982, 1984). Polachek's thesis is essentially that few jobs in professional and managerial occupations, but most jobs in clerical, sales and unskilled occupations tolerate intermittent or part-time employment. Those that do attract large numbers of women. Hence women are generally concentrated in lower grade and lower paid occupations while men are concentrated in the more demanding professional and managerial occupations which must be pursued on a continuous, full-time basis. By this time, theory attempted to explain not just why men and women do different types of work, but also why men are concentrated in higher grade occupations, while women are concentrated in lower grade occupations. However, Polachek operationalized the thesis into a statement that married women maximize their earnings or minimize the wage depreciation resulting from a career break, by choosing occupations that tolerate discontinuous work histories. England extended the thesis even further into the idea that *all* women in *all* female-dominated occupations experience lower wage depreciation after a career break than women in *all* male-dominated occupations. These reformulations offer the advantage of earnings, or earnings depreciation, being the measure of an occupation's family-friendly advantages. Using these reformulations, arguably distortions of the original idea, research results have been mixed. Polachek's studies based on several national datasets for the period 1960 to 1980 confirm the thesis, while England's studies based on similar data for the same period refute the thesis (Polachek, 1975, 1979, 1981, 1995; Goldin and Polachek, 1987; England, 1982, 1984). This is not surprising. The advantages of family-friendly occupations are not necessarily tied to earnings maximization; often earnings are traded off against other convenience factors. Teaching is attractive to mothers because the annual timetable fits in with their own children's school timetable, not because it pays more than other occupations, or pays the same after a domestic break. In effect, the thesis was distorted in order to test it with earnings data as the sole measure of an occupation's attractiveness to wives and mothers (Hakim, 2000a: 38–9).

A third approach to explaining occupational segregation argues that it is man-made: artificially created by systematic sex discrimination by employers who invariably favour men for jobs and only hire women when the supply of men is inadequate, so that men are always first in the queue for the best jobs (Reskin and Roos, 1990).[1] Paradoxically, this thesis and a related stream of research, gained popularity in the USA after the equal opportunities revolution that outlawed any overt or covert sex discrimination when selecting people for jobs or for promotion to higher grades. Reskin and Roos supported their 'job queuing' thesis with eleven case studies of occupations that feminized rapidly over the period 1970–88 in the USA. Unfortunately, as the authors themselves admit, their research evidence is equally consistent with the opposite of their preferred interpretation: that men chase money, power and status harder than women, so that any highly paid or high status occupation becomes male-dominated, while occupations with falling wages or status cease to attract men and become female-dominated (Hakim, 1998a: 64–5). For example, Reskin and Roos show that all the feminizing occupations they studied offered the alternative advantages of flexibility in hours worked and part-time/part-year work, options that were of no interest to men but of substantial value to women. The same problem of causality arises with subsequent studies seeking to validate or to challenge the job queuing thesis using cross-sectional data.

A fourth approach to explaining occupational segregation argues that it is a permanent structural feature of labour markets in modern societies (Hakim, 1998a: 236). Preference theory posits that primary and secondary earners have different sex-role preferences, different work orientations and thus seek different things from paid work. Over time, occupations become differentiated into those offering advantages for primary earners and those offering advantages for secondary earners. Equal opportunities laws ensure that all occupations and jobs remain formally open to all and any applicants. But people gravitate towards the type of occupation that is most compatible with their lifestyle preferences. In modern societies, occupational segregation is not based on sex or gender, but on the diverse lifestyle preferences emerging in a polarized labour force (Hakim, 2000a).

We test Polachek's original thesis, without focusing exclusively on earnings. Instead, we assess whether sex-role ideology and work orientations determine women's choice of occupation. More specifically, we test whether women who favour the compromise arrangement, and women who regard themselves as secondary earners, are more likely to choose female-dominated occupations rather than male-dominated occupations.

Our test of Polachek's thesis thus merges into a test of Hakim's preference theory also.

Trends in Occupational Segregation in the 1990s

The 1999 omnibus survey data was coded using the 1990 Standard Occupational Classification (SOC) employed in the 1991 Population Census and in all other British national statistics in the 1990s.[2] The classification focuses on jobs, defined as employment tasks and ignores legal employment status. It aims to rank jobs in terms of the types and level of skill required, work experience, qualifications and training usually required to do a job (Thomas and Elias, 1989). The classification is hierarchical, with three levels of aggregation: 371 occupation units, 77 minor groups, and 9 major groups. In conjunction with information on employment status, socio-economic classifications can be produced, such as the Registrar General's Social Class and Socio-Economic Group classifications (OPCS, 1990; Hakim, 1998a: 252–3). We used the most detailed 371 occupation groups for occupational segregation analysis.

There is an extensive literature on the advantages and disadvantages of various measures of occupational segregation. The vast majority of these are single number indexes, such as the Dissimilarity Index, which are popular for comparisons across societies and for studying trends over time (Hakim, 1992, 1998a; Anker, 1998; Grimshaw and Rubery, 1998; Melkas and Anker, 1998). However, single number indices are no use for our purposes, as we want to examine the particular types of occupation chosen by different groups of women. Instead, we use the three-fold classification of occupations developed by Hakim (1993, 1996a: 159, 1998a) and since used by some other researchers (Blackwell, 2001). The new approach identifies a separate category of integrated or mixed occupations straddling the dividing line between the two larger categories of male-dominated and female-dominated occupations. Mixed occupations are defined statistically as those with sex ratios close to the average for the workforce as a whole in any given year. Up to the 1991 Census, women formed about 40% of the workforce, so integrated occupations are defined as those with 25–55% female workers (40%±15%). By 1999, women formed 45% of the workforce, so mixed occupations are defined as those with 30–60% female workers (45%±15%). To allow comparisons across 1991–9, both measures are used in Table 6.1, in parts A and B respectively, and in Table 6.3. In all other tables, mixed occupations are those with 30–60% female workers.

We might expect the workforce to be divided fairly evenly between male, mixed and female occupations, given our definitions of the three groups as

<25%, 25–55%, 55%+ female workers and <30%, 30–60%, 60%+ female workers. In reality, mixed occupations form a small and select category of highly qualified and highly paid occupations, including a disproportionate share of the Service Class,[3] that is, professional and managerial occupations with the authority of senior grades and/or the independence of the self-employed professional, craftsman or business owner. In contrast, the sex-segregated male and female occupations present two parallel occupational ladders centred on the middle and lower grades of routine white-collar work, skilled and unskilled blue-collar work (Hakim, 1998a: 59).

Many of the largest occupations in which women predominate are actually gender-neutral occupations that do not draw on any special domestic or feminine skills, such as supermarket check-out operator, sales assistant and office clerical jobs. These occupations tolerate part-time work, temporary work and higher rates of labour turnover than most male-dominated and mixed occupations. Female occupations also include nurses, librarians, medical radiographers, social workers and cooks. Mixed occupations, which recruit men and women proportionately to their numbers in the workforce, include, for example, printing workers, local government officers, personnel managers, family doctors, dentists and pharmacists (Hakim, 1996a: 154–6, 1998a: 221–34). Male-dominated occupations include, for example, architects, general managers of large enterprises, police work, engineering, construction work and most occupations in mining, forestry and fishing.

Table 6.1 shows trends in the 1990s on two bases. In part A, 1999 survey data is presented on the same basis as the earlier 1991 Census analysis. In part B, the 1991 Census data is reanalysed and presented on the same basis as the 1999 survey results. On either basis, there was a small decline in the sex segregation of occupations over the decade. Male-dominated and female-dominated occupations became less exclusive, and more men worked in female occupations. However, the small group of mixed occupations shrank slightly, reversing the trend in the 1980s (Hakim, 1998a: 16). Also, the total number of people working in female occupations increased at the expense of the total number working in male occupations. This is due to the slow but steady expansion of the part-time workforce, which is concentrated almost exclusively in female occupations (Hakim, 1996a: 169, 1998a: 134).

These changes may seem relatively small, but to fully appreciate their significance we have to set trends in the 1990s in the context of trends over the whole twentieth century. From 1900 up to the 1975 legislation that prohibited sex and race discrimination, there was little or no change in the overall level of occupational segregation in Britain, although the numbers working in 100% male and 100% female occupations declined very slowly. From 1975 onwards the new equal opportunities laws stimulated a change

Table 6.1 Trends in occupational segregation, 1991–1999

		Type of occupation			
		Male	*Mixed*	*Female*	*Base = 100%*
A. Mixed occupations defined as 25–55% female					
1991	Men	67	19	14	1 439 623
	Women	9	16	75	1 085 523
	All	42	18	40	2 525 146
1999	Men	65	18	17	1 060
	Women	9	17	74	1 029
	All	38	17	45	2 089
B. Mixed occupations defined as 30–60% female					
1991	Men	71	18	11	1 439 623
	Women	11	18	71	1 085 523
	All	45	18	37	2 525 146
1999	Men	70	16	14	1 060
	Women	13	17	70	1 029
	All	42	17	42	2 089

Notes: Data for people aged 16 and over in both years. Data for people in current jobs in 1999; data for economically active people, excluding those who never had a job in the last ten years, in 1991. Both datasets employ the same classification with 371 occupations.
Sources: Hakim (1998a: Table 1.1), reporting analyses of 1991 Census, Great Britain, 10% sample data; additional analyses of published 10% sample statistics in Table 4, 1991 Census Economic Activity report; and 1999 survey data for Britain.

process. There was an immediate and substantial fall in the pay gap between men and women in the 1970s, as discriminatory pay rates were replaced by unisex pay rates. Once women were paid the same wages as men for doing the same job, there began a slow process of women entering a wide range of occupations previously dominated by men, especially as it ceased to be lawful for employers to actively exclude women. Women's massive entry into higher education eventually allowed many women to enter professional and managerial occupations, most notably the legal professions, medicine and government administration (Hakim, 1996a: 152–62). Trends in the 1990s continued the slow but steady pace of change established in the 1970s and 1980s (Hakim, 1998a: 8–20). Comparing the pace of change in Britain with trends in other European countries and the USA indicates that change in Britain is particularly sluggish, especially when compared with the USA

(Hakim, 1998a: 13–21). This suggests that women's occupational choices before the equal opportunities revolution were not in practice greatly constrained, and that the main problem was women's restricted access to professional and other higher grade occupations. The continued expansion of part-time jobs since the equal opportunities revolution, and demands for a right to work part-time in any occupation, along the lines of the recent Dutch legislation (Hakim, 2001a; Wierink, 2001), suggest that convenience factors in a job are more important to women than occupational choice *per se*. There is certainly a wealth of evidence from recent surveys showing that women value convenience factors in a job far more than do men, and this pattern continues in the younger generation (Hakim, 2000a: 139–41).

At first sight, there appears to be almost no difference in the pattern of occupational segregation in the younger and older generations (aged under 40 or 40 and over respectively) in our 1999 survey (Table 6.2). The separate results for men and women suggest rather more change between the two generations. Most notably, there is an increase in the proportion of men working in female-dominated occupations (from 10% to 18%) and a smaller increase in the proportion of women working in male-dominated occupations. However, it is unlikely that these differences show trends over time and across generations. It is more likely that they display the effects of ageing, as men and women revert to sex-typical occupations as they grow older (Hakim, 1998a: 56–9). In particular, the (part-time) jobs taken by students in full-time education are often in female-dominated occupations, and men move rapidly out of these jobs into male-dominated and mixed occupations once their education is complete (Hakim, 1998a: 57, 167–8). As early as age 33, the pattern of occupational segregation among younger people is virtually identical to the pattern in the whole workforce (Hakim, 2000a: 134).

An indisputable trend is that the feminization of the workforce is closely linked to the proliferation of part-time and other non-standard jobs (Hakim, 1996a: 166–9). As a result, the part-time workforce is now the most highly segregated section of the labour market, consisting almost exclusively of female occupations (Tables 6.2 and 6.3). Between 1971 and 1999, the concentration of women in female occupations increased from 78% to 81%, while the proportion of part-time jobs increased from 30% to 50% of jobs in female occupations (Table 6.3). Although the proportion of women in mixed occupations increased strongly from 36% to 47% over the three decades, the proportion of part-time jobs increased much more slowly, reaching 18% by 1999. In male occupations, there was little change. Thus by the start of the twenty-first century, female occupations had become an even more distinctive section of the workforce, where part-time jobs were beginning to outnumber full-time jobs. In contrast, male and mixed occupations retained

Table 6.2 Occupational segregation in Britain, 1999

| | Type of occupation | | | |
	Male	Mixed	Female	Base = 100%
All aged				
<40 years	41	16	43	1079
40 + years	43	17	40	1010
all	42	16	42	2089
Men aged				
<40 years	65	17	18	551
40 + years	75	15	10	509
all	70	16	14	1060
Women aged				
<40 years	15	16	69	528
40 + years	11	18	71	501
all	13	17	70	1029
All in				
full-time jobs	54	18	28	1506
part-time jobs	9	13	78	583
Men in				
full-time jobs	73	16	11	966
part-time jobs	32	20	48	94
Women in				
full-time jobs	20	23	57	540
part-time jobs	5	11	84	489

Note: Data for current occupations of people aged 16 and over in work.

full-time hours for the most part (Table 6.3). On the face of it, there is already strong support for Polachek's thesis.

The Impact of Sex-Role Ideology on Occupational Choice

Do women who prefer to give priority to their homemaker role or who seek an even balance between paid work and family work choose particular kinds of occupation? Surprisingly, the answer from the 1999 British survey is a resounding No. Contrary to Polachek's thesis, sex-role ideology does not determine occupational choice in Britain at the start of the twenty-first century. This result was so unexpected that the finding was thoroughly tested, using different population bases and different versions of the

Table 6.3 Feminization and polarization of the workforce, 1971–1999

		Occupational group			
		Male	Mixed	Female	All
% female	1971	7	36	78	37
	1981	7	36	80	40
	1991	9	40	81	44
	1999a	12	47	81	49
	1999b	15	51	82	49
% part-time	1971	3	11	30	15
	1981	3	11	36	18
	1991	5	15	43	22
	1999a	6	18	50	28
	1999b	6	21	52	28

Source: Hakim (1996a: Table 6.6), reporting analyses of 1971 Census, 1981 Census, and 1991 Labour Force Survey data, updated with 1999 survey data. Integrated occupations are 25–55% female in 1971, 1981, 1991 and 1999a, but 30–60% female in 1999b. Data for people currently in work, including student jobs.

occupational segregation classification. Altogether four versions of the occupational typology were applied. Integrated occupations were variously defined as those 15–45% female (30% ±15%), 25–55% (40% ±15%), 30–60% (45% ±15%) and 30–70% female (50% ±20%). The results were always similar to those presented in Table 6.4 for people in employment. Our finding is not sensitive to the particular typology applied and is robust.[4]

Ideal family model has no important and systematic impact on the occupational choices of men and women, and there are only small variations around the averages for all men and all women of working age (Table 6.4). Similarly, the type of occupation chosen does not predict or determine the preferred model of marital roles, with relatively small and non-systematic variations around the average for all persons. There is a small tendency for people in sex-atypical occupations to have more extreme views, but both these groups are small. Because people aged 65 and over are excluded from Table 6.4, the proportions choosing the role-segregated family model are somewhat smaller than when the entire population is included. However, an analysis for the whole population, thus including information on previous jobs as well as current jobs, produces much the same results as in Table 6.4, namely, of no association between the two variables. The analysis was repeated separately for the two age groups under 40 years and 40 and over,

Table 6.4 Occupational segregation by ideal family model

| | Type of occupation | *Ideal family model* | | | |
		Egalitarian	*Compromise*	*Role segregation*	*Base = 100%*
Men	male	47	41	12	717
	mixed	49	32	19	160
	female	64	26	11	144
	all	49	38	13	1022
Women	male	53	30	17	128
	mixed	45	48	7	174
	female	46	43	11	696
	all	47	42	11	997
					All
Men	male	66	77	66	70
	mixed	16	13	22	16
	female	18	10	12	14
	total	100	100	100	100
Women	male	14	9	20	13
	mixed	17	20	11	17
	female	69	71	69	70
	total	100	100	100	100

Note: Data for people currently in work of working age (16–65 years).

with the same results. Neither in the older generation, nor in the younger generation is there any important and systematic connection between people's ideal model of marriage and the type of occupation chosen by women or men.

What this means is that, by the start of the twenty-first century in Britain, the equal opportunities revolution ensured that any link between marital roles and occupational choice that existed in earlier decades had been broken completely. Whether they plan a lifelong career or a short period of employment prior to marriage and full-time homemaking, British women feel free to choose any type of occupation (assuming they obtain the relevant qualifications), whether it is typically male, typically female or one of the newly emerging mixed occupations. It also means that employers cannot assume that a woman's choice of occupation is itself a fair indicator of her long-term commitment to an employment career or else to a marriage career. On the contrary, a woman's choice of occupation is made without regard to

Table 6.5 Workrates by ideal family model and type of occupation

	Egalitarian		Compromise		Role segregation		All	
	M	F	M	F	M	F	M	F
Employment patterns:								
% in current FT job	79	53	88	26	68	41	81	40
% in current PT job	4	21	2	46	4	16	3	31
% current marginal job	1	4	*	7	*	4	1	5
% with previous FT job	16	17	9	15	24	25	15	18
% with previous PT job	*	5	*	8	1	11	*	7
% currently working full-time by type of occupation								
male	81	81	90	60	70	58	83	70
mixed	77	58	88	46	78	57	80	53
female	75	47	79	18	59	37	74	33
all jobs	79	54	89	27	71	43	82	41

Note: Data for people aged 20–59 years who have completed their full-time education, excluding people not choosing any of the three family models and people who have never had a job.

the relative priority she gives to paid work versus family work, and without regard to her long-term work plans (if any). For example, women in the highly qualified and highly paid mixed occupations are divided into two very different groups: half claim they would prefer to work throughout adult life; the other half seek a compromise arrangement in marriage in which neither career nor family life takes priority on a permanent basis. This finding has profound implications for employers' personnel and staff management policies. In the professional and managerial grades, for example, there is a general assumption that people are committed to long-term careers. This is a fair assumption for men, but it applies to barely half the women in these occupations. The majority seek a compromise arrangement. A small proportion of women in mixed occupations can be expected to drop out of the labour force at some point after marriage and never return at all unless things go seriously wrong for them.

Women's accommodation of their employment to their family responsibilities is not achieved through the careful choice of occupation today, but through the choice of job. Substantial numbers of women work part-time or on a temporary basis, in preference to the full-time year-round work typical among men (Tables 6.5 and 6.6).

Table 6.6 Labour force dropouts (%) by type of occupation

		Male	Mixed	Female	All
All men		15	15	16	15
All women		18	28	29	27
Men aged	20–39	11	7	8	10
	40–59	19	24	25	20
Women aged	20–39	14	29	30	27
	40–59	23	26	28	27
Men					
Ideal family model:					
symmetrical roles		17	19	12	17
differentiated roles		13	12	22	14
Attitude to patriarchy:					
accept/ambivalent		20	21	17	20
reject		9	9	14	10
Work orientations:					
work-centred		15	16	9	15
other reasons for a job		15	14	20	15
Women					
Ideal family model:					
symmetrical roles		8	34	24	24
differentiated roles		24	21	32	29
Attitude to patriarchy:					
accept/ambivalent		24	29	33	31
reject		12	27	24	23
Work orientations:					
work-centred		6	25	24	21
other reasons for a job		25	29	30	29

Note: Data for people aged 20–59 who have completed their full-time education, excluding people who have never had a job.

In all family models, workrates for women are substantially lower than male workrates. However, female full-time workrates are often less than half the level among men, at all ages (see Table 5.4). Women achieve a balance between paid work and family work by choosing part-time jobs, or else by moving in and out of jobs according to family needs (Tables 6.5 and 6.6). For example, 81% of men age 20–59 years are in full-time employment compared to only 40% of women. Another 31% of women have a part-time job, sometimes with such small hours per week that it can be classified as a marginal job;[5] another 25% of women have dropped out of a full-time job (18%) or part-time job (7%). Ideal family model does not determine occupational choice, but it does determine the degree of women's involvement in these occupations, as indicated by part-time work and labour force dropouts.

The proportion of women working full-time declines steadily across the three types of occupation and the three family models (Table 6.5). The only exception is the unexpected and puzzlingly high level of full-time work among women whose ideal is to be a full-time homemaker, an anomaly that was explained in Chapter 5. The pattern is repeated among women in male-dominated, female-dominated and mixed occupations. The same pattern is observed among married and cohabiting couples aged under 40 and aged 40+, with even less variation around the average than in the whole workforce. Overall, sex-role preferences determine whether women work full-time or not, but not the particular occupation they choose.

Labour Mobility

Some social scientists have assumed that sex differentials in labour mobility and employment stability are fading away, simply because female workrates are rising everywhere. In reality, sex differentials in labour market behaviour seem to be a stable and permanent feature of the workforce in the USA and across Europe, even though the size of the differentials in the 1970s, 1980s and 1990s was much lower than immediately after the Second World War (Hakim, 1996b). A variety of measures of labour mobility show that women continue to leave their employer, and quit the labour market, far more frequently than men. In Britain, for example, turnover rates[6] in 1968 were 27% for women and 18% for men; by 1991, turnover rates were still 26% for women and 17% for men (Hakim, 1996b: 5, 1998a: 54). The 50% sex differential in turnover rates is repeated in measures of job tenure, and is typical of most countries in the European Union. However, women quit the labour force two to three times more frequently than men, across the lifecycle, in Europe and the USA (Hakim, 1996b). When men leave an employer, it is usually to take up a job with another employer. When women leave an employer, it is often because they are leaving the labour market altogether to be a full-time homemaker.

Some social scientists have argued that sex differentials in labour mobility are actually attributable to the nature of the jobs women do: employers relegate women to low grade and low paid jobs, which have higher turnover rates generally. This thesis was tested carefully with population censuses, which provide datasets large enough to test for occupation effects at a detailed level as well as at the broader level of male, mixed and female occupations. These studies showed conclusively that sex differentials in labour turnover are not explained by the type of occupation, nor by occupational grade (Hakim, 1996b, 1998a: 49–56). Sex differentials in labour mobility are largest in the highest grade professional and managerial occupations, and lowest in manual occupations, in 1971 and again in 1991 (Hakim, 1996b: 6, 1998a: 50–54) and they are attributable to the substantial proportion of women who quit the labour market when they leave a job, rather than just switching employers. Sex differentials in labour mobility persist in male, mixed and female occupations. The only job characteristic associated with higher labour mobility is part-time work, and it seems to be a characteristic of part-time workers rather than part-time jobs, since the great majority of women's part-time jobs in Europe are permanent jobs (Hakim, 1990). People working in part-time jobs have higher turnover rates and lower job tenure; they are also two, three and four times more likely to quit the labour force than people in full-time jobs. These patterns have been observed in countries such as Denmark, where part-time workers have long had the same legal status and rights as full-time workers, as well as in Britain before legal rights were equalized (Hakim, 1996b).

The 1999 British survey provides an opportunity to test for the impact of sex-role preferences on labour mobility. Although research based on large scale census datasets has established that type of occupation is not a determinant of labour mobility, we include controls for type of occupation in case it has an impact in conjunction with sex-role preferences.

The only measure of labour mobility available in the British dataset is the proportion of all persons who have held a particular type of occupation who have quit the labour market, for whatever reason. Because there is no specific time reference period for the last job held, the measure captures all the women who have stayed out of the labour market since their last job. As expected, the measure displays a high sex differential: 15% of men compared to 27% of women aged 20–59 have dropped out of the workforce. However, our primary interest here is not in comparing male and female labour mobility, but in comparisons between the three groups of women and the impact, if any, of type of occupation.

Among men, there is little variation around the average, which remains relatively constant in all three types of occupation, even when ideal family model and work orientations are controlled (Table 6.6). Among women, attitudes and values have a small but systematic impact on labour mobility. Women who work for social or financial reasons, who accept patriarchal values or who prefer differentiated family roles are slightly more likely to drop out of the workforce than other women. All these differences are most systematic and pronounced among women in male and female occupations,

Table 6.7 Labour force dropouts (%) among couples

	Ideal family model						
	Symmetrical roles		*Differentiated roles*		*All couples*		
	M	*F*	*M*	*F*	*M*	*F*	*All*
Type of occupation							
male/mixed	16	21	9	23	12	22	15
female	13	21	23	31	19	27	26
All occupations	16	21	11	29	13	26	20

Note: Data for married and cohabiting couples aged 20–59, excluding students and people who have never had a job.

but by far the largest group is women in female occupations, so that, overall, female occupations produce more labour force dropouts than male and mixed occupations. In sum, sex-role preferences do not determine the occupations women enter, and they have no major impact on rates of leaving these occupations. However, women in female occupations have high labour force dropout rates, as well as the highest proportion of part-time jobs (Table 6.6). Women in mixed occupations also have high dropout rates, but in this case it is not clear that attitudes and values are contributing factors.

Once again, the picture becomes clearer when the analysis is restricted to married and cohabiting couples (Table 6.7), because it is only in this situation that women make hard choices between paid work and family work. Wives have double the labour force dropout rate: 26% compared to 13% among husbands. This sharp sex differential persists across all types of occupation and ideal family models, with some small variations. The highest dropout rate of 31% is found among wives in female occupations who prefer differentiated roles in marriage (Table 6.7). The lowest dropout rate of 9% is found among husbands in male and mixed occupations who believe in differentiated marital roles that assign them the main breadwinner role. In sum, wives working in female occupations have the highest levels of workforce dropouts, as well as the highest levels of part-time work, but this is due to a combination of attitudes and values and job characteristics rather than any single dominant factor.

The Impact of Work Orientations on Occupational Choice

The second element of our operational definition of lifestyle preferences is work orientations. Polachek's theory assumed that people working in higher grade professional and managerial occupations have greater involvement with their work than do people in lower grade and routine occupations. As noted in Chapters 3 and 4, research has already established that work commitment is highest in the higher grade occupations and falls to its lowest level in routine manual occupations. Here we assess whether work orientations are linked to people's choice of male, mixed or female occupations. There is a link, but only a weak one, and only among women.

There is no association at all between occupational choice and work commitment, for men or women, for husbands or wives. In all three types of occupation, about 60% of workers, and married people, say they would prefer to keep on working even in the absence of financial necessity. However, among men and women, those who regard themselves as primary earners tend to choose male or mixed occupation more often, and those who regard themselves as secondary earners tend to gravitate towards female occupations most often. In female occupations, a two-thirds majority of women, but only one-third of men, regard themselves as secondary earners. In contrast, in male and mixed occupations, half of all women workers regard themselves as primary earners compared to 86% of men. As noted in Chapter 3, the work orientations of men and women differ markedly, but women bring a progressively weaker personal engagement with work to their jobs when they choose male, mixed or female occupations.

Once again, the picture is clearest when analysis focuses on couples of working age (Table 6.8). Over half of all husbands are work-centred, and this does not vary by type of occupation. Only one-fifth of wives are work-centred, but the proportion is highest (27%) among women in male occupations, falls a little to 23% among women in mixed occupations, then falls to its lowest level of 15% among wives choosing female occupations. It seems clear from the second part of Table 6.8 that these sex differentiated work orientations are shaped by sex-role ideologies. The vast majority (87%) of wives who prefer differentiated family roles are not work-centred. Even among wives who claim to prefer symmetrical family roles, only one-quarter are work-centred.

As noted in Chapters 3 and 4, work centrality is not simply a reflection of actual employment status or type of job. And as shown in the following section, men and women in unisex occupations with no sex differential in earnings nonetheless maintain different work orientations, defined by their sex-role ideology rather than by their common occupation. The average hourly earnings of male, mixed and female occupations are not so very

Table 6.8 Work orientations by occupational choice in Britain

| | | *Type of occupation* | | | |
		Male	*Mixed*	*Female*	*All*
% who regard	M	93	89	77	91
themself as	F	41	35	22	27
primary earner	T	85	58	28	57
% who regard their	M	55	55	49	54
job as central	F	27	23	15	18
to their identity	T	51	37	18	35

| | | *Ideal family model* | | |
		Symmetrical roles	*Differentiated roles*	*All*
% who regard	M	86	95	91
themself as	F	36	21	27
primary earner	T	61	53	57
% who regard their	M	53	56	54
job as central	F	25	13	18
to their identity	T	39	32	35

Note: Data for couples aged 20–59 who have completed their full-time education, excluding people who never had a job, whose occupation cannot be coded.

different: £7.10, £8.65 and £5.84 for full-time employees in 1991 (Hakim, 1998a: 76). So differences in work centrality cannot be simple reflections of relative earnings levels. In particular, there is no explanation for the fact that work centrality among women declines steadily from male to female occupations, whereas mixed occupations have the highest average earnings. Consistent with all previous results, women differ in the work orientations they bring to their jobs, whereas men do not.

There is some evidence in the British survey that people in sex-atypical occupations absorb the work orientations of the dominant opposite sex. Men in female occupations are least likely to be work-centred, while women in male occupations are most likely to be work-centred. In this case it is not clear whether it is the occupation itself, and the demands it places on workers, that shapes attitudes and values, or the work culture of the largest group of workers that is communicated to and absorbed by minority groups of workers. The end result is that male and female work orientations are most dissimilar among men in male occupations and women in female occupations; male and female work orientations are most similar among men in female occupations and women in male occupations. There is no evidence that people working in mixed occupations develop similar work orientations; sex differences here are just as marked as at the national level.

Paid work is not central to everyone's identity. Even among men, only half feel this way and half work for a host of other reasons: financial necessity, social conventions, the social community of the workplace and so forth. However, all family models impose full-time work on male partners, and men bring these breadwinner work orientations to all the occupations and jobs they do in the labour market. In contrast, women's work orientations (which are linked to their sex-role ideology) do affect their choice between male, mixed or female occupations. There is no strong matching of work orientations and occupational choice for the simple reason that numerous other factors play a much greater part in occupational choice: ability, training, qualifications, accumulated work experience, accidents and good luck, geographical location and hence the industries and occupations available in someone's local labour market. Urban areas have little demand for shepherds and rural areas have few openings for ballet dancers. Given that these factors have a predominant impact on the process of matching people to occupations, it is remarkable that work orientations still play a small part in the process among women, unlike men.

Women who are not work-centred generally gravitate towards female occupations, which offer the convenience factors of part-time and temporary jobs, and the freedom to drop out of the labour market for indefinite periods of time. Women who are work-centred are more likely to choose male or mixed occupations, which generally demand continuous full-time work. However, the *majority* of women, in all three types of occupation, do not regard their work as central to their identity, and this is especially true of wives. Differences between women in male, mixed and female occupations are differences of degree rather than qualitative differences. The overriding result here is that only one-quarter of women, and one-fifth of wives, have a major involvement in their paid work, compared to over half of all men. This difference is repeated to varying degrees across the entire workforce. The reason the difference matters is because, unless they win the lottery, few men will ever have the opportunity to give up paid work, whereas the majority of women regard this as a real possibility for them if and when they marry.

One reason for this is that most women seek to marry men who are a little taller, a little older and who have higher earnings. Despite women's massive influx into higher education and the equalization of educational qualifications across Europe in recent decades, the tendency for women to marry men who are better educated and/or have more work experience has grown rather than vanished (Hakim, 2000a: 203–17). So the equalization of educational qualifications in the population as a whole does not necessarily produce an increase in educational homogamy and equality in marriage. Wives continue to regard themselves as secondary earners, almost irrespective of their level of education and earnings potential, as the next section illustrates.

One consequence of these social processes is that male, mixed and female occupations differ greatly in the relative balance between primary and secondary earners among workers within them. In male occupations, almost all (85%) workers are primary earners. The proportion falls to about half (58%) in mixed occupations and then to one-quarter (28%) in female occupations (Table 6.8). There are similar, but less extreme contrasts on work centrality. Such sharp differences in workforce composition must have a major impact on occupational cultures. It seems likely that one reason why men would feel out of place in a female occupation, and women would feel uncomfortable in a male occupation, would be these contrasting cultures created by differing levels of work centrality, which would affect informal conversations as well as work cultures.

Lifestyle Preferences and Occupational Choice

Results summarized in Table 6.9 show that there is no link between lifestyle preferences and occupational segregation in Britain at the start of the twenty-first century. Home-centred, adaptive and work-centred women are all found in male, mixed and female occupations. Home-centred, adaptive and work-centred women differ hardly at all in their choice of occupation. The only exception is that work-centred women are most likely to choose mixed occupations, while home-centred women are least likely to choose them. But the exception is relatively minor.

It is full-time workrates that reveal differences between lifestyle preference groups and types of occupation (Table 6.9). Full-time workrates are systematically high among work-centred women, no matter what type of occupation they are in. Full-time workrates are much lower among adaptive and home-centred women, especially if they are in female occupations, where part-time jobs are widely available. This is a classic illustration of the joint impact of lifestyle preferences (which generally go unmeasured in most surveys) and of social structural factors (such as the paucity or abundance of part-time jobs in an occupation). Both factors are important, but it is lifestyle preferences that determine *which* contextual factors are important, if any, so in that sense preferences are always the overriding factor.

Table 6.9 Occupational choice by lifestyle preferences

Type of occupation	Home-centred	Adaptive	Work-centred	All
All women aged				
20–59 (column %)				
Male	21	10	17	12
Mixed	12	18	22	18
Female	67	72	61	70
All	100	100	100	100
All women aged				
20–59 (row %)				
Male	22	56	22	100
Mixed	9	72	19	100
Female	13	73	14	100
All	13	71	16	100
Wives aged				
20–59 (column %)				
Male	22	9	15	12
Mixed	12	19	23	18
Female	66	72	62	70
All	100	100	100	100
Wives aged				
20–59 (row %)				
Male	24	63	13	100
Mixed	8	80	12	100
Female	12	79	9	100
All	13	78	10	100
% working FT among				
wives aged 20–59				
Male	45	64	75	60
Mixed	58	49	71	52
Female	30	25	73	29
All	37	33	73	37

Note: Data for women aged 20–59, then married and cohabiting women aged 20–59, excluding students and people who have never worked.

The analysis in Table 6.9 was repeated for the younger and older generations, with almost identical results. Only in the work-centred group is there any difference between generations: the proportion going into male occupations has doubled, with a corresponding decline in the numbers in female occupations. In effect, it is only work-centred women who are taking advantage of the equal opportunities revolution to enter non-traditional occupations. For other women, the main effect is seen in increasing demands for the right to work part-time in their existing occupations.

Case Studies: Mixed Occupations and High Achievers

Studies of mixed occupations illustrate how women and men preserve dramatically different work patterns and work orientations even when working in the same occupation. Pharmacy and translating are integrated occupations that recruit equal numbers of men and women. Within these two graduate professions, there is no sign of any sex discrimination in earnings and rates of pay. In the case of pharmacy, huge unmet demand for pharmacists has allowed women to dictate the hours and times they are prepared to work. As a result, male and female pharmacists use the profession in different ways. Men, including those from ethnic minorities, use it as a route into self-employment and ownership of their own retail business, or into management jobs with the large retail chainstores. Women use the profession as a source of family-friendly, flexible and part-time employee jobs, with limited responsibilities that do not spill over into their family time (Hakim, 2000a: 39).

Translating offers the convenience of being able to work at home, in almost any location in Europe, with work received and delivered electronically to translation agencies. There are almost no sex differences in the qualifications, characteristics and earnings of workers in this unisex occupation, but men and women still regard their jobs differently. Virtually all married women regard themselves as secondary earners, while most male translators consider themselves to be their household's main breadwinner (Hakim, 2000a: 98).[7]

Similar results are reported from a USA study of 321 young couples who were both physicians, often married to each other because they met at medical school (Hinze, 2000). The average age of the physicians was 37 when surveyed in 1996, so they all benefitted from the new scenario of options and opportunities for women. Even in this selective group of high achievers, sex differences in work histories and work orientations were prominent. Men spent more years in training than women; women interrupted their careers for 8.5 months on average for childrearing, compared to less than one month among men; women tended to choose lower prestige specialities that offer regular work hours (such as family practice or paediatrics) whereas men tended to choose higher prestige specialities such as surgery; women worked 42 hours a week on average compared to 56 hours for men; women were much more likely to report sacrificing income, work hours and availability to patients in order to give priority to their own families; and there were significant differences between men and women in annual earnings. The direct effect on earnings of career sacrifices in favour of own family was the same for men and women. But men generally gave priority to their careers, and women were almost twice as likely to sacrifice their career in favour of their family role (Hinze, 2000).

These case studies illustrate that women's sex-role ideology and work orientations do not automatically change after graduation from university. Similarly, it is not higher (or lower) earnings that determine people's adoption of a primary or secondary earner identity, but their attitudes and values formed outside the labour market.

Conclusions: A New Explanation for Occupational Segregation

It is possible that in previous decades women were obliged to choose occupations that could be fitted in with family responsibilities, as Polachek argues. It is difficult to form a view on this because Polachek's and England's tests always focused on earnings, which are not the best indicator of a family-friendly occupation. Flexibility in hours and other arrangements are the most popular family-friendly employer schemes (Hakim, 2000a: 245). Also, it is possible that things were different in the USA in the 1960s and 1970s, and maybe still are.[8] What seems certain, on the evidence of our British survey, is that women in Britain at the start of the twenty-first century are not constrained to choose occupations that are designed to fit in with family life. Whatever their attitude to career and to family work, women can choose between male-dominated, mixed and female-dominated occupations.

Polachek's thesis is not supported in Britain today, although it may possibly be validated by data for earlier decades. However, Polachek's thesis is only refuted with reference to women's choice of *occupation*; the thesis is supported if we focus instead on women's choice of *jobs* within occupations. Similarly, lifestyle preferences play almost no part at all in women's choice of occupation in the new scenario; rather, preferences determine women's choice of job and working arrangements within all types of occupation. Case studies of unisex occupations, such as pharmacy and translating, demonstrate that, within the same occupation, married women can choose jobs offering the short work hours and other convenience factors attractive to secondary earners, while men gravitate towards the managerial jobs and self-employment positions that offer higher earnings as well as longer hours. The case studies also demonstrate that married women will continue to regard themselves as secondary earners, despite working in the same occupations, with the same hourly earnings, as men who regard themselves as primary earners for their families. It is private sex-role ideology that determines whether people regard themselves as primary or secondary earners, not their occupation or earnings. Similarly, sex-role ideology determines the type of job people choose, within their chosen occupation, and this applies to university graduates in professional occupations as much as to more routine occupations.

The sex-segregation of occupations cannot be explained today with reference to the different family roles of men and women. Possibly family roles were never in fact important, even if the rhetoric that built up around masculine and feminine occupations and work cultures often referred to family roles, as well as to 'essentialist' arguments about jobs suitable for men or for women (Hakim, 1996a: 162–6). Explanations for the sex-segregation of occupations will have to rely instead on benign social processes, such as the tendency for people to choose same-sex friends[9] and hence also to prefer same-sex work groups (Hakim, 1996a: 162–6, 1998a: 56–9; Brewer and Brown, 1998; Fiske, 1998; Reskin, 2000). The emergence of mixed-sex occupations is obviously determined by women's massive influx into higher education after the education system was opened up to women. But it is testimony also to the increasing social acceptability of work groups that combine men and women, and the cross-sex friendships that inevitably arise from such work groups, along with the potential for sexual misunderstandings and harassment.[10] The contraceptive revolution has not eliminated the sexual tensions that can arise in mixed-sex workplaces and work groups, but it has eliminated the danger of heterosexual liaisons producing illegitimate children.

Humphries (1987) developed the theory that the original stimulus to the sex segregation of occupations or work groups, in nineteenth-century Britain was a concern to control sexuality, to avoid social contact between unrelated men and women in the workplace, to reduce or eliminate the potential for heterosexual liaisons (and hence illegitimate children) in social settings beyond family supervision. Concern with segregation of the sexes in the workplace was greatest in relation to young unmarried women, in a period when contraception was neither reliable nor freely available. This new explanation for the evolution of occupational segregation fits in perfectly with the theory that patriarchy also evolved primarily in order to control women's sexuality and reproductive work, not to control women's productive work *per se* (Lerner, 1986; Hakim, 2000a: 281). It follows that there is no logical need to maintain occupational segregation in order to support patriarchy now that the contraceptive revolution and other developments in reproductive technology have broken the link between sexuality and childbearing. It appears that explanations for social processes within the labour market sometimes lie in completely unrelated social fields. However, once occupations become labelled as 'female' or 'male', these classifications can become institutionalized, even rigid, until some new event disturbs the status quo and provokes change.

Adaptive women can now accommodate their paid work to their family priorities by choosing part-time jobs or by moving in and out of the labour market at different stages of their life. Women who regard themselves as secondary earners are most likely to work in female occupations, where part-time jobs are plentiful and high labour turnover is tolerated. At this point cause and effect must be disentangled with care. In line with preference theory and research evidence on how women choose their identity as primary or secondary earner, we conclude that women who prefer to give priority to their family work, in whole or in part, currently gravitate towards the female occupations because they offer plenty of part-time jobs and tolerate high turnover rates. However, male and mixed occupations are gradually increasing their share of part-time and temporary jobs as well, so that the dividing line between them is getting fainter rather than stronger over time.

These results are testimony to the impact of equal opportunities laws and policies on employers in Britain. Whatever their ambitions and lifeplans, women can now choose occupations far more freely than in the past. As part-time jobs and other forms of family-friendly flexibility gradually spread into jobs in all occupations, employers will find that they have a combination of primary and secondary earners working side by side in all types of occupation. This new type of employee diversity will pose challenges for human resource management in both the private and public sectors.

Notes

1 A more extreme version of this thesis has been presented by Hartmann (1976) and Walby (1986, 1990) who argued that occupational segregation is the primary mechanism for maintaining patriarchy, that is, male dominance in public and private life. However, Hakim (2000a: 282) has criticized the thesis as unsupported by evidence from recent research on occupational segregation and the pay gap. A historical analysis by Lerner (1986) shows that patriarchy developed first and foremost through male control of female sexuality and female reproduction, leading to an emphasis on the *physical* segregation of men and women, not on the sex segregation of occupations *per se*.

2 The 1990 Standard Occupational Classification (SOC) was updated in the SOC 2000, a revised version of SOC 1990, which was used to code occupations in the 2001 Census and forms the basis for the new ONS socio-economic classification (Rose and Pevalin, 2002).

3   The Service Class is the highest level identified in Goldthorpe's social class schema. The Service Class includes professionals, administrators and managers, high-grade technicians and supervisors of non-manual workers (Erikson and Goldthorpe, 1993: Table 2.1).

4   This is generally true of all findings in this chapter. The particular typology of occupations applied makes little or no difference to the results.

5   Marginal jobs are part-time jobs with very short hours, typically less than 10 or less than 12 hours per week and thus entail earnings low enough for wages to be paid without tax and social welfare deductions. They are popular with students as well as married women. In Britain, Germany and the Netherlands, for example, substantial numbers of part-time workers are in fact marginal workers (Hakim, 1998a: 117–19). In some countries, such as the Netherlands, these jobs are no longer included in published labour force statistics. In the British survey, marginal jobs are those that involve less than ten hours a week (N = 187). In the Spanish survey, marginal jobs are employee jobs of less than 15 hours per week (N = 10) plus all family workers (N = 3).

6   Labour turnover refers to the proportion of workers employed at the beginning of a year or some other period, who were no longer working for that employer or establishment at the end of the year, for whatever reason.

7   Some employment tribunal judges have endorsed this sex differential in work orientations when deciding that employers cannot make the same demands of secondary earners as they do of primary earners, even if they both are doing exactly the same job (Hakim, 1996a: 197)

8   The datasets used by Polachek and England cover the 1960s and 1970s, arguably the period just before and immediately after the equal opportunities and the contraceptive revolutions in the USA. So their results may now be dated.

9   Kalmijn (2002) reviews the many reasons offered for the dominance of same-sex friendships, which occurs in childhood and adolescence as well as in adult life. He finds that cross-sex friendships seem to demand greater social skills. No doubt this applies also to workplace relationships, so that same-sex workgroups are regarded as easier and more comfortable.

10   Workgroups that combine men and women probably demand greater social skills and sensitivity than same-sex workgroups. It is thus not surprising that they have emerged first and foremost among the more highly educated sectors of the workforce, who may be better able to cope with the increased demands on their social skills in the workplace.

Chapter 7

Political, Religious and Other Influences on Lifestyle Preferences

The Spanish dataset includes a rich fund of information on political and other ideologies, as well as unusually detailed information on parental characteristics. This chapter exploits this additional information to look at the *determinants* of lifestyle preferences. The focus here is thus very different from Chapters 5 and 6 which look at the behavioural *consequences* of lifestyle preferences.

Spain provides a particularly good case study for an exploration of the origins and causes of lifestyle preferences. Following a period of rapid social change, the full range of political and religious ideologies are all displayed, and are still publicly debated and tested in national and local elections. Spanish political parties and political ideologies, display greater variety and wider extremes, than in British politics. Similarly, religious beliefs present wider extremes than in the essentially secular British society. The Catholic organization *Opus Dei* is still very active in Spain, even if it no longer plays a central role in shaping social and political discourse (Pfenning and Bahle, 2000: 7, 167–76). At the other extreme, some Spaniards are beginning to openly desert the Catholic Church. This has been facilitated by the secularization process that started with the transition to democracy in 1975. Education has been secularized. Religion has ceased to be a compulsory subject in primary and secondary schools, and only one-fifth of school students now attend Catholic institutions. Marriage can now be contracted through civil procedures alone, although the proportion of young people who favour this option is actually declining in favour of marriage in church (Andrés Orizo, 1996: 149). Divorce was made possible by the 1981 divorce law, which led to a sharp rise in divorces, although Spain continues to have one of the lowest divorce rates in the EU, as noted in Table 4.10. In sum, Spain displays substantial ideological diversity.[1] It is thus an excellent choice for testing the impact of political and religious ideologies on lifestyle choices.

Our central hypothesis is that the model of the family with complete role specialization is the conservative choice while the 'egalitarian' symmetrical roles model is the liberal or left-wing choice. This means that right-wing political ideologists and extremely religious Catholics should all choose the role segregation model, while left-wing political ideologists and atheists should all choose the egalitarian model. Similarly, home-centred women should be conservatives in terms of political and religious ideology, while work-centred women should be left-wing and non-religious. In practice, the analysis reveals only weak associations between political-religious ideology and lifestyle preferences. The links are far too weak to confirm our central hypothesis.

Another possible source of contemporary sex-role ideology is parental role models: the division of labour, attitudes and values in the parental home. Of course, some people react against parental role models while others happily follow them. Our central hypothesis is that people are more likely to espouse patriarchal values if such values were dominant in their parental home. A review of the research literature on educational homogamy and its impact on marital relationships (Hakim, 2000a: 203–22) indicates that patriarchal values and practices are most likely in marriages where the husband is significantly better educated than his wife, that is, where the wife has married *up* the educational ladder. We thus assess whether the children of less-educated wives are most likely to hold patriarchal values, and whether there are also consequences for lifestyle preferences.

In practice, having a mother who married up, rather than at an equal level of education, makes only a very small difference to sex-role ideology, although it affects women more than men. Contrary to expectation, it stimulates women to reject patriarchy and to seek greater equality in their own marriage.

In addition, we explore the links between ideal family models and associated values and other ideological influences on which the Spanish survey provides information: nationalism and trade unionism.

Religiosity

Virtually everyone in the survey answered questions on religion and religious practices, with almost no refusals. This indicates that religiosity is very much in the public domain in Spain, rather than being treated as a private matter. Religiosity is surveyed just as often as political attitudes in Spain, and the decline in religiosity is regarded as a measure of the secularization process that began in 1975.

The vast majority (90%) of Spaniards are Catholic, with only 1% reporting another religion, and a surprisingly high 9% insisting they had no religion. This last group may in fact have private religious beliefs and simply object to institutional religion, but we label them 'atheists' for simplicity in this analysis. Atheism is a feature of the younger, secularized generation in Spain: 13% compared to only 5% in the older generation. It is also far more common among men (12%) than among women (4%).

The atheist group is small and distinctive, three-quarters male, mostly under 35 years old and generally well-educated: double the national average have university level education. Four-fifths hold left-wing political views, some of them extreme. This group is an ideologically consistent and coherent extreme opposite to the most devout Catholics in the survey, rather than an ill-defined group of agnostics and 'Don't knows'.

With only 1% of respondents reporting any religion other than Catholicism, they were grouped with the Catholics for convenience. They do not seem to have had any difficulty in responding to questions about the intensity of their religious practice and the frequency of their visits to church. The group is too insignificantly tiny to make any difference to the results for Catholics.

As expected, women are more religious than men, and the younger generation is far less religious than the older generation (Table 7.1). However, most Catholics are non-practising in Spain. One-quarter of women still attend church weekly, one-third in the older generation and just 7% in the younger generation. In contrast, almost two-thirds of men never or rarely attend church, half in the older generation and three-quarters in the younger generation. Two-thirds of younger women and 85% of younger men say they are effectively non-practising Catholics, compared to one-third of women and two-thirds of men in the older age cohort. The most pious Catholics tend to be older women (45%) and only rarely older men (16%). Sex differences in religiosity are greatly reduced in the younger generation.

Political conservatism and religiosity are associated, but mainly in the older generation and mainly among men. Women tend to be religious irrespective of their political ideology. Less than half of the most devout Catholic women consider themselves to be right-wing and one-third hold left-wing views. In the younger generation, over half define themselves as left-wing, irrespective of their religious involvement. Overall, the link between political conservatism and religiosity is moderate, and declining rapidly over time.

Putting aside the well-established sex and age differences in religious practice, there are no sex or age differences at all in the small impact of religiosity on ideal family model and on other values. So the overall picture presented in Tables 7.2, 7.3 and 7.4 applies broadly to men and women, younger and older generations. The only exception is of course work centrality, where sex differences are marked. However, here too religiosity has little or no impact on values. Table 7.2 shows the impact of religious and political ideology on ideal family model, to test our central hypothesis.

Table 7.1 Religious and political ideology by age

	Men			Women		
	<40	*40 +*	*All*	*<40*	*40 +*	*All*
% atheist	16	10	12	10	2	4
Church attendance:						
% weekly	4	14	10	7	37	26
% rarely/never	75	49	60	49	19	30
Religious practice:						
% little/none	85	64	73	69	33	46
% very devout	6	16	12	14	45	35
1996 vote:						
Partido Popular	20	37	29	22	34	29
PSOE	25	37	32	24	40	33
UI	6	3	5	4	3	4
others	9	9	9	13	7	9
non-voters	40	14	25	37	16	25
Political ideology:						
left	59	47	52	43	41	41
centre	27	26	27	35	28	31
right	14	27	22	22	31	28
Nationalism:						
% regional identity	24	21	22	22	16	18
% Spanish identity	36	39	38	30	35	34

Note: Data for people aged 18 and over who have completed their full-time education. The three main parties in the 1996 elections were Partido Popular, Partido Socialista Obrero Español (PSOE) and Izquierda Unida (IU), a left-wing coalition.

However, we can equally well be interested in the obverse: the religious and political composition of the three family model preference groups, so this is also shown in Table 7.3.

Roughly half of the people who define themselves as extremely religious and fully practising Catholics prefer the egalitarian model of the family, only slightly less than the two-thirds average. One-quarter of people who attend church weekly prefer the role-segregated model of the family, but so do 10% of people who rarely or never attend church (Table 7.2). Religiosity does make a difference, but a relatively small one, and the association is stronger among older people who are more religious and also prefer the role segregation model of the family. The link is not causal, otherwise it would persist among the most pious group in the younger generation as well. As a

Table 7.2 Impact of religious and political ideology

	Ideal model of the family			
	Egalitarian	*Compromise*	*Role segregation*	*Base = 100%*
All 18 +				
excluding students	64	20	16	931
Catholics	62	22	16	481
Atheists	86	5	9	74
Church attendance:				
weekly	51	23	26	191
rarely/never	70	20	10	462
Religious practice:				
little/none	71	19	10	617
very pious	54	21	25	245
1996 vote:				
Partido Popular	59	22	19	275
PSOE	60	22	19	303
UI	79	13	8	39
others	76	17	7	82
non-voters	70	19	12	232
Political ideology:				
left	67	19	14	381
centre	66	20	14	236
right	60	22	18	205
Nationalism: identity is				
mainly regional	62	25	13	213
mainly Spanish	66	20	14	377

result, the religious differences between the three ideal family model groups are not large (Table 7.3). For example, one-third of the group preferring role segregation is extremely religious, but another one-third does not practice at all. Two-thirds of the egalitarian group does not practice at all, but one-fifth are extremely observant. The overall conclusion is that there is no more than a weak link between religiosity and ideal family model. Religion does not shape sex-role preferences to any major degree at the start of the twenty-first

Models of the Family in Modern Societies

Table 7.3 Religious and political characteristics by ideal family model

	Ideal model of the family			
	Egalitarian	Compromise	Role segregation	Total
% atheists	10	4	4	8
Church attendance:				
% weekly	14	21	31	18
% rarely/never	48	44	29	44
Religious practice:				
% little/none	64	56	38	59
% very devout	19	25	38	23
1996 vote:				
Partido Popular	27	32	36	30
PSOE	30	35	39	33
UI	5	3	2	4
others	11	7	4	9
non-voters	27	23	19	25
Political ideology:				
left	48	44	43	46
centre	29	28	27	29
right	23	28	30	25
Nationalism: identity is				
mainly regional	19	25	18	20
mainly Spanish	36	36	32	36
Base = 100%	698	216	163	1077

century and probably never did. In the past, some of the most pious women avoided marriage altogether in order to found religious orders that provided an alternative career to the marriage career for women.

Religiosity is not linked to work centrality, either for men or women (Table 7.4). There is an association between patriarchal values and religiosity, but it is small, with no sex differences. Once again, the link is largely due to age and is coincidental, not causal: older people tend to be religious and are more inclined to support patriarchy, but the link does not persist in the younger generation.

In sum, Catholic religiosity does not, in practice, have an important impact on lifestyle preferences. Catholic, but secularizing Spain is an excellent test case for this question.

Political Ideology

The Spanish survey provides three indicators of political ideology: a simple self-classification as left-wing or right-wing, a statement of which political party they voted for in the last general election of March 1996, and responses to a question about regional versus Spanish identity. Up to one-quarter of survey respondents chose not to answer at least one of these questions (usually the self-classification as left- or right-wing), most of them women, suggesting that lack of interest in politics contributed to lower response rates.

Women are divided relatively evenly between left-wingers, centrists and right-wingers, while a small majority of men label themselves as left-wing (Table 7.1). However, sex differences vanish when it comes to voting, and age differences also vanish once non-voters[2] are excluded. Similarly, there are no sex and age differences in regional versus Spanish identities (Table 7.1). It is notable that only one-third of Spaniards feel a predominantly Spanish nationalistic identity, and regional identities are strongest in the younger generation, implying a revival. Most Spaniards feel that their regional national identity is of equal importance to their Spanish national identity, reflecting a semi-federalized political culture and a history in which several regions had independent monarchies. To avoid confusion and repetition, the term national identity will be used here to refer to people whose identity is predominantly Spanish, and the term regional identity will be used to refer to people whose identity is predominantly regional. A strong regional identity does not necessarily inform voting behaviour. The question asking about people's vote in the 1996 elections listed a large number of nationalist regional parties,[3] but only 8% of respondents (9% after excluding refusals) voted for them. Minority party voters are found in all age groups.

Surprisingly, there is no association between education and political ideology in Spain, in the younger and older generations, among men and women. The least-educated groups are just as likely to be left-wing as the university graduates. The recent massive expansion in access to education appears to have had no effect at all on the political climate. Despite the tendency for everyone to report themselves as middle-middle class, there is a link between social class and political ideology. The small minorities of people who define themselves as upper-middle or lower-middle class hold distinctively right-wing or left-wing views respectively.

Political ideology and nationalism have no impact at all on ideal family model. Similarly, there is no difference at all between the supporters of the two main political parties as regards family models. There are no sex differences at all in the overall picture shown in Table 7.2. The only departure from the average distribution is found among supporters of the minority political parties: the Izquierda Unida left-wing coalition; regional nationalist parties of the right, centre and left; and the mainly young non-voter group. These groups are more likely to choose the egalitarian family model but, apart from the non-voters, they are too small in size to have any appreciable impact on the overall picture. Contrary to expectation, political ideology has no impact at all on how people choose between the three models of family roles.

Political ideology has a slightly more visible impact on patriarchal values (Table 7.4), but again the main departures from the average response are among the tiny groups of supporters of the minority political parties. The pattern is duplicated among men and women.

Somewhat surprisingly, political ideology has some impact on work orientations (Table 7.4). Supporters of the two main political parties are undifferentiated, with work centrality high among men and low among women, as usual. However, work centrality rises sharply among women and falls sharply among men who vote for the minority parties, thus achieving an equalization of work-centrality in these small parties. Why this should happen is not clear, but it only occurs in the younger generation of minority party supporters. It appears that youthful idealism leads men to avoid the primary earner role, while pushing women to adopt it.

To conclude, ideal family model and sex-role ideology are generally separate from and not shaped by political and religious values. There is no evidence that people choosing the role-segregated model of the family are all ideological conservatives, nor that people choosing the 'egalitarian' model are all liberals and left-wingers. In all three ideal family model groups, there is the full spectrum of religious and political opinion. As a result there are only small differences in the political and religious composition of the three lifestyle preference groups (Table 7.5). Work-centred women in Spain are slightly more left-wing than home-centred women, but almost indistinguishable in their voting patterns. The largest difference is in religiosity. Most work-centred women are non-practising Catholics and 8% are atheists. Most home-centred women are devout Catholics and 42% attend church weekly. But these differences are due largely to the differing age structure of the three groups, and often shrink to nothing in the younger generation.

Table 7.4 Impact of religious and political ideology on patriarchal values and work centrality

	% who reject patriarchy	% who are work-centred		
		M	F	T
All 18 + excluding students	54	40	16	28
Catholics	52	42	15	27
atheists	69	30	23	28
Church attendance:				
weekly	38	47	14	22
rarely/never	61	33	17	27
Religious practice:				
little/none	58	39	17	30
very devout	41	40	15	22
1996 vote:				
Partido Popular	47	47	16	32
PSOE	46	46	14	30
UI	75	26	33	29
others	75	30	30	30
non-voters	62	29	10	20
Political ideology:				
left	59	39	18	30
centre	58	38	14	26
right	46	49	20	33
Nationalism: identity is				
mainly regional	59	43	23	34
mainly Spanish	52	37	13	26

Table 7.5 Ideological characteristics of lifestyle preference groups

	Home-centred	Adaptive	Work-centred	All
Political ideology:				
left	31	42	50	41
centre	35	31	24	31
right	34	27	26	28
1996 vote:				
Partido Popular	35	29	26	30
PSOE	39	31	31	33
UI	1	4	8	4
others	5	8	19	9
non-voters	20	28	16	25
Nationalism:				
% regional identity	18	17	29	19
% Spanish identity	27	35	30	33
% atheist	2	4	8	4
Church attendance:				
% weekly	42	23	21	26
% rarely/never	20	32	37	30
Religious practice:				
% little/none	28	49	58	46
% very pious	53	29	28	34
Base = 100%	97	387	71	555

Note: Women aged 18 +, excluding students

Trade Unionism

The Spanish survey provides just one indicator of trade union activism: trade union membership. Only 6% of respondents refused to answer the question, so trade unionism is not a sensitive subject. Trade union membership enjoyed a revival in the first decade of democracy, then declined again. Today, it is very rare indeed in Spain, at 7% of all respondents aged 18 and over. Trade union membership is found across the entire age spectrum,

Table 7.6 Political ideology of trade unionists

	Trade unionists	Others	All
1996 vote:			
Partido Popular	11	27	26
PSOE	36	30	31
UI	4	6	5
others	22	9	10
non-voters	27	28	28
Political ideology:			
left	59	49	50
centre	29	29	29
right	12	22	21
Base = 100%	55	415	469

Note: Data for all aged 20–59, excluding students.

roughly in proportion to the age distribution. There is no bunching in the older or younger generations, as with most other subjects.

Most people are members of trade unions only while they are of working age, so the following analysis is limited to people aged 20–59 years, excluding full-time students.[4] Trade union membership is more common among men (13%) than women (9%). In consequence, three-quarters of all trade union members are male and only one-quarter are female.

Spanish trade unionists are more likely to vote for minority regional nationalist parties, and less likely to vote for the Partido Popular, which was in power at the time of the survey (Table 7.6). However, there is only a very small tendency for trade unionists to be more left-wing than non-unionists (Table 7.6). All these results are equally valid for men and women. In sum, Spanish trade unionists tend to have slightly more extreme political views, but not necessarily left-wing views. Male trade unionists do not differ from non-unionists in terms of religiosity and nationalistic values. Female trade unionists are less religious than non-unionists, but no different in terms of regional versus national Spanish identity.

Trade unionism, albeit rare, is still a normal aspect of the world of work for men. Among women, trade unionism is yet another aspect of the self-selection process that characterizes all female employment in Spain. As a result, male

Table 7.7 Impact of trade unionism on sex-role ideology

	Men			Women		
	Trade unionists	Others	All	Trade unionists	Others	All
Ideal family model:						
egalitarian	77	69	70	89	73	73
compromise	11	19	18	5	17	16
role segregation	12	12	12	6	10	10
% work-centred	43	38	38	39	16	17
% reject patriarchy	70	60	61	83	64	65
% regard woman responsible for housework	11	22	20	5	15	14
% regard man as responsible for income	11	23	21	11	17	17
Base = 100%	40	263	302	15	152	167

Note: Data for all aged 20–59, excluding students.

trade unionists are only very slightly more work-centred than non-unionists, but work centrality is markedly higher among the minority of female trade unionists. Apart from this, trade unionism has virtually no impact on sex-role ideology, for men or women. Trade unionists are just slightly more egalitarian, less supportive of strict role segregation and more likely to reject patriarchy. Given the small base numbers, especially for women, these results are not totally reliable, but they are all consistent (Table 7.7).

To summarize, trade unionism has an impact on work-centrality among women, but this is probably due to selection effects. Trade unionism has virtually no impact on other aspects of sex-role ideology.

Parental Cultural Capital

The Spanish survey provides information on the educational qualifications of both parents, and on the number of books in the parental home when the respondent was aged 15 years. These are all indicators of parental cultural capital, which might be expected to have an impact on their children's attitudes and values. As noted in Chapter 4, own education only has an impact on attitudes and values in the older generation; education has little or no impact on the younger generation's values, except for patriarchal values. However, higher education is linked to greater work-centrality among women, probably due to selection effects. It thus seems unlikely that parental cultural capital could have much impact on sex-role ideology, as any impact would necessarily be even weaker than the impact of the respondent's own education. But the question still seems worth asking. For example, parental cultural capital might enhance the impact of own education, or might substitute for it.

In the past, it was unusual for Spanish children to be significantly better-educated than their parents. Access to education was determined primarily by family wealth. The expansion of state education under democracy has changed this. In the younger generation, a good third of children are better-educated than their parents (Marí-Klose and Nos Colom, 1999: Table 2.2). Three-quarters of parents had no more than primary education, at best, compared to one-third of our survey respondents. Only 3% of mothers and 8% of fathers had university level education, compared to 22% of respondents.[5] Low levels of parental cultural capital are indicated also by the number of books in parental homes: 37% had 0–10 books, 19% had around 20, 19% had around 50 and 25% had 100 or more.

The number of books in the parental home is strongly associated with respondents' educational attainment in the older generation, those aged 40 and over. In the younger generation, large numbers of books and university education, are both more common and the association is weaker. The association with subjective social class is weaker still, due to the universal popularity of the middle-middle class label.

Parental cultural capital, as indicated by books in the home, has no impact at all on ideal family model, some impact on patriarchal values and some impact on work centrality. The impact on work centrality seems to be due entirely to books acting as a proxy for family wealth. Richer families produce sons who are *less* work-centred and daughters who are *more* work-centred, the exact opposite of poor families. The impact on patriarchal values is limited to the older generation of respondents who generally had only primary level education. There is no impact in the younger generation, who are better educated, and among whom their own education is the only determinant of patriarchal values. It appears that, among people with little education, access to books in the family home can provide a substitute source of information and ideas, which helps to shape attitudes and values, most notably on patriarchy. But parental cultural capital ceases to be important in the younger generation, whose values are shaped partly by their own education and partly by wide access to the mass media and other sources of information and socialization processes that homogenize values.

Results are much the same when the indicators of parental cultural capital are father's education and mother's education. The main impact of parental education is on their offspring's education and thus, very indirectly, on their attitudes and values. In line with many other studies, mother's education is found to be most important in Spain, both for sons' and daughters' educational attainment. Both parents push sons harder than daughters, but the mother's education is a stronger determinant of outcomes than the father's education. However, parental education only influences attitudes and values for those respondents who fail to replicate (or surpass) their parents' education.

Parental Educational Homogamy

When the vast majority of people had no more than a basic education, it was inevitable that most spouses would be equally, if poorly, educated. A decline in the educational homogamy of spouses only appears when people achieve higher levels of secondary and tertiary education (Hakim, 2000a: 193–222). The wider the range of potential educational qualifications, the greater the scope for women to marry up, to a man who is even better educated than they are. The most obvious example is a woman with secondary level qualifications who marries a university graduate. A less obvious example is the woman university graduate who marries a man with a doctorate. Given that most surveys group everyone with tertiary level education into a single category, the second example of a woman marrying up is virtually never identified in research analyses. Our survey thus understates the full extent of women marrying up.

Most research on trends in educational homogamy is concerned with social mobility processes, in particular with whether own education is replacing social class of origin as the dominant factor in assortative mating. A quite different reason for looking at trends in and levels of, educational homogamy is because of its impact on family relationships and role-segregation in marriage (Hakim, 2000a: 217–220). Studies show that role specialization is far more common in marriages where the wife is significantly less educated than the husband. In such cases, it makes more sense for the husband to be a full-time breadwinner while the wife is a homemaker. When spouses are equally educated, there is greater potential for moving towards symmetrical family roles, and even for role reversal.[6]

The Spanish survey provides information on spouses' employment status, which was particularly useful in Chapter 5. Unfortunately, it does not provide information on spouses' educational qualifications. However, the information on parental education is detailed enough to allow us to study the impact of *parental* educational homogamy on respondents' attitudes and values.[7]

The central hypothesis here is that women whose mother was less educated than their father will seek equality in their own marriage. Daughters will tend to conflate the disadvantages of a less educated wife with the role segregation model of the family, leading them to reject any form of role specialization in favour of the symmetrical roles model. Similarly, we expect women whose mothers married up to be more likely to reject patriarchy. Studies of marital relationships suggest that male dominance is more likely in couples with a less educated wife than in couples with equally educated spouses. So the rejection of patriarchal values should be stronger among daughters whose mothers achieved social mobility by marrying a better educated man. The implicit assumption here is that parents who were educationally homogamous are more likely to have had an egalitarian relationship irrespective of the particular division of labour they adopted. The problem is that a mother who married a more educated husband may also have presented a positive image to her daughters. For example, such women may have been exceptionally attractive, clever, competent and delighted with the social mobility they had achieved through marriage, thus projecting a positive image of this situation, even if they were full-time homemakers. So such women might also present role models to be admired and copied rather than rejected.

Nationally, about four-fifths of parents were educationally homogamous, and 15% had a less-educated wife. Wives who marry down are exceptionally rare among parents in Spain, just 2%, although this seems to be increasingly common in the younger generation of highly educated women.[8] For reasons that are not clear, Spanish men consistently report a higher percentage of less-educated mothers: 18% compared to 13% among women (Table 7.8). There is a clear pattern of parental educational homogamy declining across ten-year age groups in Spain, with an increasing percentage of wives marrying up, as is the case in most western European countries (Hakim, 2000a: 203–17).[9] The more educated a father was, the more likely it is that he married a less-educated wife. Paradoxically, the more educated a mother was, the more likely it is that she married up.

As can be seen in Table 7.9, parental homogamy does not have a major impact on attitudes and, in turn, women's workrates. In fact, the impact is relatively small. The results are still of interest because they shed some light on the origins of family model preferences and work centrality. An earlier review of the research evidence (Hakim, 2000a: 185–9) failed to uncover any early experiences, personal or family characteristics that might explain why some women develop a preference for role specialization in the family

Table 7.8 Parental educational homogamy

		Mother married up	Homogamy	Mother married down	Base = 100%
All 18 +		15	83	2	1139
Men	all	18	80	2	554
	<40	21	75	3	254
	40 +	14	84	2	300
Women	all	13	85	2	585
	<40	16	81	3	244
	40 +	10	88	2	341

while others prefer symmetrical roles, why some women are home-centred while others are work-centred.[10] The experience of growing up with parents who were equally educated, with all that entails for personal relationships, or with a mother who was significantly less educated than her husband, with all that entails, seems to leave a mark on children, daughters especially. Compared to the children of women who married a better-educated man, sons and daughters of educationally homogamous marriages are more comfortable with the idea of complete role specialization, they are less likely to reject patriarchy, and daughters especially are the least work-centred. The experience of having a mother who was significantly less educated than her husband seems to push women towards greater emphasis on 'egalitarian' relationships in their own marriage, and thus towards employment as a defining feature of lifestyle. In particular, women with such mothers are almost twice as likely to be work-centred and almost twice as likely to have full-time jobs. There are similar effects among men, but they are very small indeed.

The experience of a mother who married up is clearly not overwhelming. Most women in this group are no different from the great majority who had equally educated parents. But there is enough of an impact to suggest that this finding merits further exploration. Unfortunately we have no further information on parents' characteristics, for example whether the mother worked or not, so we cannot explore this result further with the Spanish data.

These results on the impact of parental educational homogamy complicate what we already know about the impact of mother's and father's education on the educational achievements of daughters: more educated mothers produce more educated daughters and sons. However, the Spanish

Table 7.9 Impact of parental educational homogamy on values and workrates

	Mother married up		Parental homogamy	
	M	F	M	F
Ideal family model:				
egalitarian	70	78	62	64
compromise	21	14	20	21
role segregation	9	8	18	15
% regard man as ultimately responsible for income	18	17	31	26
% regard woman as ultimately responsible for housework	19	14	28	25
% reject patriarchy	63	71	51	52
% work-centred	44	26	39	14
% work full-time	67	37	58	21
% work at all	70	46	62	28
Women's lifestyle preferences:				
home-centred		11		19
adaptive		62		70
work-centred		27		11
Base = 100%	83	66	421	466

Note: Data for all aged 18 +, excluding students.

survey also shows that the more educated a woman is the more likely she is to marry up. In Britain, cross-sectional surveys show the opposite: that women are more likely to marry *down*, the greater their own education (Hakim, 2000a: Table 7.4). So the results for Spanish women suggest that the impact of a mother's increasing education on her daughter's aspirations might be reinforced by the impact of having a mother who also married up and demonstrated the disadvantages of this situation to her daughter.

Conclusions

Attempts to identify the early experiences which lead women to be home-centred or work-centred in their aspirations and values have generally failed. The only experiences that emerge regularly in research results as promoting a work-centred lifestyle among women are attendance at all-women schools and colleges, and a strong bond with their father (Hakim, 2000a: 188). Attendance at all-women schools and colleges is probably of declining importance, in the long run, because single-sex establishments are gradually disappearing in most modern societies. However, a strong bond between father and daughter is of increasing importance, in the long run, because families are getting smaller and smaller. Couples who have only one or two children may have an only daughter or no sons and this increases the likelihood of a strong bond between father and daughter.

Our exploratory analysis suggests a third factor which also seems to be of increasing importance: daughters' responses to a mother who married *up* the educational ladder. Paradoxically, as women take advantage of improved access to higher education, the proportion of women who marry up, to an even better-educated man, is increasing in the long run (Hakim, 2000a: 221). Educational institutions function as marriage markets as well as training centres, and are used by women to achieve upward social mobility through marriage as well as through the labour market. When a woman marries up, it is almost guaranteed that the couple will adopt a clear division of labour in the family, with the husband's marked advantage in cultural capital and earnings potential giving him the main or sole income-earner role, while the wife becomes a full-time homemaker or a secondary earner. The Spanish survey suggests that having a mother who married up the educational ladder spurs women to seek greater 'equality' in their own marriage, and thus to seek full-time employment. This process could help explain the increasing popularity of the 'egalitarian' model of the family, with symmetrical roles and merits further research.

Otherwise, parental cultural capital seems to be generally unimportant. The results of this chapter reinforce the conclusions in Chapter 4 that education, the most common indicator of cultural capital, is not a key determinant of lifestyle preferences.

Finally, the key finding of this chapter is that lifestyle preferences are *not* closely linked to, or shaped by, political and religious values. It is not true that home-centred women are all right-wing conservatives, while work-centred women are all left-wing liberals. In all three lifestyle preference groups, there is a mixture of political views. The study shows that links between ideological conservatism and a home-centred lifestyle preference are restricted mainly to the older generation, aged 40 and over, and are coincidental, not causal. The younger generation of women are far less conservative in political and religious ideology, but many of them still regard some degree of role specialization in the family as attractive.

Notes

1 Social scientists devote as much attention to changing social attitudes in Spain as to changes in behaviour. The government-funded Centro de Investigaciónes Sociológicas (CIS) publishes a continuous stream of survey reports on attitudes on political, social, economic and religious topics, as illustrated by Cruz Cantero and Cobo Bedia (1991), Cruz Cantero (1995) Andrés Orizo (1996), Delgado and Castro Martín (1998) and Marí-Klose and Nos Colom (1999).

2 Non-voters are predominantly those who did not vote in the 1996 election, 22.5% of the sample. However, we included in this category the small number of people who participated but returned a null vote, 1.5% of the sample. Non-voters are concentrated in the younger generation, especially among people aged 18–21 years who would have been too young to vote in the 1996 election. There are about 10–15% non-voters in all ten-year age groups, rising to around 30% among people aged under 35 years.

3 The regional nationalist parties listed on the interview showcard were: Convergencia i Unió (CiU), Partido Nacionalista Vasco (PNV), Eusko Alkartasuna (EA), Coalición Gallega (CG), Partido Aragonés Regionalista (PAR), Partido Andalucista (PA), Unión del Pueblo Navarro (UPN), Unión Valenciana (UV), Coalición Canaria (CC), Esquerra Republicana de Cataluña (ERC), Herri Batasuna (HB), Bloque Nacionalista Gallego (BNG), plus a write-in option for others.

4 Given high rates of unemployment in Spain, we decided not to limit the analysis to people in employment.

5 As noted in note 7 to Chapter 1, survey respondents with PREU-COU were classified within the higher education category because the COU is taken only by those proceeding on to higher education. However, less than 1% of respondents' mothers and fathers had PREU-COU qualifications and they were classified within the secondary education category. So there is a tiny discrepancy between the educational classifications used for parents and for respondents.

6 Even when spouses have the same *level* of education, the wife may still have much lower earning power, so that fully symmetrical roles are still not advantageous. Although women are now taking advantage of free access to higher education, women continue to choose courses that are less vocational and less likely to lead to remunerative careers as compared with men. In Spain, as in many other European countries, women take degree courses in the humanities, arts and social sciences (particularly in teaching and nursing), whereas men are more likely to take courses in engineering, business and law.

7 The parental educational homogamy classification was obtained by grouping their education into four bands: illiterate and some primary education (42%); primary complete (27%); secondary education (13%); university and other higher education (2%). Wives who married up, or down, the four levels, thus had a significantly lower or higher level of education than their husband.

8 Without quoting any evidence, Garrido (1992: 23) states that women marrying men with significantly lower education or occupational grade dates only from 1989 in Spain, and is found only among the youngest people. In effect, it is a phenomenon of the 1990s and beyond.

9   The trend towards more wives marrying up the educational ladder is consistent with an increasing age gap between spouses in Spain. From 1900 up to 1970–75, the average age gap between spouses in Spain was 1.9 years; it rose to 2.7 years by 1981–5 (del Campo, 1991: 52).

10 The social science literature underlines the impact of sex-role socialization (Losh-Hesselbart, 1987). However, it fails to explain why the socialization process is successful with some children and not with others. While socialization appears to explain the average case, it cannot explain extreme outcomes, nor can it explain outcomes when children are exposed to conflicting messages from different sources. Finally, research shows that most parents seek to inculcate relatively androgenous behaviours (Losh-Hesselbart, 1987).

Chapter 8

The Polarization of Housing and Women's Employment in Britain

Chapter 5 suggested that housing can have almost as much impact on women's employment decisions as their lifestyle preferences. Housing debt can force up workrates, although apparently only among work-centred women (see Table 5.10). Public sector rented housing seems to depress workrates for men and women. This chapter explores the interaction between women's lifestyle preferences and housing type more fully. It examines the link between the polarization of lifestyle preferences and the social polarization of housing, a very different type of polarization that occurs in Britain, but not necessarily in all modern societies.

Britain is just one of the countries where housing became polarized in the late twentieth century. It provides an apposite case study because the link to fertility differentials and to female employment patterns emerges clearly, and has been the subject of several studies. The exact nature of the links between type of housing, women's fertility and women's employment patterns will of course differ between countries, due to institutional differences in the supply, control and funding of housing and due to institutional differences in the links between housing, and public sector income support policies for the unemployed and other low-income groups. These institutional variations are too large for us to take the discussion beyond the single case of Britain, where a link between the social polarization of housing and the polarization of female employment patterns emerged in the 1990s.[1] This case study illustrates one of the predictions of preference theory, namely that the polarization of lifestyle preferences and hence of household employment profiles leads to widening inequalities between families (Hakim, 2000a: 84–127). We first review trends in housing, female employment and fertility toward the end of the twentieth century, and then examine recent developments in the light of our 1999 survey results.

Table 8.1 Stock of dwellings by type, 1914–1995 (row %)

	Owner occupied	Public rented	Private rented and other	Total (millions = 100%)
1914	10	–	90	7.9
1938	32	10	58	11.4
1960	44	25	32	14.6
1971	53	29	19	17.1
1979	57	30	13	18.7
1971	49	31	20	NS
1981	54	34	12	NS
1991	67	24	9	NS
1995	67	18	15	NS

Sources: First half of table extracted from Murphy and O'Sullivan (1983: Table 1.1), reporting data from several sources; second half of table extracted from ONS (1997: Table 3.1), reporting General Household Survey data.

The Social Polarization of Housing

In Britain, private sector rented accommodation constituted the dominant form of housing at the beginning of the twentieth century. After the Second World War, private renting was gradually eliminated – partly by greater controls on private rented housing that reduced profitability for landlords and owners and partly by a succession of government policies favouring home purchase through mortgages on the one hand, and public sector rented housing supplied and controlled by local government councils on the other hand. The combined effect of these policies meant that up to 1981, housing became increasingly dominated by just two types, owner-occupier and public rented housing, known also as council housing, local authority housing and housing association housing (Murphy and Sullivan, 1985; Holmans, 1987). Private rented accommodation was virtually squeezed out of the picture to leave these two categories dominant (Table 8.1). After the election of a Conservative government in 1979, which lasted until 1997, the public rental sector then shrank rapidly in favour of owner-occupation due to consistent government policies favouring home ownership over public sector housing. An important element of these policies was the Right-to-Buy policy introduced in 1980, which encouraged council housing tenants to buy the home they had been renting from the local council at significantly reduced prices, with discounts of about 50%. Almost one-third of tenants did so.

In the post-war period, public rented and owner-occupier housing became the two stable and permanent forms of housing, which most people entered early in married life or early in adult life and normally maintained for the remainder of adult life (Madge and Brown, 1981). In practice, privately rented housing became a tenure used on a temporary or short-term basis by people in transition between regions, between jobs or between stages in the lifecycle. In 1995, for example, the majority of people living in privately rented accommodation had been in that home for no more than two years: 80% in the case of people in furnished accommodation and 50% for people in unfurnished accommodation (ONS, 1997). This and other minority types of housing are ignored in the remainder of this chapter. We also focus on people of working age, excluding retired groups wherever possible.

As they grew in importance in the 1960s and 1970s, owner-occupation and council housing became increasingly differentiated and socially segregated in terms of the social class composition and earnings levels of the two tenure groups (Hamnett, 1984). Even in the 1970s, public sector housing was already becoming a 'residual' sector for people who could not afford to buy a home – mainly semi-skilled and unskilled workers, the unemployed and poor retired. The social polarization process continued throughout the 1980s and 1990s when the council housing sector was reduced in size. As families that could afford to buy switched to home ownership, public sector housing became increasingly 'residualized', with access to a smaller stock of housing further restricted to low-income groups (Ford *et al.*, 1995: 1–4; Hogarth *et al.*, 1996; Murie, 1997: 139). Increasingly, this has meant people who are not in employment, including people living on a state pension (Holmans, 1993) as well as people in insecure jobs with a high risk of periodic unemployment (Hogarth *et al.*, 1996). The proportion of households in public rented housing with no member in employment increased slowly from 11% to 30% between 1962 and 1978, and then shot up from 30% to 63% between 1978 and 1991 (Table 8.2). By the 1990s, council housing costs were typically covered by the social welfare payments given to households that had no earners or very low incomes.

The two almost invisible aspects of the social polarization of housing that concern us here are the employment and fertility of the wives and cohabiting partners of male heads of households.[2] Virtually all housing research has so far focused on the employment, social class, education, earnings and other characteristics of 'heads of household', in effect, the men who were the main breadwinners.[3] Women's contribution as secondary earners was not regarded as sufficiently important to merit any attention. If women were studied at all, it was normally with reference to their reproductive activities, as noted below. There is hardly any mention, in housing research, of the

Table 8.2 Number of earners in each household by housing tenure, 1962–1991 (row %)

	None	*One*	*Two*	*Three or more*
Owner-occupiers				
1962	17	45	28	9
1971	19	38	36	7
1978	19	30	40	11
1982	21	34	36	9
1988	23	29	39	9
1990	24	29	38	9
1991	26	29	36	8
1993	29	28	35	7
Public renters				
1962	11	34	33	22
1971	23	34	28	15
1978	30	30	28	12
1982	44	30	19	7
1988	60	22	13	4
1990	60	23	12	5
1991	63	24	11	2
1993	66	21	11	3

Sources: Extracted from Holmans (1993: Table 9.1), reporting Family Expenditure Survey data and other sources and Holmans (1995: Table 9.6).

significance of wives' employment for housing finance and housing choice and this topic only attracted researchers' attention in the 1990s (Holmans, 1993; Hogarth *et al.*, 1996). Similarly, only in the 1990s did labour market analysts notice how housing choices can lock wives into regular employment or non-employment (Hakim, 1998a: 93–7). A close association between women's employment, fertility and housing choice only crystallized at the very end of the twentieth century in Britain.

Women living in public rented housing were found to have significantly higher fertility than women in owner-occupied homes, an association that attracted a good deal of attention as to what was cause and effect. In the 1990s, it was also discovered that women who were buying their homes, jointly with a partner or alone, had significantly higher employment rates than women in public rented housing. More important, the polarization of women in the two housing groups increased sharply in the 1980s and 1990s, at the same time that female employment patterns were polarizing (Hakim,

2000a: 84–156). The two following sections set out the research evidence on this recent polarization of women's lifestyles in the two main types of housing. We then discuss explanations for these new trends before presenting analyses of the 1999 British survey.

Housing Type and Women's Fertility

It is well-established that fertility is higher among working-class couples than in higher social classes. Working-class women marry at younger ages, have higher ideal family sizes, are more likely to want to start childbearing immediately after marriage, are more likely to be pregnant at the time of marriage, and produce more children than women in professional, managerial and other white-collar classes (Cartwright, 1976; Dunnell, 1979). Marriage and childrearing have a more central place in the lives of working-class women than in the lives of middle-class women, and working-class women have few other aspirations (Dunnell, 1979: 23).

Class-related education and employment differences do not completely account for these differences; additional powerful cultural and attitudinal factors are clearly involved (Dunnell, 1979: 21). One key factor isolated in the 1976 Family Formation Survey was the propensity to plan ahead or to 'just let things happen'. The majority of women in the non-manual classes were planners, while the majority of women in the manual classes just let things happen. Planners had fewer children, on average, than non-planners. Couples who had experienced the husband's unemployment or job insecurity had more children than couples who had never experienced these difficulties. Dunnell (1979: 25–6) concluded that economic insecurity and higher fertility were linked in some way. An alternative explanation for these results is that fertility differentials between planners and non-planners, between couples with and without employment problems, were in fact due to lifestyle differences between the two housing groups that were already manifest in the 1970s.

It was repeatedly observed in the 1970s that fertility is markedly higher among people in public rented housing than among people in owner-occupied housing with a mortgage still being paid off (Cartwright, 1976: 114–17; Madge and Brown, 1981: 136). (Home owners without such a loan are very often retired rather than people of working age and thus of no direct interest here.) For example, Madge and Brown (1981: 136) found that 2.5 years after marriage, three-quarters of young couples in owner-occupied accommodation were still childless whereas three-quarters of young couples in public rented housing already had children. Initially, the housing differential in fertility was explained by the social polarization of housing

Table 8.3 Distribution of live-births among married women by social class and housing tenure

	Non-manual workers		Manual workers	
Number of births	Owner-occupiers	Public renters	Owner-occupiers	Public renters
0	24	17	23	13
1	20	17	21	21
2	38	37	40	31
3	15	20	12	17
4 +	3	9	4	18
Base = 100%	1277	160	1116	847

Source: Special analyses of the 1977 General Household Survey data reported in Murphy and Sullivan (1983: Table 4.2). Percentages have been rounded.

and the higher concentration of working-class families in public housing. However, careful analyses of GHS data showed substantial fertility differentials between the two main housing groups, even after social class and wife's education were controlled (Murphy and Sullivan, 1983). For example, women aged 40–44 years in 1977 had on average two children if they were owner-occupiers and three children if they were living in public housing; this differential persisted across social classes, with some variation. Fertility differentials were even larger among young women aged 20–24 (Murphy and Sullivan, 1983: 30). Couples who owned their homes were very unlikely to have three or more children, and almost one-quarter had none at all in 1977, irrespective of the husband's social class (Table 8.3). In contrast, few couples in public sector housing had no children at all, and one-third had three or more children, again irrespective of the husband's class (Murphy and Sullivan, 1983: 56). Among women aged 40–49 years in 1976 and with a husband in a manual occupation at marriage, half of those in public sector housing had three or more children, while two-thirds of those in owner-occupied homes had less than three children (Murphy and Sullivan, 1985: Table 8). It seems clear that cultural or attitudinal factors, plus self-selection into housing groups, are more important than economic circumstances as determinants of fertility patterns.

Evidence of the *increasing* polarization of reproductive behaviour between the two housing groups comes from the 1986 SCELI survey (Reidy, 1994). Among couples aged 30 and over, at five years after

**Table 8.4 Number of children born to young married couples after five
years of marriage**

	Cohort's year of birth						
	1926–31	*1932–36*	*1937–41*	*1942–46*	*1947–51*	*1952–56*	*Total*
Owner-occupiers							
0	21	21	27	35	35	32	29
1	42	40	38	43	38	32	38
2	32	34	31	20	22	32	29
3 +	5	5	4	2	5	4	4
Public renters							
0	14	9	8	12	6	4	10
1	29	39	29	36	33	29	35
2	44	38	50	40	51	49	43
3 +	13	14	13	12	10	18	12

Source: Extracted from Reidy (1994: Table 6.2), reporting special analyses of 1986 SCELI
survey data for couples aged 30 and over and still married after five years of marriage (N =
3713). Percentages have been rounded.

marriage, there is a sharp difference in fertility between the two housing
groups, with more than one-quarter of the owner-occupiers remaining
childless while half the couples in public rented housing had two or more
children (Table 8.4). More important, differences between the two groups
increased across age cohorts in the post-war decades. The largest differences
in fertility are within the two youngest age cohorts, who benefitted from the
contraceptive revolution of the mid-1960s. Among couples born between
1952 and 1956, who entered the labour market in the 1970s and were aged
30–34 years in 1986, one-third of owner-occupiers had remained childless
and only 4% had three or more children; in contrast, one-fifth of the couples
in public housing already had three or more children and only 4% remained
childless (Table 8.4).

Housing Type and Women's Employment Patterns

Another type of social polarization in housing took place in the 1980s, partly
as a result of the Conservative government's sales of public sector housing
to the existing tenants, usually at prices well below market value. As a result

of this policy over 1.6 million homes were transferred out of the public rented sector into owner-occupation. The council housing sector shrank to only 18% of the total housing market by 1995 (Table 8.1). People who bought their homes were self-selected, but they also had to meet mortgage requirements. In effect, the population of council housing tenants was split into those who chose to switch from renting to buying their homes, and those who remained renters. The unanticipated effect of this popular and successful policy was that couples of working age who continued to live in public rented housing became sharply differentiated, in terms of *wives' workrates*, from their counterparts who had changed to owner-occupied housing.

Our analysis draws on two independent research reports on trends in the 1980s, one by Alan Holmans for the Department of the Environment, the other by a team at the Institute for Employment Research (IER) for the Joseph Rowntree Foundation (Holmans, 1993; Hogarth *et al.*, 1996). Holmans analysed the 1977–8 National Dwelling and Housing Survey and the 1984, 1990 and 1991 LFS. The IER team analysed the 1984 and 1991 LFS, using data for households where the head of household was of working age (16–59 for women, 16–64 for men). Holmans used data for all households, including the retired, but in many cases it is possible to recalculate figures to exclude this group. Small differences in methods between the two studies produce small discrepancies in the results, most noticeably for 1991, but the results are generally consistent and sometimes identical. The two studies have complementary strengths.

Holmans' (1993) careful analysis identified the selection process which split the council tenants into two groups. There was no difference between the two housing groups in wives' workrates in 1977–8, before the council house sales policy was initiated, with 57–58% of wives of working age in employment. By 1991, the two housing groups had polarized in terms of wives' workrates: only half (47%) of wives in rented public sector accommodation were in work compared to a clear majority of 71% of wives in owner-occupied housing (Table 8.5). By 1991, wives' workrates were 50% higher among couples in owner-occupied housing than among couples in council housing and *full-time* workrates were twice as high among owner-occupier wives (Holmans, 1993: 78–109).

Between 1962 and 1991, an increasing proportion of owner-occupier households found it necessary to have two incomes in order to reliably pay off their mortgage (Table 8.2). Holmans shows that couples in public sector housing who took advantage of the Right-to-Buy policy already had a wife in employment at the time of the purchase, or else had a wife who was prepared to go back to work after the purchase, in order to help ensure loan repayments were secure. There is evidence of both selection factors

Table 8.5 Employment patterns of wives of working age, 1977–1991

	Full-time work	Part-time work	Unemployed	Not in workforce	Total
Owner-occupiers					
1977–8	29	29	1	41	100
1984	30	34	5	31	100
1990	33	38	4	26	100
1991	34	37	4	25	100
Public renters					
1977–8	21	36	2	41	100
1984	16	29	8	47	100
1990	17	30	8	45	100
1991	15	32	6	47	100

Source: Calculated from Holmans (1993: Table 9.18), which reports special analyses of the 1977–78 National Dwelling and Housing Survey and of the 1984, 1990 and 1991 Labour Force Surveys and linked LFS Housing Trailers.

operating, with workrates rising steadily among purchaser wives, in parallel with rising workrates among the wives of other owner-occupiers. By 1991, employment rates among public sector home purchasers were identical with workrates among other owner-occupiers: three-quarters of both groups had two or more earners compared with 38% of couples who remained public sector renters (Holmans, 1993: 94, 103). The council tenants who took advantage of the Right-to-Buy scheme differed in other respects as well: the men had longer job tenures, were better qualified and were more likely to be skilled manual workers rather than unskilled manual workers and, not surprisingly, they were in employment rather than unemployed. However, the financial contribution of a working wife and, sometimes, sons and daughters was clearly a major factor helping a distinctive group of public sector renters to buy the homes they had previously rented and become owner-occupiers. Holmans' (1993) analysis of this process in the 1980s is sufficiently detailed to indicate that the decision to remain in council housing was linked to a preference for a well-defined sexual division of labour in the home which went beyond the well-known preference of working-class women to start childbearing early in life, as noted above. For example, Holmans carried out careful comparisons of couples aged 30–34 years and 45–59 years, both with and without dependent children, to show that in all four groups there were sharp differences in wives' workrates (and in wives' full-time workrates) between the public sector renters who chose *not* to buy their homes and those who did buy their homes. The latter group were almost identical to other owner-occupiers in having three-quarters to four-fifths of wives in employment (Holmans, 1993: 104).

By 1991, there were fundamental differences in employment patterns between women of working age in owner-occupied housing and in public rented housing. For example, among women aged 25–34 years, 70% of women owner-occupiers were in employment and another 23% had held a job within the previous ten years. In contrast, among women living in public housing, only one-third were doing any paid work, one-third had given up work within the previous ten years, and another one-third had not had any paid work for over a decade (Hakim, 1998a: 96). Employment is a dominant feature of the lives of women owner-occupiers but has become a minority activity among women in public housing.

The IER study also displayed the selection process which took people with more secure jobs and more reliable earnings out of public housing into home ownership. By 1991, for the first time, home owners[4] were more numerous than council tenants among unskilled and semi-skilled manual workers (Social Classes IV and V together). But the authors admit that motivational factors must also have been important in the self-selection process (Hogarth *et al.*, 1996: 20–21). It is important to remember that the people who made the change did not move house. They remained living in the same accommodation as before, but with ownership of the property transferred to them. Payments of rent to the local council were replaced by payments of interest and capital on the mortgage that funded the purchase. The change was social-psychological and legal, but did not force anyone to move home. Years later, some couples did move home, for other reasons. So the change of housing tenure involved a commitment to a greater degree of financial self-reliance, given that the welfare state safety net was far less generous to home owners than to families in public housing at that time. Since then, it has become even more restrictive, effectively making it impossible for mortgage-holders to remain unemployment benefit claimants without running the risk of losing the home they may have spent years paying for because they cannot meet mortgage payments.

The IER study also reveals that the differences in wives' workrates between the two housing groups in the 1990s are not due simply to compositional differences which strengthened in the 1980s. For example, they are not due to the increasing concentration of working-class families in public rented housing, while middle-class families became concentrated in owner-occupied housing. The IER analyses included the most systematic controls for social class, as indicated by the head of household's occupational grade and for household composition (Hogarth *et al.*, 1996: Table 4.2, Figures 4.3 and 4.4). They found that having a child under school age (that is, under 6 years old) at home temporarily depresses female workrates among *both* home owners and council tenants. In 1991, having a pre-school child at home compared to no children at home reduced wives' workrates by about 30 percentage points, from about 80% to 50% among home owners and from about 60% to about 30% among council tenants. Surprisingly, social class had virtually no impact at all on wives' workrates *within* each housing group, after taking account of the presence of pre-school children. This is another instance of the declining importance of social class and the rising importance of lifestyle groups as the principal determinant of behaviour.

Overall, among couples of working age living in public rented housing, about two-thirds were dual-earner and about one-third had a single male breadwinner with a full-time homemaker wife. Among home owners, about three-quarters of couples were dual-earner. Curiously, these proportions remained fairly stable between 1984 and 1991, showing that the incoming group of new home owners from the public sector must have had, or adopted, the higher workrates of wives in the home ownership sector.

By the mid-1990s, employment patterns had polarized even further. Holmans' analysis of the 1993/94 Survey of English Housing found that, among married and cohabiting couples of working age, 64% of owner-occupier households had both partners in employment, 28% had a single earner and 8% had no earner. In contrast, among married and cohabiting couples of working age in public sector rented housing, 30% of households had both partners in work, 35% had a single earner and 35% had no earner (Holmans, 1995: Table 9.4). These differences are further magnified by differences in wives' *full-time* workrates. A two-thirds majority of the working wives in council housing are working part-time hours only, some of them working very short hours in marginal jobs (Hakim, 1998a: 118). The most telling indicator is the fact that one-third of the owner-occupier wives had a full-time job compared to 15% of wives in council housing (Table 8.5).

One of the stereotypes associated with a couple owning their own home is of feminine domesticity, a full-time homemaker role and the start of childbearing. In reality, this stereotype characterizes couples in rented public housing far better than couples who have bought their home. Indeed, the substantial debts required to finance home purchase mean that wives usually delay childbearing, if possible, and continue in full-time work far longer than wives in public rented housing. This polarization of family employment profiles has regularly been overlooked in studies of housing polarization, where the emphasis has usually been on political attitudes and affiliation (Saunders, 1990; Murie, 1997).

Links between Housing, Fertility and Employment

Attempts to explain these developments have focused on the impact of housing type on fertility and the impact of fertility on housing choice (Cartwright, 1976; Murphy and Sullivan, 1983, 1985). What has been left out of the picture is women's sex-role ideology and work orientations, which determine _both_ fertility patterns and the financial strength to afford home ownership. By the end of the twentieth century in Britain, couples who were buying their home had significantly higher (full-time) workrates for wives than couples living in rented public housing, half of whom remained single breadwinner families. It seems likely that this polarization of wives' employment patterns reflects an equivalent polarization in lifestyle preferences. A combination of institutional factors, location and other factors discourage many wives and partners of men in council housing from becoming equal joint earners. However, these factors were clearly unimportant for the wives in couples who bought their homes from the local council and adopted higher workrates, so they cannot be conclusive.

We were interested to see if preference theory helps to explain these social processes, particularly given the fact that a close association between women's employment, fertility and housing choice only crystallized in the 1980s and 1990s, with polarizing trends on all these behaviours. Public sector housing is the natural haven for women (married or not) for whom childrearing and family life are the central focus of adult life, who need little inducement to bring forward the start of childbearing (and thus become eligible for public housing on grounds of need) but who could not be induced to postpone childbearing in favour of market work and the status and consumption benefits it buys.[5] Work-centred women, who often remain childless anyway, are the first to achieve home ownership, alone or in partnership. They are followed by adaptive women who respond quickly to public policy favouring home ownership as well as market work, as happened in the 1980s, with both being promoted by a consumption-oriented culture and the equal opportunities movement. Preference theory might help to explain the _increasing polarization_ of women's activities in the two housing sectors, and to make sense of the different social processes that lead to the two different types of housing and associated lifestyles.

These processes linking lifestyle preferences and housing are contingent rather than necessary. They depend heavily on the institutional and policy context. However, preference theory could provide a more complete explanation for the process of polarization on several fronts, and for the diversity of decision-making processes, than do previous attempts at explanation. It also exposes the limitations of male-biased studies of housing that have so far tended to look only at the behaviour and characteristics of male heads of household. Just as a wife's secondary contribution to the household's income can lift some families out of relative poverty, a wife's contribution can lift other households into relative affluence and a higher standard of living.

However, it is clear that preference theory alone cannot provide a complete explanation for the social processes described above. Other factors are also important. The IER study concluded that public sector housing in Britain limits market work in some way, among both men and women. Even after controlling for the main correlates of employment rates, heads of household who are council tenants are more likely to be unemployed and have a non-working partner (Hogarth *et al.*, 1996: 42). Overall, unemployment rates among people in the public rented sector are six times higher than among owner-occupiers: 25% versus 4% (Table 8.6).[6] The usual explanation given for this is that people in unskilled and semi-skilled occupations are concentrated in council housing and they are also more at risk of unemployment than people with better qualifications and those in higher grade occupations, who invariably get priority in job queues. However, this can no longer be the main explanation for differences in unemployment rates as dramatic as those in Table 8.6. Across all occupational grades, and across all types of household, people in public housing have unemployment rates two to eight times larger than people in owner-occupied housing. Interestingly, there are virtually no differences between 1984 and 1991, despite the large housing transfers that took place in this period. It seems obvious that there are differences in motivation and self-reliance between the two housing groups. Taken at face value, Table 8.6 reveals a culture of welfare dependency in the council housing sector which affects everyone, in all grades of occupation and in all types of household. Welfare dependency is weakest among unskilled manual workers, because their unemployment rates in the two housing groups are the closest, suggesting that motivational factors are least important in this group. The culture of welfare dependency is suggested more emphatically in the figures for single people without dependent children. Ill-health seems to be another factor. The ONS LS shows higher mortality rates among people in public sector rented accommodation than among people who own their own homes, even after controlling for social class. It appears that a (self)selection process means that the healthiest people become owner-occupiers, while people with health problems, who are more likely to be unemployed, become public sector housing tenants. However, this cannot be the main

Table 8.6 Unemployment rates (%) of heads of household in the two main housing groups by social class and household composition, 1984 and 1991

	Owner occupiers with loans		Public rented housing	
	1984	*1991*	*1984*	*1991*
Total	4	4	24	25
Social class/Occupational grade				
Professionals	1	2	17	6
Managers	2	3	10	10
Skilled white-collar	2	3	12	15
Skilled blue-collar	4	5	15	18
Partly skilled manual	5	5	19	18
Unskilled manual	10	7	21	23
Household composition				
Single, no children	4	5	29	33
Single, with children	8	6	25	24
Couple, no children	3	3	16	18
Couple, youngest child aged 0–5	4	4	33	29
Couple, youngest child aged 6–15	3	3	23	22
Couple, youngest child aged 16 +	3	4	13	15
Other households	5	5	22	26

Source: Hogarth et al. (1996: Tables 2.3, 3.1 and 3.2), based on LFS data for people of working age. Percentages have been rounded.

explanation for such high unemployment rates among council tenants, and attitudinal factors must also contribute to these results. This is shown by Buckingham's (1999) study of young men aged 33 years in the NCDS cohort study. He found large differences in work orientations between an 'underclass' group of young men living in public sector housing and other working-class men. The 'underclass' men varied in intellectual ability and were just as successful as other young men in getting jobs, but they were far more likely to leave them.

A full explanation for the results shown in Table 8.6 go beyond our concerns here. However, it does seem likely that low workrates among wives and solo women in public sector housing could be explained by the surrounding culture of welfare dependency as well as their own preference for a life centred on family work rather than market work. A third factor would be the work disincentives unintentionally built into the way the welfare safety net works, especially as regards housing costs. Most studies focus on this last factor (Ford *et al.*, 1995; Hogarth *et al.*, 1996). We propose that lifestyle preferences are another factor here.

Finally, it is notable that the attractions of home ownership are sufficient to tie many women into regular and even full-time employment. The attractions of home ownership are also sufficient to persuade some women to delay childbearing and to have fewer children. This suggests that it might be home ownership, rather than commitment to a career, that ties some women to their jobs. We would expect this to happen most often among adaptive women, who do not have any pronounced preference for employment careers. But it might also be a more general phenomenon.

Sex-Role Ideology and Housing Tenure

People in Spain are more likely to own their home than people in Britain: 81% compared to 67% (see Table 1.5). The proportion of home owners in our British survey is a little higher at 75%, suggesting some non-response among people renting their accommodation. Overall, the sample divides into 1010 people (28%) who own their accommodation outright, 1701 (47%) who own their home but are still repaying the purchase loan, 628 people (17%) who are renting from a public sector body, mainly council renters, and 305 people (8%) renting from a private person or firm. Given our focus on the relationship between sex-role ideology, employment and home purchase, we compare people with a mortgage for house purchase with people in all other tenures grouped together. This effectively splits the sample into two halves of roughly equal size.

Contrary to expectation, there are no large and consistent differences in attitudes between the two housing groups, even though there are large differences in full-time workrates among men and women in the two groups (Table 8.7). Men and women who have a mortgage are slightly more likely to favour a working wife and flexibility in the sexual division of labour in the family; people in other tenures are slightly more likely to favour complete role segregation. Men and women who are purchasing their home are less work-centred than men and women in other tenures. The only clear difference between the two housing groups concerns attitudes to patriarchal values in public and private life: half of people with a mortgage accept patriarchal values compared to almost three-quarters of people in other tenures. Table 8.7 show that this lack of distinctive differences is repeated across the three tenures in the 'other' housing group. In addition, there are virtually no sex differences within tenure groups, apart from the usual differences in work centrality.

Table 8.7 Sex-role ideology and work orientations by housing tenure

| | Mortgage holders | | All other tenures | | | | | | | |
| | | | Total | | Outright owners | | Public renters | | Private renters | |
	M	F	M	F	M	F	M	F	M	F
% who regard man as responsible for income-earning	23	19	38	31	41	35	39	30	23	19
% who regard woman as responsible for housekeeping	22	24	33	40	37	45	34	39	17	23
Ideal family model:										
egalitarian	47	42	43	40	38	34	51	46	48	48
compromise	40	44	32	41	36	45	27	36	26	39
role segregation	13	15	25	19	26	21	22	18	26	13
% who accept patriarchal values	51	50	72	70	74	77	78	71	51	46
% work-centred	49	22	54	29	51	23	60	37	55	31
% working full-time	86	44	37	16	30	12	35	13	66	37

Note: Data for people aged 16 and over who have completed their full-time education.

The absence of any major differences between the two tenure categories is due to the heterogeneous composition of both the mortgage-holders group and the all other tenures group. Both groups include a wide range of ages, occupations and household types. People who own their home outright tend to be older, but private renters tend to be young. People in public sector subsidized housing tend to have low incomes, but outright owners tend to have high incomes. So the 'all other tenures' group provides a fair comparison with the mortgage holders group.

The analysis of women's workrates must be restricted to married and cohabiting couples aged 20–60, so Table 8.8 shows attitudes in the two tenure groups for this subgroup. Here, there are even smaller differences between the two tenure groups in attitudes, and also in full-time workrates. Even the marked difference in attitudes to patriarchy is reduced to a smaller level.

There is a substantial difference in full-time workrates between couples with a mortgage to pay off and couples in other housing tenures (Table 8.9). What is remarkable here is that the difference is large among men as well as

Table 8.8 Attitudes among couples by housing tenure

| | Mortgage holders | | All other tenures | | | | | | | |
| | | | Total | | Outright owners | | Public renters | | Private renters | |
	M	F	M	F	M	F	M	F	M	F
% who regard woman as responsible for housekeeping	21	24	31	33	35	35	35	36	16	21
% who regard man as responsible for income-earning	22	19	33	23	35	23	36	25	22	19
Ideal family model:										
egalitarian	45	38	49	39	43	35	54	48	51	31
compromise	43	49	29	46	29	51	26	38	32	50
role segregation	12	13	22	15	28	14	20	14	17	19
% who accept patriarchal values	51	50	65	62	59	69	78	63	53	41
% work-centred	53	17	59	18	53	15	65	23	59	17
% working full-time	91	41	66	25	65	23	58	17	82	44

Note: Data for married and cohabiting couples aged 20–59 who have completed their full-time education.

women. Almost all (91%) the husbands with a housing loan are in full-time work compared to a bare two-thirds of husbands in other tenures, a difference of 26 percentage points. The difference is slightly smaller for wives: 42% and 25%, or a difference of 17 percentage points, but this represents an increase of two-thirds on 25%. The attractions of owning your home are sufficient to force both men and women to maintain consistent full-time employment.

Within the two tenure groups, attitudes still have a big impact on female workrates but not on men's rates (Table 8.9). Among mortgage-holders, for example, three-quarters of work-centred women work full-time compared to only one-third of women who work for social and financial reasons. There is a smaller contrast among wives in other tenures. Among mortgage-holders, a preference for egalitarian family roles raises wives' full-time workrates from a low of 26% to a high of 64%. Sex-role ideology has a much smaller impact on wives in other housing tenures, where workrates are generally low. It is notable that having a mortgage to pay off has a sharp impact even

Table 8.9 Full-time workrates (%) by housing tenure and values among couples

	Mortgage holders		All other tenures		Total	
	M	F	M	F	M	F
All couples	91	42	65	25	84	36
Ideal family model:						
egalitarian	89	64	59	33	80	53
compromise	95	26	77	19	92	24
role segregation	85	40	64	24	76	34
Patriachal values:						
accepts	91	33	62	21	81	28
rejects	91	50	75	33	87	45
Work orientations:						
work-centred	93	76	66	52	84	68
other reasons for job	89	34	67	19	83	29
Women's lifestyle preferences:						
work-centred		82		42		63
adaptive		42		23		35
home-centred		47		32		41
Base = 100%	572	616	232	313	805	930

Note: Data for married and cohabiting couples ages 20–59 who have completed their full-time education.

among women who would normally prefer to be full-time homemakers: 40% have full-time jobs compared to only 24% in other tenures. The pattern of results in Table 8.9 is replicated, with small variations, in the younger generation of couples aged under 40 as well as in the older generation aged 40 and over.

In sum, the rewards of home ownership and the constraints of having a home loan mortgage to repay are sufficient to ensure that men and women in this situation maintain higher full-time workrates than people in other tenures. The effect of housing tenure is observed in all lifestyle preference groups, but is generally small (Table 8.9). It is much larger in the small group of work-centred women. For women in particular, housing tenure can have almost as large an impact on full-time workrates as attitude variables. No doubt there is an element of self-selection here. But as the studies reviewed earlier demonstrate, once people have chosen to become owners of their accommodation, the continuing debt forces them to maintain high levels of full-time employment, whereas people in other tenures can allow themselves to drop out of the workforce. Overall, the impact of a mortgage on workrates is smaller than the impact of lifestyle preferences. But it is a separate and parallel effect. Differences between housing tenure groups do not reduce to differences in the attitudinal composition of the two groups, which we have already found to be trivial or non-existent.

Differences in workrates are not explained by large differences in fertility between women who are mortgage-holders and women in other tenures. The polarization of fertility rates as well as workrates that was observed throughout the 1970s and 1980s seems to have disappeared by the end of the twentieth century. On the contrary, mortgage-holders collectively are more likely to have school age children (aged under 16 years) at home than people living in other tenures: 36–41% compared to 11–19% of people in other tenures. They are also more likely to have pre-school age children (aged 0–4 years) at home: 17% compared to 7% of people in other tenures. These differences are concentrated within the younger generation aged under 40 years. There is little evidence here of women postponing childbearing in order to pay for a mortgage. They may still be doing this, but they are nonetheless more likely to have children and to have young children, than people in other tenures, including people renting council housing. The financial pressures of home ownership *and* of a young family are combined for about two-fifths of all mortgage-holders. In sum, there is no evidence here that women are choosing between home ownership and having children: they expect to do both and are prepared to go out to work to finance them.

Women who are married or cohabiting have the option of becoming full-time homemakers or secondary earners. Women without partners who have dependent children do not have this choice and are necessarily primary earners responsible for ensuring an income sufficient for their household to live on. There is only a small group of solo mothers in the British survey sample, and most of them are living in public sector subsidized accommodation. In this group of women, housing tenure has a large impact on workrates, but sex-role ideology has no impact at all (Table 8.10). Two-thirds of solo mothers in owner-occupied homes are in work compared to one-third of solo mothers in public rented homes. Despite the small numbers, this analysis further confirms that housing tenure has an independent influence on lifestyle choices or reflects lifestyle choices made at an earlier stage in the lifecycle. Alternatively, these dramatically different workrates reflect a culture of dependency among public sector tenants and a culture of self-reliance among people in owner-occupied housing.

Table 8.10　Workrates (%) among solo mothers

	Family role preferences			Base
	Symmetrical roles	Differentiated roles	All	= 100%
Owner-occupiers	70	67	69	36
Council renters	35	30	33	57

Note: Data for lone parent women with children aged 16 or younger at home.

Conclusions

Contrary to expectation, preference theory contributes little to the explanation of the polarizing trend in women's workrates and housing tenure. There is no difference of any importance between the sex-role ideology and work orientations of women who have taken on a loan for home purchase and women in other housing tenures. However, the two tenure groups have substantially different workrates, especially full-time workrates, among women and men. The attractions of home ownership and the constraints of the necessary loan which has to be repaid are sufficient to raise male full-time workrates by some 25 percentage points and female full-time workrates by 17 percentage points. The effect of housing tenure, and the lifestyle choice it implies, is separate from the impact of lifestyle preferences on female workrates.

In some cases, the desire for home ownership outweighs lifestyle preferences. For example, women who prefer complete role segregation in the family and would normally become full-time homemakers after marriage, are nonetheless prompted to work full-time in two-fifths of cases, in order to ensure that loan repayments are maintained in the context of spouses with insecure employment and relatively low workrates.[7] These women can be classified as involuntary workers, or purely instrumental workers, as they maintain relatively high full-time workrates despite preferring to be out of the labour market altogether and have no commitment to careers. It appears that the demands of a mortgage and house purchase, plus a husband's insecure employment, are sufficient to override lifestyle preferences and raise workrates among women who would normally have exceptionally low levels of paid employment.

Feminists have argued that housewives find the home oppressive, a view that has been challenged by Saunders (1990), who pointed out that most men and women regard their home as a safe haven. There is now greater willingness to recognize that women are generally more emotionally attached to their homes than are men, that the home is a more salient part of their identity for women than for men (Darke, 1994). At the same time, women periodically resent the time taken up by housework, the loss of control over their time after children are born and, by the 1990s, the financial burden of mortgage repayments (Darke, 1994). Overall, women are more likely to use the home as an avenue for self-expression, to display and define social status, and they are more likely to regard it as a personal domain. Wives who were asked whether they missed having a personal space of their own in the home failed to understand the question, because they regarded the whole house as their personal domain (Darke, 1994: 20).

The social and psychological processes linking the home with women's personal identity in modern society seem to be strengthened by home ownership as compared with rented accommodation. Several of the contributors to Duncan's (1982a) collection describe this process. Home ownership is an indicator of social status, a depository of value and a source of personal autonomy due to control over a private space; it testifies to the creditworthiness and trustworthiness of the mortgagee and is a symbol of self-sufficiency and independence (Agnew, 1982). One consequence of home ownership is greater community consciousness, because people seek to ensure changes in the neighbourhood do not erode the value of their property investment (Agnew, 1982). In prosperous modern societies, the home ceases to be a production unit or a simple container for the family and becomes dedicated to consumption, the display of wealth and self-expression. The new trend towards home-based market work does not seriously alter this primary function of the home today. Home ownership thus enhances women's role in the home, as manager of consumption, display and related leisure activities (Loyd, 1982; see also Galbraith, 1975: 45–53). This aspect of home ownership is most pronounced among upwardly mobile and migrant groups, in meritocratic and individualistic societies where the educational system serves as the mechanism for selection and accreditation. In these social groups and societies, consumption and display become individualized rather than collective, with the home providing a principal vehicle for status display and self-expression (Duncan, 1982b; Pratt, 1982).

Surveys show that the great majority of people in Britain regard home ownership as preferable to renting. However, home ownership seems to have particular psychological attractions for many women. This may explain why some wives are prepared to delay childbearing and many spend longer years in regular, full-time employment in order to achieve home ownership. This seems to have been a crucial factor contributing to the success of the public housing sales policy of the 1980s. It also means that the decision to buy a home can tie women into continuous employment as effectively as work-centred attitudes.

The case study also illustrates the thin dividing line between attitudinal and social structural factors. The initial catalyst is the aspiration to be a homeowner, with the social status and lifestyle that this represents. Once a mortgage is taken and the property is bought, home ownership becomes a relatively permanent 'structural' factor that shapes other decisions, about jobs and working hours for example. Women who remain continuously in full-time work may be career-oriented or they may simply be prepared to make sacrifices in order to achieve home ownership. In both cases, employment decisions are driven by lifestyle aspirations, albeit of a different nature. Whether these two different aspirations have similar implications for women's work histories and career trajectories must remain a question for future studies.

Notes

1   Finland is another country where fiscal and institutional support for home ownership is strong, and the desire to achieve home ownership becomes an additional factor driving up women's employment. Finland has high female employment rates despite low levels of part-time work (see Table 1.3). Apart from the tradition of women's employment in agriculture, this is explained by a housing policy which favours owner occupancy, even at low income levels, which means that households need to have two wages in order to cope with their mortgages (Nikander, 1998: 5).

2   Social scientists have devoted more attention to the idea that the polarization of housing produced a polarization of social and political attitudes (Saunders, 1990; Murie, 1997). Several studies suggest there are also differences between home owners and public renters in attitudes to claiming welfare benefits and to self-reliance (Ford *et al.*, 1995). These differences in perspective and the large gap in average income between public renters and home owners are reinforced by the fact that the welfare safety net treats home owners much less generously than it does people in public rented housing, when they become unemployed (Hogarth *et al.*, 1996: 5).

3   The datasets used in this research usually identify the husband or male partner, as the head of household. In practice, men are usually the main breadwinner, as noted in Chapters 4 and 5. Women are only identified as the head of household if they live without a male partner, and the proportion of such households is small.

4   The focus throughout this discussion is on home owners with a mortgage, excluding the minority without a loan to repay.

5   For example, in 1993/94, three-quarters of all lone parents without jobs in England, almost all of them women, were living in public sector housing (Holmans, 1995: Table 9.1).

6   The true level of unemployment among owner-occupiers in 1991 must be higher than shown in Table 9.6. Unemployment rates for owner-occupiers are understated, to an unknown extent, because some of them lose their home as a result of being unable to continue mortgage repayments. Some of these dispossessed households return to rented housing (thus boosting unemployment rates in this sector), but many go to live as part of another household (Holmans, 1995: 117).

7   We assume that wives who prefer role segregation in the family are married to husbands with the same preferences, that is, that couples generally have consistent lifestyle preferences. Research indicates that this is generally the case. Unfortunately, our survey does not allow us to know just what proportion of wives and husbands have spouses with different preferences.

Chapter 9

Conclusions: Rhetoric and Reality in Lifestyle Preferences

Studies based on depth interviews can achieve a richness of understanding that generally eludes surveys based on structured interviews. The challenge of our project was to identify the three lifestyle preference groups among women within the constraints of large, nationally representative interview surveys, instead of the finely crafted study based on long personal interviews that has so far been necessary, as illustrated by Gerson's classic study of women's *Hard Choices* (Gerson, 1985; Hakim, 2000a: 149–54). Overall, the project was a success, but there are lessons for future research in this field.

Identifying Lifestyle Preference Groups

A principal objection to preference theory is that the three lifestyle preference groups cannot be identified by other researchers – in national surveys (McRae, 2002), in case study research (Crompton and Harris, 1998) or in studies based on repeated depth interviews (Proctor and Padfield, 1999). They conclude that the groups cannot exist. This study has demonstrated that preference theory is relatively easy to operationalize, using the right questions.

Placing our core questions in two omnibus surveys constitutes a stringent test of their utility as classificatory questions that might be inserted in any national survey or other study. The success of the British and Spanish surveys confirms that a tiny number of questions can be sufficient to identify the three lifestyle preference groups among women. Identifying preference groups among men will require an extra question or two. But the main difficulty here is that we do not yet have any qualitative research, similar to Gerson's study, that might inform the development or selection of suitable questions. There is almost no research that asks men what they want, in quite the same way as the voluminous literature on what women want (Hakim, 2000a: 254–72). Given these difficulties, national estimates of the distributions of preference groups among men (see Table 3.15) must be

Table 9.1 Distribution of women's lifestyle preferences, Britain and Spain

	Home-centred	Adaptive	Work-centred
Britain			
Women aged 16 +	17	69	14
Women aged 20–59			
excluding FT students	14	70	16
Spain			
Women aged 18 +	17	70	13
Women aged 20–59			
excluding FT students	12	72	16

regarded as tentative. In contrast, the distribution of women's lifestyle preferences (Table 9.1) is reasonably robust. In line with preference theory, the majority of women, in both countries, are adaptive. Home-centred and work-centred women form small minorities of the adult female population, although together they form a relatively substantial one-third.

In order to permit comparisons between men and women throughout this study, most analyses in previous chapters utilize the constituent indicators of lifestyle preferences. A question on family roles (F in Table 3.1) identifies home-centred women and most adaptive women. Two questions on work orientations (E and G in Table 3.1) identify work-centred people. Combining the three questions allows us to identify all three groups of women at the national level and also at the micro-level. All three questions have been used before in national surveys and for cross-national comparisons within Europe, so they can be regarded as tried and tested, producing robust results. Two weaknesses remain, however.

First, questions on work orientations are particularly sensitive to social and cultural context and are prone to a social desirability bias. This is perhaps more true of question E on work commitment than question G on the breadwinner role. So our two indicators of work centrality may not necessarily work well in all cultural contexts and other questions may need to be devised, whether alternatives or additions.

Second, question F as currently formulated does not identify home-centred and adaptive men. It could be extended to include role reversal couples as a fourth option.[1] Alternatively, another, more explicit question could be devised to identify home-centred and adaptive men directly. Preference theory was developed first and foremost to explain women's choices between family work and market work. Similarly, our two surveys were designed primarily to operationalize, test and develop the theory in relation to women. Now that the success of the theory and the feasibility of translating it into national empirical studies are demonstrated, it will be necessary to expand the scope of future research to cover men more completely.

All three classificatory questions are needed in surveys in order to identify the three lifestyle preference groups. The question on ideal family models is not sufficient by itself, even for women. In addition, many analyses must be limited to married women and preferably to married women of working age, which we defined narrowly as 20–59 years. The two questions to identify work centrality are only really meaningful for people of working age. All surveys show that people of pensionable age can and do answer the questions, but the substantive import of the questions fades after retirement, when paid work becomes a distant memory, often bathed in the rosy glow of nostalgia.

However, it is crucial that certain analyses are limited to married people, in particular analyses of employment patterns. All the analyses in this study included the small number of cohabiting couples within the very much larger group of married couples, because this has become the convention in survey analysis, as illustrated by the General Household Survey in Britain. With the benefit of hindsight, we regard this procedure as misinformed and mistaken. Cohabiting couples are qualitatively different from married couples, in their relationships, time horizons, financial arrangements and the family division of labour (Morgan, 2000; Waite and Gallagher, 2000). Our surveys also show them to have attitudes and values that place them closer to single people than to married couples. Future analyses to extend and develop preference theory should be restricted to married couples, if possible, because the preference to give up paid work to become a full-time homemaker or to adopt the work patterns of a secondary earner, can only realistically be implemented after marriage to a breadwinner spouse.[2] Before that, lifestyle preferences remain aspirations, ambitions, hopes and desires that may or may not be implemented in reality.[3]

There is no reason why all three questions have to be located together, in a single sequence in a survey. We did this, setting them within the context of other, related questions in our survey module. However, the three questions could be dispersed in a survey questionnaire, as suits the other topics covered. What is essential is for a study to include questions that explicitly address work centrality, lifestyle priorities and lifeplans. None of our critics did this, so it is not surprising that they had difficulty identifying women's lifestyle preferences in their studies. Public opinion attitude questions are no substitute for direct questions about *personal* preferences and priorities, as this study has demonstrated.

Finally, the full range of lifestyle preference groups will only be observed in studies that provide reasonably representative data on *all* women of working age or *all* adult women. This point should be obvious, but it is regularly ignored, even by experienced researchers. Studies that focus selectively on the subgroup of women who are in the labour market will exclude virtually all home-centred women. Thus Crompton and Harris' (1998) early challenge to preference theory focused selectively on doctors and bank managers. Their study thus excluded home-centred women completely and even many adaptive women, if not currently in work and they did not bother to classify work-centred women separately due to small base numbers (Hakim, 1998b). Virtually all the women in these case studies were adaptives, who displayed some variation in attitudes and behaviour, as expected, given the size and diversity of the group (Hakim, 2000a: 165–8). Studies that focus selectively on women who have just given birth, or on mothers generally, will exclude the large proportion of work-centred women who remain voluntarily childfree. Studies that focus selectively on women who have recently given birth *and* who worked during their pregnancy should exclude most home-centred women and many work-centred women, to focus primarily on adaptive women. Thus McRae's maternity rights studies and subsequent follow-up surveys, cover adaptive women mainly and exhibit the variation expected within this large group (McRae, 1991, 2002; Hakim, 1996a: 127–30, 2000a: 120–22, 130).[4]

Sample selection bias may of course occur also in qualitative research, but in this type of study it is much easier to conceal it in reports and harder to detect it. However, as studies by Gerson (1985) and Proctor and Padfield (1999) demonstrate, it is feasible for samples to be drawn widely enough to display all three preference groups. In both these studies, the authors' reports focus on the twists and turns of life to which adaptive women responded. However, an independent reading of the results easily identified the three lifestyle preference groups in each study (Hakim, 2000a: 149–56).

Another objection to preference theory is that there are 100 shades of grey, that the world is more complex than the classification of three preference groups allows. Of course. But at the two extremes there are black and white, two polar opposites on either side of the 100 shades of grey. This is the essential feature of female heterogeneity – the two polar opposites of home-centred and work-centred women at either end of the adaptive continuum.

Macro-Level and Micro-Level Perspectives

Two nationally representative surveys of Britain and Spain allow us to draw comparisons between the two countries, as well as making comparisons between groups within each country. Our research design thus permits conclusions at the macro-level, on between-country differences, and at the micro-level, on differences between individuals within countries. Unfortunately, these two levels of analysis have often been treated as competing theoretical paradigms, instead of complementary perspectives – as illustrated by the debates reviewed in *Were They Pushed or Did They Jump?* (Gambetta, 1987).

There is no doubt that social and economic structures, history and culture are all important at the aggregate level. Cross-national comparative studies of nations will always find differences that are readily 'explained' by some variant of societal effect theory, although 'nation as object' and 'nation as context' studies often shade into each other (Kohn, 1989: 21; Hakim 2000b: 202). The European Union and the OECD promote cross-national comparisons of European and other modern societies and thus indirectly promote interest in macro-level theories and classifications of societies that purport to explain differences between member states.

Currently, the most fashionable theory is Esping-Andersen's classification of welfare states (1990). Originally intended purely for studies of social policy, the classification is routinely stretched into a multi-purpose classification of European societies, as illustrated by Blossfeld (1997) and Blossfeld and Drobnic (2001). The main alternatives are Lewis' typology of welfare states (1992) with weak, moderate or strong support for the male breadwinner model of the family and the societal effect theories first developed in France for comparisons of labour markets, employment institutions and labour processes (Maurice *et al.*, 1982; see also Benoit-Guilbot, 1989; Marsden, 1999), which again run the risk of being stretched into multi-purpose classifications in their applications. Advocates of societal effects theories and classifications routinely dismiss explanations that focus on individual choice and individual action (Blossfeld and Drobnic, 2001: vi; Benoit-Guilbot and Clémencon, 2001; Hakim, 2001a). Social science theorizing about the relative importance of individual motivation and aspirations and social structural effects amounts to a long-standing cold war, with neither side gaining ascendancy.

This dichotomous, either-or approach to sociological theorizing is of course a waste of effort, since both perspectives are necessary, are indeed complementary, as they contribute at two different levels of analysis. This is neatly illustrated by the two systems X and Z shown in Figure 9.1. Small differences between the two systems lead to dramatically different

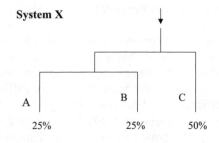

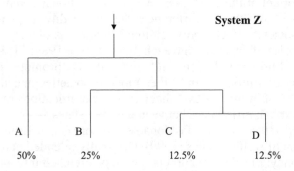

Figure 9.1 Structure and individual choice

outcomes. Even though X and Z are very simple structures compared to the enormous complexity of social structures and social processes, they produce significantly different outcomes *at the aggregate level*. In system X, 25% of people end up in position A compared to 50% in system Z. In system X, 50% of people end up in position C compared to only 12.5% in system Z, and position D exists only in system Z. The two systems might be two societies, two regions in the same society or two industries in the same regional labour market. Tiny structural differences produce substantively different outcomes for the people whose lives or careers pass through them. But these differences only emerge at the aggregate level, when comparing outcomes for thousands of people moving through each system.

Where any individual person ends up in each system appears to be a matter of chance, but in fact depends on small differences in how decisions are taken, at each junction, to turn left or right. This is obvious if each system is perceived as a pinball machine: where each ball ends up depends on small differences in the angle and speed at which the ball reaches each junction. There is no way of predicting where any individual ball or individual person will end up in each system. No matter what the overall structure is, an individual person could end up in *any* position A, B, C or D, if it exists. Societal effects theories are helpful in predicting that most people end up in position C in system X, while most people end up in position A in system Z. But this is only half the story. It is not the same as predicting where each individual will end up in the two systems. Most is not all.

Social scientists rarely do research on people who are exceptions to the general rule. One rare study of this type is Pilling's (1990) study of people from poor and socially disadvantaged families who were nonetheless high achievers by their mid-twenties. She found that all of them explained their success by their own determination and hard work. She also found that high aspirations in adolescence were not simply a reflection of ability and that adolescent aspirations and motivation had a powerful influence on achievements in adult life. A study with the opposite focus concluded that work orientations and other attitudes were important correlates, possibly predictors, of young men's membership of the underclass at age 33 (Buckingham, 1999). People who insist on the primacy of structural constraints are looking at the fence rather than what the cows do within it (Elster, 1979: 114, quoted in Gambetta, 1987: 8) or, to use our framework, they are describing the system rather than the choices of individuals within it.

Using qualitative research methods for her study of recruitment to the 'Moonies' (Unification Church) rather than the quantitative methods chosen by Gambetta (1987), Barker (1984) also addresses the question of coercion or choice, the relative importance of social structural factors and individual agency. She concludes that, on balance, rational choice and active self-determination are the main features of the decision to join a religious movement. Barker's study is perhaps most valuable for pointing out that when people make choices that seem incomprehensible to an observer, because they would not themselves make such a choice, there is a tendency to argue that the person cannot be 'in their right mind', that some sort of coercion or forced choice must have occurred (Barker, 1984: 235). The same process leads female academics, who have worked all their lives, to argue that women cannot ever make an authentic choice to be full-time homemakers, that the decision must have been forced on them in some way.[5]

Chaos theory is the only theory that begins to address the unpredictability of outcomes at the individual level, by showing that small differences in initial conditions can lead to large differences in outcomes (Kiel and Elliott, 1996; Ormerod, 1998; Byrne, 1999). Person-centred analysis is the only approach that pays as much attention to extreme cases as to the central tendency in a group (Magnusson and Bergman, 1988; Cairns *et al.*, 1998;

Models of the Family in Modern Societies

Magnusson, 1998). Preference theory points to some of the small differences in motivation and aspirations at the start of lives that can produce large differences in outcomes in later years. At the same time, it identifies five key social and economic features of societies that are major determinants of how the system treats women, what options and opportunities it offers them and what barriers are put in their way. Preference theory thus seeks to combine societal effects theory with micro-level theory focusing on agency and individual choice. But even without it, we should be able to accept that the two types of theory are complementary, not mutually exclusive alternatives, as has so often been argued in the social science cold wars of agency *versus* structure. Agency and choice are clearly important if we want to explain the heterogeneity of outcomes *within* societies, as well as identifying macro-level differences *between* societies.

The distinction between agency and structure may be fading anyway in the long term due to the globalization of labour markets and high volumes of international migration. There are increasing differences between countries built on immigration and with continuing active immigration policies, such as Australia, Canada or the USA (which has over 1 million legal immigrants every year, in addition to the illegal immigration which attracts most media attention), and countries of mass emigration, such as Ireland and Spain in the past. International migrants are young and self-selected for high motivation to succeed and a belief that individual effort can surmount major obstacles. They also choose to go to societies that appear to value and reward individual effort and achievement. In the long run, societies built on immigration can become expressions of individual agency transformed into social structure, culture and collective values. So in some societies, most notably the USA and to a much lesser extent Britain, agency and structure can become conflated within a meritocratic and opportunistic culture. We might also expect the reverse: that countries of low immigration or net emigration, would have cultures that emphasize the dominance of social structure and collective values over individuality. This merits further research, but goes well beyond our current research subject.

There are substantial differences between the British and Spanish labour markets, particularly as regards women's opportunities. For example, female unemployment is twice as high as male unemployment in Spain and almost five times higher than among British women. However, in both countries, personal goals and lifestyle preferences still have the same huge impact on women's full-time workrates, which are in that sense individually determined.

Results for Britain

Throughout the analyses of attitudes and values, sex differences are either tiny or non-existent. There is a remarkable degree of unanimity, across men and women, about models of the family and the sexual division of labour. The survey offers little support for the idea that women are well ahead of men in adopting an 'egalitarian' sex-role ideology and that men are more 'traditional', as has been argued repeatedly from opinion poll research. Nor is there any evidence of patriarchal men seeking to restrict women's access to jobs and their economic self-reliance. On the contrary, there is evidence of men being slightly ahead of women in the adoption of 'egalitarian' attitudes, particularly as regards sharing the income-earning role.

Sex differences only emerge in work centrality, because the vast majority of men regard themselves as primary earners throughout adult life, while the vast majority of women regard themselves as secondary earners as soon as they get married. There is nothing natural or inevitable about this automatic assumption of different roles and it is not imposed by a reified 'society'. The majority of black British women regard themselves as primary earners, whereas the majority of white women regard themselves as secondary earners. Black women adopt the primary earner identity despite being subject to greater discrimination in the labour market, not because they have any special advantages in British society. Full-time workrates are thus 20 percentage points higher among black women than among white women in Britain. Women's enthusiasm for an egalitarian division of labour in the family does not extend, in practice, to sharing responsibility for income-earning. Less than 15% of couples of working age report joint responsibility for income-earning. Up to 15% report the wife to be the main income-earner, but this usually appears to be a temporary situation, prompted by the husband's unemployment, rather than a permanent choice of role-reversal. In three-quarters of couples of working age, wives and husbands are agreed that it is the husband alone who is the principal earner. A three-quarters majority of wives still regard themselves as secondary earners, if they work at all.

What has changed is the idea that family roles are rigidly allocated by sex and are immutable. The great majority of Britons today accept that partners can and should substitute for each other, *in extremis*. Sex-role ideology has become more open and flexible, admitting of change and accepting diversity in preferences. What has not changed much is personal preferences. Most reports on opinion poll results make the mistake of conflating public opinion with personal preferences and individual choice. Majority opinion now accepts that 'anything goes', that the rigid differentiation of roles by sex is outdated, that rules are mostly redundant, that 'society' or public opinion should no longer seek to impose the same rules on everyone. However, people still have to make choices for their own lives and most people find the existing models of family roles perfectly acceptable. The most dissatisfied group appears to be divorcees, who are most likely to challenge the three existing models of the family, although only 4% do so. So the changes in public opinion reported by the BSAS and ISSP do not necessarily mean any change in personal choices.

In sum, secondary earners have become and will remain, a substantial element in the workforce, particularly in the female workforce. There is no substantively important difference in the level of work commitment between primary earners and secondary earners, but their interest in work is of a different nature. This implies a permanent diversity in attitudes to employment within the labour force, of a more fundamental nature than the cultural, religious and ethnic differences that are currently treated as the main sources of diversity. This new diversity may be helpful in facilitating the redistribution of work and reducing unemployment. But it may also require more complex social insurance and social welfare arrangements than the present system predicated on the lifelong employment of self-supporting primary earners, which the European Commission believes should be the basis for future policy-making. Our research results should thus inform future European social policy on the family, fiscal policy and labour market policy.

Surveys that have collected public opinion style attitude data on women's employment have generally found little or no association between attitudes and behaviour. The best known example in Britain is the 1980 Women and Employment Survey, which collected extensive attitude data but never asked about personal preferences and life goals. Repeated analyses of the results found only weak associations between general approval for women's employment and women's own employment choices (Martin and Roberts, 1984: 172–6; Dex, 1988: 124).[6] The same problem appears again in the BHPS, which also used generalized attitude statements as a proxy for women's personal work orientations (Corti *et al.*, 1995: 65–9).

In contrast, our indicators of women's lifestyle preferences predict their employment choices very strongly, whereas being in employment, even as a full-time worker, does not predict attitudes and values. Lifestyle preferences are not the only major predictor of women's workrates. Aspirations to home ownership (or the absence of them) emerge as a second key predictor of high female workrates, partly because mortgage debts 'lock in' wives' financial contribution to their household budgets. The two key findings for Britain are, first, that it is possible to fully predict women's workrates with just a handful of variables and, second, that lifestyle preferences are an important predictor. Our analysis also shows that childcare responsibilities are only important among home-centred women and, to a much lesser extent, adaptive women. Lifestyle preferences determine *which* practical constraints are regarded as important enough to have an impact on women's choices.

Lifestyle preferences also predict what type of job women choose when they go out to work, especially the choice between full-time and part-time hours. Polachek's thesis, that women's family responsibilities lead them to choose particular family-friendly occupations, is not supported in Britain today. These results are testimony to the impact of equal opportunities laws and policies on employers in Britain. Whatever their ambitions and lifeplans, women can now choose occupations far more freely than in the past. In effect, employers are being obliged to provide family-friendly arrangements in most occupations. Many non-standard types of job provide greater flexibility than full-time permanent employee jobs, so they are attractive to adaptive and home-centred women. Women who regard themselves as secondary earners are most likely to work in female-dominated occupations because part-time jobs are plentiful in this sector of the labour market and higher labour turnover is tolerated. It is the type of job that attracts them rather than the occupation *per se*. As such jobs become available in integrated occupations, such as pharmacy and in male-dominated occupations, such as bus and coach driving, secondary earners will be found side by side with primary earners in all occupations.

Results for Spain

Spaniards embraced modern social and political values with alacrity after the transition to democracy in 1975. Francoist ideology emphasized women's role as mothers and homemakers and public policy discouraged women's employment. Yet by 1987, just one year after joining the EU, Spain displayed similar views to Britain on the division of labour in the family: 30% and 19% respectively preferred complete role specialization, while 50% and 49% felt the ideal was fully symmetrical roles (see Table 1.1). In the next decade, the egalitarian model of the family rapidly became the stated ideal of the majority of Spaniards, men and women. By 1999, two-thirds claimed this as their ideal, even though in practice Spain still had the lowest female employment rates in the EU (see Table 1.3). Women's overall employment rate has been raised significantly by the large numbers of single women who now work before marriage. Married women have much lower workrates of around one-third, but virtually all of them work full-time, due to the paucity of part-time jobs in Spain, so that female full-time workrates are similar to those in Britain.

The two key findings for Spain are the tremendous enthusiasm for modern social values, including the European Commission's favoured Scandinavian model of the symmetrical roles family and the wide gulf between rhetoric and reality for most married couples. Because there are few part-time jobs, the compromise model of the family is not seen as a realistic option by most people. The change in sex-role ideology thus took the form of a sharp jump from the role segregation model of the family championed by Francoist ideology to the symmetrical roles model. The ideological U-turn was encouraged by the new emphasis, within democracy, on equality for everyone and in all contexts. Thus, by 1999, Spaniards were ahead of Britons in rejecting patriarchal values and in rejecting rigid sex-role ideology. The survey offers contradictory evidence on how far these attitudes and values shape women's behaviour.

On the one hand, there is a huge gap between the majority stated preference for an egalitarian family model and the reality of most wives being out of employment. This gap is narrowing in the younger generation, but remains substantial. The reality in Spain is that the great majority of couples are dependent on a single male breadwinner, irrespective of stated lifestyle preferences (see Table 5.17). On the other hand, lifestyle preferences have the same impact on wives' full-time workrates in Spain as in Britain (see Tables 5.18 and 5.7), and this impact seems to be stronger in the older generation rather than the younger generation. The Spanish survey is a little too small for these results to be completely reliable, but they present conflicting accounts of the relative importance of lifestyle preferences, possibly because women's lives are still undergoing a process of social transformation.

Qualitative research carried out with younger generation urban working mothers in 1995 and 1996 by Tobío (2001) shows that sex-role ideology and work orientations are still in flux.[7] Even working wives still regard men as providers, still take it for granted that men's primary obligation is to earn the family's income; any contribution husbands make to family work is seen as an optional extra. Women's primary obligation is still seen as domestic work and family work. As Tobío puts it, Spanish women are living a romance with paid work. It is still a novelty, not yet regarded as routine and certainly not an obligation. They all feel they could stop working if they wanted,[8] because it is only their husbands who must work as an obligation. Working wives treat their earnings as their own personal money, to spend as they wish, rather than as a contribution to the routine household budget. In sum, younger generation working wives in Spain do not adopt the responsibilities of a joint breadwinner, even though most are working full-time, and even though they defend their right to work on the grounds that their family needs the second salary in order to maintain their standard of living (Tobío, 2001).

There is a tendency to regard jobs almost as a personal hobby rather than a taken-for-granted sharing of the income-earning role. This is also one reason why women feel obliged to continue to do virtually all domestic work and childcare themselves. In short, younger working wives still have highly ambivalent, even contradictory perceptions of family roles and responsibilities, despite accepting the rhetoric of 'egalitarian' relationships. This probably explains why sex-role ideology, as measured in our surveys, has such a variable association with women's employment.

It may also help to explain the lack of any consistent relationship between sex-role ideology and other ideologies in Spain. One of the key findings of this study is that lifestyle preferences are formed independently of political and religious ideologies. The assumption that home-centred women are all right-wing conservatives and that work-centred women are all left-wing liberals is simply unfounded. In the older generation, these values tend to coalesce. In the younger generation, their independence of each other becomes obvious. Lifestyle preferences cut across political groups, religious and non-religious groups, just as they cut across social class, education and income groups.

The Spanish survey is much smaller than the British survey, but in some respects it is a richer dataset, particularly as regards parental characteristics. There is a tradition in research on women's employment of looking at the mother's employment status, to see if she provided a role model for her daughters. Instead, we looked at parental *education*, to see what impact educational homogamy had on sons' and daughters' sex-role ideology.[9] Base numbers in the analysis were too small for the results to be more than indicative, but they all point in the same direction. Women whose parents were equals, in terms of their educational level, are more comfortable with role specialization in the family, are less likely to reject patriarchal values and are less work-centred. The experience of having a mother who was significantly less educated than her husband, with all that entails for personal relationships, pushes women to seek greater equality in their own marriages, for example through an independent career, and to reject patriarchal values.

Paradoxically, as more women achieve higher levels of education, the proportion of women who marry *up* the educational ladder, to an even better educated husband, is increasing in most European societies (Hakim, 2000a: 203–17). The results of our Spanish survey suggest that this trend must boost the proportion of women seeking egalitarian relationships in their own marriages.

Preference Theory

The analyses in preceding chapters have been guided by preference theory, both as to general perspective and in more specific questions. Overall, preference theory has been validated by the results of the surveys in Britain and Spain. Britain provides an example of the situation in a country that has already achieved the new scenario for women, while Spain provides an example of a modern European society undergoing rapid social change but without having yet achieved the new scenario for women. The similarities and contrasts between them provide a stronger test of the utility of preference theory than if a single new scenario society had been studied.

The most important, central tenet of preference theory is that women are heterogeneous in their lifestyle preferences and priorities once they have genuine choices to make. The three groups of home-centred, adaptive and work-centred women were identified in both surveys, using just three survey questions. The distribution of three lifestyle preference groups in Britain and Spain is almost identical and very close to that posited by preference theory (Table 9.1), whether we focus on the entire adult population or the narrower working age population. Because our surveys were designed to focus on women primarily, they could not easily be stretched to cover men adequately. Estimates of the distribution of the three preference groups among men are far more tentative, due to data limitations and are given in Table 3.15.

The preference theory profiles of home-centred, adaptive and work-centred women are also confirmed in Britain, in relation to employment patterns and personal characteristics, whether we focus on women of working age narrowly defined (Table 9.2) or the entire adult population (Table 9.3). A striking feature of both tables is that work-centred women are distinctively different from the other two groups on many personal and attitudinal characteristics. Adaptive women and home-centred women do not differ to the same degree, at least on the indicators available in Tables 9.2 and 9.3. For example, work-centred women are least likely to be married; the majority are living without a partner. They are less likely to have children at home, and much more likely to be living alone or as a lone parent. The sex-role ideology of work-centred women is also distinctively different from that of adaptive and home-centred women. For example, only a one-quarter minority accept patriarchal values in public and private life, compared to over half of the other two groups. Almost none of the work-centred women still believe that ultimate responsibility for housework and income-earning lie with women and men respectively, compared to around one-quarter of the other two groups. Finally, the majority of work-centred women are working full-time, in contrast to the other two groups.

Differences between home-centred and adaptive women are less dramatic, in ideology and behaviour. Home-centred women are more likely to have never had a paid job, they have a larger number of children and one-third still believe in rigid role segregation in the family. They have the lowest workrate of all three groups, but they are no less educated than adaptive women, who are the vast majority. Home-centred women have by far the lowest personal incomes.

Ideological and other differences between the three lifestyle preference groups are even more marked in Spain (Tables 9.4 and 9.5). For example, the vast majority of work-centred women reject patriarchal values and rigid role allocation in the family, whereas the majority of home-centred women accept patriarchy and rigidly specialized family roles. The groups also differ in personal characteristics. Work-centred women tend to be highly educated, whereas home-centred women typically have only primary education. Work-centred women are least likely to be married or to have children. Differences between the three groups in political ideology, religiosity and nationalism are small or non-existent, so preferences regarding private lives are clearly quite separate from other ideologies. Work-centred women are twice as likely to have a mother who married a better-educated man, which implies that she achieved upward social mobility through marriage, usually at the expense of becoming a full-time homemaker wife. However, the major difference between the three groups is in employment rates. The great majority of work-centred women have full-time jobs, while the great majority of home-centred women do no paid work at all. Adaptive women fall between the extremes. Interestingly, the three groups report almost identical distributions of family income (Table 9.4).

Preference theory is also confirmed by negative results from the British and Spanish surveys: the failure to find differences between the three lifestyle preference groups. Preference theory states that the three lifestyle preference groups cut across social class, education and ability differences (Hakim, 2000a: 2, 94–9, 155–6, 275). Actual behaviour will not be totally independent of education, class and income because work-centred women will invest more time and effort in gaining educational qualifications (or equivalent work-related training) and will therefore have higher occupational status and income, on average, than other women. But this relationship will remain weak because women can invest in educational qualifications without necessarily planning a career. In fact, one well-established reason for women entering higher education is because this gives access to a superior marriage market, both during the educational process itself and later through the professional and other occupations attained through higher education (Hakim, 2000a: 193–222). In effect, for women who pursue the marriage career, and for adaptive women, the returns

Table 9.2 Profiles of three lifestyle preference groups in Britain, women aged 20–59

	Home-centred	Adaptive	Work-centred
% who are work-centred	20	12	100
Ideal family model:			
egalitarian	–	40	100
compromise	–	60	–
role segregation	100	–	–
% accept patriarchy	60	55	28
Believes that ultimate responsibility			
for housework lies with woman	33	25	13
for income lies with man	29	20	6
% left full-time education at age:			
by age 16	54	55	42
17–20 years	28	28	32
age 21 +	18	17	26
% employed in:			
full-time job	41	35	63
part-time job	16	37	15
any job	56	72	78
% never had a job	7	2	2
% workforce dropouts	37	26	20
Current/last occupation type:			
male	21	10	17
mixed	12	18	22
female	67	72	61
Composition by socio-economic groups:			
professional & managerial	14	16	25
intermediate white collar	21	20	25
junior white collar	33	34	20
skilled manual	6	6	7
semi-skilled/unskilled manual	26	24	23
Personal gross income:			
up to £4 000	35	30	12
£4 000–£8 000	24	27	19
£8 000–12 000	13	17	18
£12 000–£15 000	7	8	11
£15 000–£25 000	18	13	26
£25 000–£40 000	2	4	12
£40 000 +	2	*	3
Preferences among:			
whites	14	71	15
ethnic minorities	19	61	21

	Home-centred	Adaptive	Work-centred
% ethnic minority	9	6	8
Age structure:			
16–24	10	9	6
25–39	39	43	46
40–54	35	40	44
55 +	16	8	4
% who are:			
single	15	12	26
married/cohabiting	71	80	45
ex-married	14	8	29
% who have:			
child(ren) <16 at home	41	43	33
child(ren) 0–4 at home	18	19	13
Average number of dependent children at home	1.28	1.02	.61
Household type:			
living alone	11	5	21
couple, no dependent children	37	36	27
couple, with dependent children	40	46	19
lone parent	5	5	24
other	7	8	9
% whose housing is:			
owned outright	19	16	11
owned with mortgage	56	61	52
public renters	16	14	26
private renters	9	9	10
% with			
1 + car(s)	80	87	79
3 + cars	4	8	3
Preferences by region:			
North	16	67	17
Midlands/East	13	73	14
London	14	67	19
South East	18	70	12
South West	13	70	17
Wales	9	75	16
Scotland	6	78	16
Base = 100%	171	870	194

Notes: Data for women aged 20–59, excluding full-time students. Dependent children are those aged 0–15 living at home. Lone parents do not necessarily have children who are still dependent. The average number of dependent children is presented for women aged 20–55 years, as virtually none of those aged 55–60 had school-age children at home.

Table 9.3 Profiles of three lifestyle preference groups in Britain, women aged 16 +

	Home-centred	Adaptive	Work-centred
% who are work-centred	20	12	100
Ideal family model:			
egalitarian	–	38	100
compromise	–	62	–
role segregation	100	–	–
% accept patriarchy	75	63	38
Believes that ultimate responsibility			
for housework lies with woman	46	32	18
for income lies with man	43	26	8
% left full-time education at age:			
by age 16	68	63	51
17–20 years	20	24	27
age 21 +	12	13	22
% employed in:			
full-time job	24	26	49
part-time job	11	29	14
any job	35	55	63
% never had a job	6	3	2
% workforce dropouts	59	42	35
Current/last occupation type:			
male	16	10	14
mixed	15	18	21
female	69	72	65
Composition by socio-economic group:			
professional & managerial	11	14	21
intermediate white collar	17	18	26
junior white collar	32	33	22
skilled manual	8	6	7
semi-skilled/unskilled manual	32	29	24
Personal gross income:			
up to £4 000	41	36	15
£4 000–£8 000	30	30	26
£8 000–12 000	12	15	20
£12 000–£15 000	5	6	9
£15 000–£25 000	11	10	20
£25 000–£40 000	1	3	9
£40 000 +	1	*	2
Preferences among:			
whites	17	69	14
ethnic minorities	16	66	18

	Home-centred	Adaptive	Work-centred
% ethnic minority	5	5	7
Age structure:			
16–24	7	9	8
25–39	22	30	35
40–54	19	28	33
55 +	52	33	25
% who are:			
single	13	12	23
married/cohabiting	64	72	42
ex-married	23	16	35
% who have:			
child(ren) <16 at home	24	31	25
child(ren) 0–4 at home	10	14	11
Household type:			
living alone	22	12	29
couple, no dependent children	44	41	29
couple, with dependent children	25	35	14
lone parent	3	4	19
other	7	8	9
% whose housing is:			
owned outright	34	28	20
owned with mortgage	39	47	42
public renters	20	17	27
private renters	7	8	11
% with			
1 + car(s)	70	80	72
3 + cars	5	6	2
Preferences by region:			
North	18	66	16
Midlands/East	17	70	13
London	14	70	16
South East	19	69	12
South West	19	66	15
Wales	15	72	13
Scotland	13	73	14
Base = 100%	308	1245	258

Notes: Data for women aged 16 +, excluding full-time students. See notes to Table 9.2.

Table 9.4 Profiles of three lifestyle preference groups in Spain, women aged 20–59

	Home-centred	Adaptive	Work-centred
% who are work-centred	0	2	100
Ideal family model:			
egalitarian	–	79	100
compromise	–	21	–
role segregation	100	–	–
% accept patriarchy	66	33	17
Believes that ultimate responsibility			
for housework = woman	47	11	2
for income = man	60	12	2
Education level:			
primary	45	31	17
secondary	51	56	37
higher	4	13	47
% employed in:			
full-time job	13	30	72
part-time job	4	12	8
any job	17	42	80
% trade union member	2	4	12
Subjective social class:			
upper middle/upper	4	2	10
middle-middle	71	64	76
lower middle/lower	25	34	14
Husband's employment status:			
full-time work	90	87	80
part-time work	2	1	0
unemployed	3	4	3
retired, etc.	5	8	17
Family income (pesetas):			
up to 100 000	15	13	14
100–150 000	26	29	18
150–200 000	21	22	18
200–275 000	20	21	20
275–500 000	15	14	26
500 000 +	3	1	4
Size of locality:			
% in most rural areas	13	15	13
% in Madrid-Barcelona	6	14	18
Age structure:			
16–24	13	10	12
25–39	25	44	50
40–54	49	37	28
55 +	13	9	10

	Home-centred	Adaptive	Work-centred
Marital status:			
single	9	17	30
married	85	74	50
cohabiting	2	3	7
ex-married	4	6	13
% who have child(ren) at home	74	82	63
Household type:			
living alone	–	–	10
2 + adults, no children	19	16	24
2 + adults, with children	66	76	50
lone parent	9	6	13
other	6	2	3
Political ideology:			
left	30	41	51
centre	33	35	27
right	37	24	22
Vote at last election:			
Partido Popular	26	27	24
PSOE	41	28	32
IU	3	5	6
nationalist parties	5	10	21
non-voter	25	30	17
Nationalism:			
mainly regional identity	17	16	31
equally Spanish and regional	51	46	41
mainly Spanish identity	32	38	28
% atheist	4	6	10
Church attendance:			
weekly	26	17	16
monthly	17	16	14
yearly	46	54	49
never	11	13	21
Religious practice:			
% not at all	27	34	44
% very devout	9	7	5
Parental education:			
mother married up	13	13	27
homogamy	87	85	71
mother married down	0	2	2
Base = 100%	47	273	61

Note: Base is women aged 20–59, excluding full-time students.

Table 9.5 Profiles of three lifestyle preference groups in Spain, women aged 18 +

	Home-centred	Adaptive	Work-centred
% who are work-centred	5	3	100
Ideal family model:			
egalitarian	–	74	100
compromise	–	26	–
role segregation	100	–	–
% accept patriarchy	77	41	20
Believes that ultimate responsibility			
for housework = woman	57	18	6
for income = man	66	18	3
Education level:			
primary	68	45	24
secondary	30	45	30
higher	2	10	46
% employed in:			
full-time job	6	18	43
part-time job	3	9	8
any job	9	27	51
% trade union member	1	4	12
Subjective social class:			
upper middle/upper	2	3	12
middle-middle	60	59	74
lower middle/lower	38	38	14
Husband's employment status:			
full-time work	55	69	70
part-time work	1	1	0
unemployed	1	3	2
retired, etc.	42	27	28
Family income (pesetas):			
up to 100 000	41	28	18
100–150 000	19	25	18
150–200 000	19	17	15
200–275 000	11	18	18
275–500 000	9	11	27
500 000 +	1	1	3
Size of locality:			
% in most rural areas	14	16	11
% in Madrid-Barcelona	4	16	18
Age structure:			
16–24	7	9	10
25–39	12	31	41
40–54	24	25	24
55 +	57	35	25

	Home-centred	Adaptive	Work-centred
Marital status:			
single	5	16	28
married	73	67	49
cohabiting	1	2	5
ex-married	21	15	18
widowed			
% who have child(ren) at home	50	67	57
Household type:			
living alone	1	1	10
2 + adults, no children	34	24	25
2 + adults, with children	43	60	46
lone parent	6	7	11
other	16	8	8
Political ideology:			
left	31	42	50
centre	35	31	24
right	34	27	26
Vote at last election:			
Partido Popular	35	29	26
PSOE	39	31	31
IU	1	4	8
nationalist parties	5	8	19
non-voter	20	28	16
Nationalism:			
mainly regional identity	18	17	29
equally Spanish and regional	55	48	41
mainly Spanish identity	27	35	30
% atheist	2	4	8
Church attendance:			
weekly	42	23	20
monthly	21	19	15
yearly	32	48	47
never	5	10	18
Religious practice:			
% not at all	15	27	37
% very devout	17	11	7
Parental education:			
mother married up	8	11	25
homogamy	90	87	73
mother married down	0	2	2
Base = 100%	98	393	73

Note: base is women aged 18 and over, excluding full-time students.

to education consist of their husband's career and earnings rather than their own. For the husband, too, there can be major benefits to having a graduate wife, whether she works or not (Waite and Gallagher, 2000: 104). Recent research has started to acknowledge the mutual benefits to couples who are educationally homogamous (Hakim, 2000a: 159–61, 166, 191, 195–6).

In Britain, the three lifestyle preference groups differ remarkably little in educational level and socio-economic status. Personal incomes differ due to the variations in employment rates and working hours, and we have no information on family incomes. Using number of cars in the household as a proxy indicator for wealth, there are virtually no differences between the three preference groups.

In Spain, family income differs hardly at all between the three groups. There are tiny differences in social class composition, but there are substantial differences in education (Table 9.4), largely due to historical changes. Apart from this very last finding for Spain, the survey results are all in line with preference theory. Cultural, economic and social capital do not determine lifestyle preferences.

Preference theory proposes that there is a polarization of women's lifestyles, that the differences between work-centred women and home-centred women are becoming stronger over time (Hakim, 2000a: 155, 175–8). In particular, younger women, whose adult lives are lived entirely within the new scenario and who benefit from free contraception, equal opportunities policies and other social changes will display more divergent lifestyles and activities than the older generation of women, who did not benefit from these new developments and whose lives were shaped primarily by social and economic circumstances, rather than by personal choices. There is no doubt about women's lifestyles being polarized, even on the limited evidence available in our two surveys. In Britain, for example, home-centred women have twice as many children as work-centred women and work-centred women are twice as likely as other women to be in full-time employment. In Spain, there are dramatic differences in workrates between the three groups. No doubt qualitative research would reveal the polarization of lifestyles and priorities in richer detail. There is also no doubt that there are notable differences between the two generations in both countries. There is generally greater consistency and coherence in attitudes and values in the generation aged under 40 than in the older generation, suggesting greater deliberation and well-defined goals and motivation. In both countries, there is also greater consistency between preferences and behaviour in the younger generation, implying greater freedom to implement goals. If anything, the change is greater in Spain than in Britain, due to the sudden opening up of the education system and the labour market to women, which affected younger women more than older women. Overall, there is polarization of women's lifestyles, but the pace of change varies and is not necessarily faster in new scenario countries. It appears that social change has powerful effects on older women as well as on the younger generation; its effects are not selective, but pervade the whole of society to a greater or lesser extent. In sum, differences between the two generations are relatively small, in both countries. Our thesis that the younger generation displays the effects of social change more fully is not supported by the evidence. Similarly, differences between the two countries are smaller than expected. It seems that Spanish women have changed in advance of the new scenario being fully achieved in that country.

In contrast, men's lives have changed little. Among men, sex-role ideology has almost no impact on employment patterns, in either Britain or Spain, because men do not yet have genuine choices to make about their role in the family. One of our key conclusions is that social change gives women real choices as to how to live their lives, choices that men do not yet have but will soon start to demand.

The absence of sex differences in lifestyle preferences and in closely related values confirms another tenet of preference theory: that differences between lifestyle preference groups are becoming more important than differences between men and women (Hakim, 2000a: 279–80). This has important implications for public policy. At present, social, family and employment policies are discussed in terms of their benefits for men or women, poorer or richer families. We should instead be assessing policies in terms of their bias towards work-centred or home-centred people, towards single-earner families or dual-earner couples. We should also be seeking to make policies more neutral between these groups rather than favouring only one (Hakim, 2000a: 223–53).

Our surveys reconfirm the findings of earlier studies showing that lifestyle preferences are not determined by social, economic or cultural capital. The three lifestyle preference groups cut across social classes, income groups and educational levels. In addition, preferences regarding family lifestyle seem to cut across all shades of political opinion, religious groups and atheists and other ideological positions. This is consistent with the idea that lifestyle preferences concern *private* lives and *personal* identity, as distinct from the public issues addressed by political and other ideologies.

Finally, all our results confirm the crucial distinction between personal preferences and public opinion attitudes, between what people choose for themselves and what are thought to be good general rules for society as a whole. It is perfectly possible for people to believe that women are just as able as men and can perform equally competently in any occupation and yet personally choose to be full-time homemakers or secondary earners who give priority to their families. It is entirely feasible for people to believe women generally should have the right to work as surgeons or politicians, without necessarily wanting to do either of these jobs themselves. Most attitude surveys collect data on public opinion, on what 'society' or 'the general public' thinks, but not on personal preferences and choices – as illustrated by the British Social Attitudes Survey, the International Social Survey Programme, the World Values Survey and almost certainly also the new European Social Survey running from 2002 onwards. There are good reasons to document the climate of public opinion on women's position in society and women's employment. But we need also to collect data on personal choices and personal preferences, if only because our ultimate interest is in the relationship between behaviour and attitudes and values.

Other Aspirations: Home Ownership

Lifestyle preferences are becoming increasingly important determinants of behaviour, but they are never the sole determinant. Preferences do not express themselves in a vacuum, but within a particular social and economic context, within a particular system, to use the macro-level terminology adopted earlier and this system will help to determine overall outcomes. Housing and housing policies form part of the context within which couples implement their preferences. Analyses in Chapters 5 and 8 show that housing aspirations form a separate, parallel determinant of female employment in Britain, one that is sufficiently powerful to override lifestyle preferences in certain circumstances.

First, home ownership aspirations seem to be an especially powerful motivator among women. The home becomes a symbol of family life as well as containing it. Because of the way the mortgage system works in Britain, wives can find themselves locked into continuous employment in order to safeguard mortgage repayments. Recent decades have seen a polarization of women's workrates by housing tenure. A two-thirds majority of wives in owner-occupied homes are in work and one-third work full-time. In contrast, less than half of wives in public rented homes are in work and only 15% work full-time. The polarization becomes even sharper when we compare women in our survey who still have a mortgage on their home with women in public rented housing: 44% and 13% respectively are in full-time employment. This substantial difference in behaviour occurs despite the fact that the two groups of women do not differ in lifestyle preferences. As a result, having a mortgage debt on one's home emerges as a second, separate major determinant of female full-time employment, almost as powerful as lifestyle preferences.

Second, home ownership aspirations and responsibility for a mortgage can in certain situations override lifestyle preferences. Thus we found that women with mortgages and a husband with low or precarious earnings, as a result of redundancy or unemployment, would put aside their preference for being full-time homemakers and take full-time jobs in order to safeguard mortgage repayments.

Home ownership aspirations are particularly interesting because they illustrate the thin dividing line that sometimes exists between personal values and social or economic structural factors. Values can be transformed into structural factors, once choices are locked in. After a home has been bought and a mortgage obtained, the need to keep up payments becomes a fixed 'external' factor, even though it is aspirations to home ownership and the status and lifestyle that entails, that create this burden in the first place. Thus responsibility for a mortgage could be labelled either as a structural determinant of women's workrates or as a personal aspiration and value that pushes women's employment up to a higher level and then locks it in. Which of these two accounts is offered seems to vary between men and women. Men's accounts of their lives tend to emphasize agency and their own determination to overcome difficulties. Women's accounts tend to emphasize contextual 'structural' factors or chance events, to which they accommodate themselves (Hakim, 2000a: 16–17).

Extending Preference Theory

This study has demonstrated that home-centred, adaptive and work-centred women constitute meaningful ideological groups in two very different European countries. Preference groups constitute more than just diversity. The groups sometimes have *conflicting* values, as illustrated by contrasting attitudes to patriarchy. However, the minimalist approach adopted for our surveys means that we were not able to fully explore ideological differences between the three preference groups. Future research might do this. The three lifestyle preference groups differ on their priorities as to time allocation as between market work and family work. However, lifestyle preference groups also differ in value systems.

Home-centred people have what can loosely be called 'family values', with an emphasis on the sharing, caring and non-competitive values of private family life. It is not clear whether this is necessarily the same thing as Gilligan's (1993) 'ethic of care' on which there have been few empirical studies.

Work-centred people have marketplace values, with an emphasis on competitive rivalry, achievement orientation and individualism rather than collectivism. These are the values that most often dominate the workplace, competitive sport and commercial art.

As Talcot Parsons pointed out a long time ago, these two value systems are often incompatible and potentially in conflict,[10] even more than any potential conflict between the quite different time budgets of home-centred and work-centred people. Adaptive people, who divide their time and efforts between the public world of the marketplace and the private world of the family, must also juggle with two competing value systems. Just how they do this deserves closer study. It seems likely that the jobs they choose (as distinct from their occupations) must be ones which permit some balance between competitive values and collectivist family values. It may be that part-time jobs are attractive to adaptive women not only because they facilitate the combination of family work with market work in terms of time budgets, but also because part time jobs have a culture that explicitly prevents workplace values becoming dominant at the expense of family values, especially if they are in the public sector. Thus adaptive women can work as pharmacists just as well as work-centred men, but they choose part-time jobs in state hospitals rather than long hours as a self-employed entrepreneurial owner of a private retail pharmacy (Bottero, 1992; Hakim, 1998a: 221–34; Hassell *et al.*, 1998; Tanner *et al.*, 1999). Similarly, raising children may be less attractive to work-centred people not only because they constitute a competing life priority in terms of time allocation, but also because they entail a change of emphasis, from competitive, achievement values to caring and sharing values.

The distinctive feature of integrated occupations like pharmacy is that, because they employ roughly equal numbers of men and women, they employ roughly equal numbers of primary earners and secondary earners, albeit in different types of job. In contrast, male-dominated occupations employ primary earners almost exclusively and female-dominated occupations employ secondary earners almost exclusively (see Table 6.8). Work-centrality thus varies strongly between workers in male, mixed and female occupations. This would be consistent with the idea that the institutions and culture of male occupations emphasize competitive rivalry whereas the culture and institutions of female occupations do not, with integrated occupations somewhere in between. Thus, women who switch from male or mixed occupations to female occupations after childbirth (Dex, 1987: 122–30; McRae, 1991; Hakim, 1998a: 56–9) are not only obtaining jobs that offer increased time flexibility and convenience, they may also be choosing occupations and jobs with cultures that are much less competitive and aggressive, much less work-centred and thus far more compatible with family values.

These questions merit further attention, but they serve to underline the point that the three preference groups are not merely different, but potentially in conflict on several fronts. The challenge for policy-makers is to make space for all three groups and to support them all equally instead of pretending, as does the European Commission, that only one lifestyle group has legitimacy.

A Unisex Future of Work?

What are the implications of our results for the future of work? Most social science research is backward-looking in the sense that it describes the social situation in the recent past and places it in the context of a social science literature for the last century. The ESRC Future of Work Research Programme was explicitly designed to look ahead to developments over the next 20–30 years.

The virtual absence of differences between men and women in attitudes and values throughout this study suggests we are moving rapidly towards a unisex workforce, with unisex workrates and unisex employment patterns. This development is reinforced by the European Commission's determination to ensure that all workers have the same legal rights, terms and conditions of employment. This objective has already been achieved throughout the EU in relation to part-time workers, who now benefit from the same rights to pensions, holidays and other benefits as full-time workers. Part-timers have also been given the same employment protection rights as full-timers. In 2002, the European Commission proposed a new Directive giving temporary and fixed-term workers the same rights and benefits as permanent employees. In the long term, these policies will ensure a fairly homogeneous workforce as regards legal status and employer benefits.

Paradoxically, these developments ensure that the only cleavages that will matter within the workforce in the twenty-first century will be the continuing differences between primary and secondary earners and the widening differences between lifestyle preference groups among both men and women. Sex and gender will cease to be important factors and are already being replaced by lifestyle preferences as the only important differentiating characteristic in labour supply.

The improved legal status, rights and benefits of non-standard workers will make all these jobs more attractive, not only to women but to men also. The effects can already be seen in Britain, where there is a long tradition of part-time jobs and temporary contracts. Most part-time jobs have the security of a permanent contract and many mothers choose these jobs in preference to full-time permanent jobs. Improvements to legal rights and benefits simply increase the attraction of non-standard jobs, as illustrated by the huge upsurge in part-time employment in the Netherlands in the 1970s and 1980s. Secondary earners who are currently forced to choose full-time jobs in order to achieve adequate pay rates and benefits will switch to part-time or temporary jobs instead. In Britain, three-quarters of part-time workers are secondary earners and the vast majority (90%) of women part-time workers are not work-centred (see Table 5.6). Two-thirds of secondary earners have little or no involvement with paid work: one-third do no paid work and one-third have a part-time job. However, one-third of all secondary earners are still in full-time jobs, so there is great scope for the further expansion of part-time working, even in Britain. Similar developments can be expected in relation to temporary jobs.

We can thus expect lifestyle preference groups to become the principal characteristic differentiating workers, informing their choice of occupation and job and shaping their employment histories. Even if the logic of preference theory fails to persuade, it is undeniable that the distinction between primary and secondary earners is becoming clearer and causes qualitatively different employment choices and career patterns. This is illustrated most forcefully by the differing career choices of men and women in graduate professions such as pharmacy, which now recruit men and women in equal numbers in many modern societies. Women in pharmacy tend to prefer part-time and even temporary employee jobs, either in state hospitals or neighbourhood retail pharmacies. Men in pharmacy generally choose full-time work, either as a self-employed entrepreneur in their own retail pharmacy or else they aim for management posts in the large chainstores. As a result, the pay gap continues even in integrated occupations (Hakim, 1998a: 221–34).

In sum, the future of work will be unisex and we can expect homogenization of the terms and conditions offered to all workers. However, these equalities will only highlight the profound and continuing differences between primary and secondary earners and between lifestyle preference groups. Men and women are in agreement that some role specialization in the family is beneficial, even if both partners have paid jobs. The debate is now about how each family organizes their division of labour, in a situation where there are no rigid rules or fixed guidelines and all options are open. The challenge for employers is to design jobs so that secondary earners and primary earners can work side by side even in the same occupation. The challenge for national governments is to reorganize fiscal policy, family policy and employment policy so as to avoid discriminating against any preference group.

Notes

1   The danger here is that this might prompt some men to facetiously choose this option as a joke. In 1999, only 3% of respondents in Britain and Spain were unable to choose between the three family models offered in question F. In Britain, 2% said they would not choose any of them and another 1% gave a don't know response. In Spain, only 1% were unable to choose between the three family models and another 2% gave a don't know response. So there is currently little evidence that heterosexual people in Europe actively contemplate role reversal or any other arrangement, as the preferred alternative to the three existing models of the family. Nonetheless, it may be desirable to include a role reversal fourth option in future surveys, to anticipate the time when this becomes a personal choice for some couples even if not yet a widely accepted alternative model of marriage.

2   This is not necessarily the case, but true in practice, simply because most people have to earn their living themselves or find someone else to do it for them. Millionaires do not require a breadwinner spouse, but few people are millionaires.

3   Analyses for married couples only (excluding cohabiting couples) in our survey were generally more sharply defined and showed stronger differences between lifestyle preference groups, but also ran into the problem of small base numbers for the two extreme groups of home-centred and work-centred women, as illustrated by analyses in Hakim (2003b).

4   McRae's 1999 survey (2002) suffered organizational errors that restrict the representativeness of the sample of 1500 mothers. Even so, the 1999 survey results for women who were in work in 1987 and were first-time mothers in 1988 confirm preference theory predictions very clearly. Due to sample selection bias, only 10% were work-centred (with continuous full-time work after childbirth), and only 9% were home-centred (with no paid employment after childbirth and larger numbers of children born); the remaining 81% of mothers were adaptives, with varied patterns of employment after childbirth.

5   Brown (1995: 73) and Rose (1999: 269) offer a somewhat different analysis: that women's politicized identity becomes attached to its own exclusion. Feminist ideology insists on women's victimhood and historical suffering; in the process it denies the possibility of change or of authentic choice in the future.

6   McRae's 1999 survey also used attitude questions taken from the 1980 WES and, not surprisingly, she found only weak associations between attitudes and behaviour (McRae 2002).

7   Tobío's conclusions are based on several studies carried out in 1995 and 1996, plus a national survey of working mothers in 1998. The qualitative research was carried out in the four main cities – Madrid, Barcelona, Valencia and Bilbao – and thus covers women in the most cosmopolitan urban centres, who would be at the leading edge of attitude change in Spain. Their views are likely to be well ahead of attitudes in small towns and rural areas.

8   Partly because of long-term high unemployment, it is difficult, even impossible, to re-enter the workforce once one has dropped out of it. So exits are usually permanent in Spain. Women who work generally work continuously.

9   Once of the advantages of looking at spouses' or parents' education rather than employment is that the information is available for everyone and is a constant. Whether or not a mother or wife works can vary according to her age or the child's age, so is not a fixed parameter. In addition, employment itself is not homogeneous and varies between full-time and part-time work, permanent, fixed-term or seasonal work, and so on.

10   Parsons was right to highlight the distinctive and incompatible value systems of family life and the marketplace. However, he was wrong in assuming that these were essentially female and male value systems, rather than characteristics of particular social settings. Gilligan (1993) makes the same essentialist error in assuming that the 'ethic of care' is peculiarly and necessarily female, in contrast to the more abstract male ethical values she describes.

Bibliography

Abramson, P. R. and Inglehart, R. (1995) *Value Change in Global Perspective*, Ann Arbor: University of Michigan Press.

Agnew, J. (1982) 'Home ownership and identity in capitalist societies', in J. S. Duncan (ed.) *Housing and Identity: Cross-Cultural Perspectives*, New York: Holmes & Meier, pp. 60–97.

Alba, A. (2000) *La Riqueza de las Familias: Mujer y Mercado de Trabajo en la España Democrática*, Barcelona: Editorial Ariel.

Albrecht, J. W., Edin, P. A. and Vroman, S. B. (1995) 'A cross-country comparison of attitudes towards mothers working and their actual labor market experience', Working Paper 1995: 28, Department of Economics, Uppsala University.

Alcobendas Tirado, P. M. (1983) *Datos sobre el Trabajo de la Mujer en España*, Madrid: CIS.

Andrés Orizo, F. (1996) *Sistemas de Valores en la España de los 90*, Madrid: Siglo XXI for CIS.

Andrisani, P. J. (1978) *Work Attitudes and Labor Market Experience: Evidence from the National Longitudinal Surveys*, New York and London: Praeger.

Anker, R. (1998) *Gender and Jobs: Sex Segregation of Occupations in the World*, Geneva: ILO.

Barker, E. (1984) *The Making of a Moonie: Brainwashing or Choice?*, Oxford: Basil Blackwell.

Becker, G. S. (1981, 1991) *A Treatise on the Family*, Cambridge, MA: Harvard University Press.

Benoit-Guilbot, O. (1989) 'Quelques réflexions sur l'analyse sociétale: l'exemple des régulations des marchés du travail en France et en Grande-Bretagne', *Sociologie du Travail*, 2: 217–25 (special edition on *International Comparisons: Theories and Methods*).

Benoit-Guilbot, O. and Clémencon, M. (2001) 'Emploi féminin, natalité et tâches maternelles: comparaison Européenne', *Revue de l'OFCE: Observations et Diagnostiques Economiques*, No. 77: 259–96.

Bernard, J. (1981) 'The good-provider role: its rise and fall', *American Psychologist*, 36: 1–12. Reprinted in E. D. Salamon and B. W. Robinson (eds) *Gender Roles*, New York: Methuen, 1987, pp. 177–92.

Bielby, D. D. V. and Bielby, W. T. (1984) 'Work commitment, sex-role attitudes and women's employment', *American Sociological Review*, 49: 234–47.

Blackwell, L. (2001) 'Women's work in UK official statistics and the 1980 reclassification of occupations', *Journal of the Royal Statistical Society A*, 164: 307–25.

Blau, F. D. and Ferber, M. A. (1992) *The Economics of Women, Men and Work*, Englewood Cliffs, NJ: Prentice-Hall.

Blossfeld, H.-P. (1997) 'Women's part-time employment and the family cycle: a cross-national comparison', in H.-P. Blossfeld and C. Hakim (eds) *Between Equalization and Marginalization: Women Working Part-time in Europe and the USA*, Oxford: Oxford University Press, pp. 315–24.

Blossfeld, H.-P. and Drobnic, S. (eds) (2001) *Careers of Couples in Contemporary Society: From Male Breadwinner to Dual-Earner Families*, Oxford: Oxford University Press.

Blossfeld, H.-P. and Hakim, C. (eds) (1997) *Between Equalization and Marginalization: Women Working Part-time in Europe and the USA*, Oxford: Oxford University Press.

BMRB (1988a) *A Plain Man's Guide to the TGI*, London: British Market Research Bureau.

BMRB (1988b) *Your Lifestyle*, London: British Market Research Bureau.

Borreguero, C., Catena, E., de la Gándara, C. and Salas, M. (eds) (1986) *La Mujer Española: De la Tradición a la Modernidad 1960–1980*, Madrid: Editorial Tecnos.

Bottero, W. (1992) 'The changing face of the professions? Gender and explanations of women's entry into pharmacy', *Work Employment and Society*, 6: 329–46.

Bourdieu, P. (1984) *Distinction: A Social Critique of the Judgement of Taste*, trans. R. Nice, London: Routledge.

Bourdieu, P. (1997) 'The forms of capital', in A. H. Halsey, H. Lauder, P. Brown and A. S. Wells (eds) *Education: Culture, Economy and Society*, Oxford: Oxford University Press, pp. 46–58. trans. Richard Nice.

Brewer, M. B. and Brown, R. J. (1998) 'Intergroup relations', in D. T. Gilbert, S. T. Fiske and G. Lindzey (eds) *Handbook of Social Psychology*, New York: McGrawHill, pp. 554–94.

Brown, R., Curran, M. and Cousins, J. (1983) *Changing Attitudes to Employment?*, Research Paper No. 40, London: Department of Employment.

Brown, W. (1995) *States of Injury: Power and Freedom in Late Modernity*, Princeton, NJ: Princeton University Press.

Bryson, A. and McKay, S. (1997) 'What about the workers?', in R. Jowell *et al.* (eds) *British Social Attitudes – the 14th Report*, Aldershot: Ashgate, pp. 22–48.

Bryson, C., Budd, T., Lewis, J. and Elam, G. (1999) *Women's Attitudes to Combining Paid Work and Family Life*, London: Cabinet Office Women's Unit.

Buckingham, A. (1999) 'Is there an underclass in Britain?', *British Journal of Sociology*, 50: 49–75.

Byrne, D. (1999) *Complexity Theory and the Social Sciences*, London: Routledge.

Cairns, R. B., Bergman, L. R. and Kagan, J. (eds) (1998) *Methods and Models for Studying the Individual*, London and Thousand Oaks, CA: Sage.

Carrasco, C. (1991) *El Trabajo Doméstico y la Reproducción Social*, Madrid: Ministerio de Asuntos Sociales, Instituto de la Mujer.

Cartwright, A. (1976) *How Many Children?*, London: Routledge.

Castaño, C. and Palacios, S. (eds) (1996) *Salud, Dinero y Amor: Cómo Viven las Mujeres Españolas de Hoy*, Madrid: Alianza Editorial.

Chappell, N. L. (1980) 'Paid labor: confirming a conceptual distinction between commitment and identification', *Work and Occupations*, 7: 81–116.

Charles, N. (2001) *The Gender Dimensions of Job Insecurity: An Ethnographic Study*, End of Award Report to the ESRC.

Cohen, P. N. (2002) 'Cohabitation and the declining marriage premium for men', *Work and Occupations*, 29: 346–63.

Coleman, D. (1996) 'New patterns and trends in European fertility: international and sub-national comparisons', in D. Coleman (ed.) *Europe's Population in 1990*, Oxford: Oxford University Press, pp. 1–61.

Corti, L., Laurie, H. and Dex, S. (1995) *Highly Qualified Women*, Research Series No. 50, London: Employment Department.

Cox, B. D., Huppert, F. A. and Whichelow, M. J. (eds) (1993) *The Health and Lifestyle Survey: Seven Years On*, A longitudinal study of a nationwide sample, measuring changes in physical and mental health, attitudes and lifestyle, Aldershot: Dartmouth.

Crompton, R. and Harris, F. (1998) 'Explaining women's employment patterns: orientations to work revisited', *British Journal of Sociology*, 49: 118–36.

Cruz Cantero, P. (1995) *Percepción Social de la Familia en Espana*, Madrid: CIS.

Cruz Cantero, P. and Cobo Bedia, R. (1991) *Las Mujeres Españolas: Lo Privado y Lo Publico*, Madrid: CIS.

Dale, A. and Holdsworth, C. (1998) 'Why don't ethnic minority women in Britain work part-time?', in J. O'Reilly and C. Fagan (eds) *Part-Time Prospects*, London: Routledge, pp. 77–95.

Darke, J. (1994) 'Women and the meaning of home', in R. Gilroy and R. Woods (eds) *Housing Women*, London and New York: Routledge, pp. 11–30.

Davis, J. A. (1982) 'Achievement variables and class cultures: family, schooling, job and forty-nine dependent variables in the cumulative GSS', *American Sociological Review*, 47: 569–86.

Davis, K. (1984) 'Wives and work: the sex role revolution and its consequences', *Population and Development Review*, 10: 397–417.

del Campo, S. (1991) *La Nueva Familia Española*, Madrid: Eudema.

Delgado, M. and Castro Martín, T. (1998) *Encuesta de Fecundidad y Familia 1995 (FFS)*, Opiniones y Actitudes No. 20, Madrid: CIS.

DeMaio, T. J. (1984) 'Social desirability and survey measurement: a review', in C. F. Turner and E. Martin (eds) *Surveying Subjective Phenomena*, vol. 2, New York: Russell Sage, pp. 257–81.

de Miguel, A. (1974) *Sexo, Mujer y Natalidad en España*, Madrid: Cuadernos para el Dialogo.

Dex, S. (1987) *Women's Occupational Mobility: A Lifetime Perspective*, London: Macmillan.

Dex, S. (1988) *Women's Attitudes Towards Work*, London: Macmillan.

Díez Nicolás, J. and de Miguel, J. M. (1981) *Control de Natalidad en España*, Barcelona: Fontanella.

Duncan G. J. and Dunifon, R. (1998) 'Soft skills and long run labor market success', *Research in Labor Economics*, 17: 123–49.

Duncan, J. S. (ed.) (1982a) *Housing and Identity: Cross-Cultural Perspectives*, New York: Holmes & Meier.

Duncan, J. S. (1982b) 'The house as an expression of social worlds', in J. S. Duncan (ed.) *Housing and Identity: Cross-Cultural Perspectives*, New York: Holmes & Meier, pp. 36–59.

Dunnell, K. (1979) *Family Formation 1976*, London: HMSO.

Elster, J. (1979) *Ulysses and the Sirens*, Cambridge: Cambridge University Press.

England, P. (1982) 'The failure of human capital theory to explain occupational sex segregation', *Journal of Human Resources*, 17: 358–70.

England, P. (1984) 'Wage appreciation and depreciation: a test of neoclassical economic explanations of occupational sex segregation', *Social Forces*, 62: 726–49.

Erikson, R. and Goldthorpe, J. H. (1993) *The Constant Flux*, Oxford: Clarendon Press.

Esping-Andersen, G. (1990) *The Three Worlds of Welfare Capitalism*, Cambridge: Polity Press/Princeton, NJ: Princeton University Press.

Esser, H. (1996) 'What is wrong with variable sociology?' *European Sociological Review*, 12: 159–66.

European Commission (1987) *Eurobarometer*, No. 27, Brussels: DGV.

European Commission (1991) *Lifestyles in the European Community: Family and Employment within the Twelve*, Eurobarometer special report, DGV.

European Commission (1998) *Equal Opportunities for Women and Men in Europe?* Eurobarometer No. 44. 3, Luxembourg: OOPEC.

European Commission (2000) *Employment in Europe 2000*, Luxembourg: OOPEC.

European Commission, Employment and Social Affairs Directorate (2001) *EU Employment and Social Policy 1999–2001*, Luxembourg: OOPEC.

Eurostat/European Commission (2001) *The Social Situation in the European Union*, Luxembourg: OOPEC.

Fiske, S. T. (1998) 'Stereotyping, prejudice and discrimination', in D. T. Gilbert, S. T. Fiske and G. Lindzey (eds) *Handbook of Social Psychology*, New York: McGrawHill, pp. 357–411.

Ford, J., Kempson, E. and England, J. (1995) *Into Work? The Impact of Housing Costs and Benefits on People's Decision to Work*, Layerthorpe: YPS for the Joseph Rowntree Foundation.

Galbraith, J. K. (1975) *Economics and the Public Purpose*, Harmondsworth: Penguin.

Gallard, O. *et al.* (2000) 'La jeunesse dans quatre pays de l'Europe', *Revue de l'OFCE*, No. 72: 185–228.

Gallie, D. and White, M. (1993) *Employee Commitment and the Skills Revolution*, London: Policy Studies Institute.

Gallie, D., White, M., Cheng, Y. and Tomlinson, M. (1998) *Restructuring the Employment Relationship*, Oxford: Clarendon Press.

Gambetta, D. (1987) *Were They Pushed or Did They Jump? Individual Decision Mechanisms in Education*, Cambridge: Cambridge University Press.

García-Osuna, C. (1993) *La Mujer Española, Hoy: Ante la Salud, el Sex., el Dinero y el Poder*, Madrid: Nuer Ediciones.

Garrido, L. J. (1992) *Las Dos Biografías de la Mujer en España*, Madrid: Ministerio de Asuntos Sociales, Instituto de la Mujer.

Geerken, M. and Gove, W. R. (1983) *At Home and At Work: The Family's Allocation of Labor*, Beverly Hills, CA: Sage.

Gerson, K. (1985) *Hard Choices: How Women Decide about Work, Career and Motherhood*, Berkeley and Los Angeles: University of California Press.

Gilligan, C. (1982, 1993) *In a Different Voice: Psychological Theory and Women's Development*, Cambridge MA, and London: Harvard University Press.

Goldin, C. and Polachek, S. (1987) 'Residual differences by sex: perspectives on the gender gap in earnings', *American Economic Review*, 77: 143–51.

Grimshaw, D. and Rubery, J. (1998) *The Concentration of Women's Employment and Relative Occupational Pay: A Statistical Framework for Comparative Analysis*, Labour Market and Social Policy Occasional Papers No. 26, Paris: OECD.

Grundy, E. and Murphy, M. (1999) 'Looking beyond the household: intergenerational perspectives on living kin and contact with kin', *Population Trends*, 100: 21–5.

Hakim, C. (1990) 'Workforce restructuring in Europe in the 1980s', *International Journal of Comparative Labour Law and Industrial Relations*, 5, part 4: 167–203.

Hakim, C. (1991) 'Grateful slaves and self-made women: fact and fantasy in women's work orientations', *European Sociological Review*, 7: 101–21.

Hakim, C. (1992) 'Explaining trends in occupational segregation: the measurement, causes and consequences of the sexual division of labour', *European Sociological Review*, 8: 127–52.

Hakim, C. (1993) 'Segregated and integrated occupations: a new framework for analysing social change', *European Sociological Review*, 9: 289–314.

Hakim, C. (1996a) *Key Issues in Women's Work: Female Heterogeneity and the Polarisation of Women's Employment*, London: Continuum.

Hakim, C. (1996b) 'Labour mobility and employment stability: rhetoric and reality on the sex differential in labour market behaviour', *European Sociological Review*, 12: 1–31.

Hakim, C. (1997) 'A sociological perspective on part-time work', in H.-P. Blossfeld and C. Hakim (eds) *Between Equalization and Marginalisation: Women Working Part-Time in Europe and the USA*, Oxford: Oxford University Press, pp. 22–70.

Hakim, C. (1998a) *Social Change and Innovation in the Labour Market*, Oxford: Oxford University Press.

Hakim, C. (1998b) 'Developing a sociology for the twenty-first century: Preference Theory', *British Journal of Sociology*, 49: 137–43.

Hakim, C. (1999a) 'Models of the family, women's role and social policy: a new perspective from Preference Theory', *European Societies*, 1: 25–50.

Hakim, C. (1999b) 'Diversity and choice in the sexual contract: models for the 21st century', in G Dench (ed.) *Rewriting the Sexual Contract*, New Brunswick, NJ: Transaction Publishers, pp. 165–79.

Hakim, C. (2000a) *Work-Lifestyle Choices in the 21st Century: Preference Theory*, Oxford: Oxford University Press.

Hakim, C. (2000b) *Research Design: Successful Designs for Social and Economic Research*, London: Routledge.

Hakim, C. (2001a) 'Les femmes obtiennent-elles ce qu'elles veulent ou se contentent-elles de ce qu'on leur propose?' (Do women get what they want, or accept what they are offered?), *Revue de l'OFCE – Observations et Diagnostics Economiques*, No. 77: 297–306, April 2001, Paris: Observatoire Francais des Conjonctures Economiques. Reprinted July 2001 in *Problèmes Economiques*, No. 2721: 25–8.

Hakim, C. (2001b) 'Taking women seriously', *People and Place*, 9, 4: 1–6.

Hakim, C. (2002) 'Lifestyle preferences as determinants of women's differentiated labour market careers', *Work and Occupations*, 29: 428–59.

Hakim, C. (2003a) 'Lifestyle preferences and patriarchal values: causal and non-causal attitudes and values' in J. Z. Giele and E. Holst (eds), *Changing Life Patterns in Western Industrial Societies*, New York: Elsevier.

Hakim, C. (2003b) 'A new approach to explaining declining fertility: preference theory', *Population and Development Review*, 29.

Hakim, C. and Jacobs, S. (1997) *Sex-Role Preferences and Work Histories: Is There a Link?*, Working Paper No. 12, London School of Economics, Department of Sociology.

Haller, M., Höllinger, F. and Gomilschak, M. (1998) 'Family and gender roles in macrosocial constraints and cultural contradictions: a comparative analysis of attitudes and their recent changes in twenty countries', in S. Supper and R. Richter (eds) *New Qualities in Family Life*.

Hamnett, C. (1984) 'Housing the two nations: socio-tenurial polarisation in England and Wales, 1961–81', *Urban Studies*, 21: 389–405.

Hartmann, H. (1976) 'Capitalism, patriarchy and job segregation by sex', in M. Blaxall and B. Reagan (eds) *Women and the Workplace: The Implications of Occupational Segregation*, Chicago: University of Chicago Press, pp. 137–79. Reprinted 1976, *Signs*, 1: 137–69. Reprinted in Z. R. Eisenstein (ed.) *Capitalist Patriarchy and the Case for Socialist Feminism*, 1979, New York and London: Monthly Review Press.

Hassell, K., Noyce, P. and Jesson, J. (1998) 'White and ethnic minority self-employment in retail pharmacy in Britain: an historical and comparative analysis', *Work, Employment and Society*, 12: 245–71.

Hedström, P. and Swedberg, R. (1996) 'Rational choice, empirical research and the sociological tradition', *European Sociological Review*, 12: 127–46.

Himmelweit, S. (2001) *Women's Decisions about Employment and Childcare*, End of Award Report to the ESRC.

Hinze, S. W. (2000) 'Inside medical marriages: the effect of gender on income', *Work and Occupations*, 27: 464–99.

Hofstede, G. (1980) *Culture's Consequences: International Differences in Work-Related Values*, New York and London: Sage.

Hofstede, G. (1991) *Cultures and Organisations*, London: HarperCollins.

Hogarth, T., Elias, P. and Ford, J. (1996) *Mortgages, Families and Jobs*, Coventry: University of Warwick Institute for Employment Research.

Holmans, A. (1987) *Housing Policy in Britain: A History*, London: Croom Helm.

Holmans, A. (1993) 'The changing employment circumstances of council tenants' and 'Sales of houses and flats by local authorities to sitting tenants' in Department of the Environment, *Housing in England: Housing Trailers to the 1988 and 1991 Labour Force Surveys*, London: HMSO, pp. 78–109.

Holmans, A. (1995) 'The changing relationship between tenure and employment', in H. Green and J. Hansbro, *Housing in England 1993/94*, London: HMSO, pp. 105–17.

Holt, D. B. (1997) 'Poststructuralist lifestyle analysis: conceptualizing the social patterning of consumption in postmodernity', *Journal of Consumer Research*, 23: 326–50.

Holt, D. B. (1998) 'Does cultural capital structure American consumption?', *Journal of Consumer Research*, 25: 1–25.

Houston, D. (2001) *Employment Choices for Mothers of Pre-School Children: A Psychological Perspective*, End of Award Report to the ESRC.

Humphries, J. (1987) 'The most free from objection ... the sexual division of labour and women's work in nineteenth-century England', *Journal of Economic History*, 47: 929–49.

INE (Instituto Nacional de Estadística) (1982) *Metodología de la Encuesta de Salarios*, Madrid: INE.

Inglehart, M. R. (1991) 'Gender differences in sex-role attitudes: a topic without a future?', in K. Reif and R. Inglehart (eds), *Eurobarometer: The Dynamics of European Public Opinion,* London: Macmillan, pp. 187–200.

Inglehart, R. (1977) *The Silent Revolution: Changing Values and Political Styles*, Princeton, NJ: Princeton University Press.

Inglehart, R. (1990) *Culture Shift in Advanced Industrial Society*, Princeton, NJ: Princeton University Press.

Inglehart, R. (1997) *Modernization and Postmodernization: Cultural, Economic, and Political Change in 43 Societies*, Princeton, NJ: Princeton University Press.

Inglehart, R., Basañez, M. and Moreno, A. (1998) *Human Values and Beliefs: A Cross-Cultural Sourcebook – Political, Religious, Sexual, and*

Economic Norms in 43 Societies: Findings from the 1990–1993 World Values Survey, Ann Arbor: University of Michigan Press.

Inner (1988) *Los Hombres Españoles*, Madrid: Ministerio de Asuntos Sociales, Instituto de la Mujer.

Jacobsen, J. P. (1994) *The Economics of Gender*, Cambridge, MA and Oxford: Blackwell.

Janssens, A. (ed.) (1998) *The Rise and Decline of the Male Breadwinner Family*, Cambridge: Cambridge University Press.

Jones, E. L. (1983) 'The courtesy bias in South-East Asian surveys', in M. Bulmer and D. P. Warwick (eds) *Social Research in Developing Countries*, New York: John Wiley, pp. 253–60.

Jones, T. (1993) *Britain's Ethnic Minorities: An Analysis of the Labour Force Survey*, London: Policy Studies Institute.

Jowell, R. *et al.* (1997) *The British Social Attitudes Survey – the 14th Report*, Aldershot: Ashgate.

Kahle, L. R. (ed.) (1983) *Social Values and Social Change: Adaptation to Life in America*, New York: Praeger.

Kalmijn, M. (2002) 'Sex segregation of friendship networks: individual and structural determinants of having cross-sex friends', *European Sociological Review*, 18: 101–17.

Kiel, L. D. and Elliott, E. (eds) (1996) *Chaos Theory and the Social Sciences: Foundations and Applications*, Ann Arbor: University of Michigan Press.

Kiernan, K. (1992) 'Men and women at work and at home' in R. Jowell *et al.* (eds), *British Social Attitudes: the 9th Report*, Aldershot: Dartmouth, pp. 89–112.

Kohn, M. L. (1989) 'Cross national research as an analytic strategy', in M. L. Kohn (ed.) *Cross-National Research in Sociology*, London: Sage pp. 77–102.

Kuechler, M. (1998) 'The survey method: an indispensable tool for social science research everywhere?', *American Behavioural Scientist*, 42: 178–200.

Kuhn, T. (1962, 1970) *The Structure of Scientific Revolutions*, Chicago: University of Chicago Press.

Ladipo, D. (2000) 'The demise of organisational loyalty?' in K. Purcell (ed.), *Changing Boundaries in Employment*, Bristol: Academic Press, pp. 186–208.

Lamont, M. (1992) *Money, Morals and Manners*, Chicago: University of Chicago Press.

Lawlor, T. and Rigby, M. (1998) *Contemporary Spain*, London and New York: Longman.

Lerner, G. (1986) *The Creation of Patriarchy*, New York and Oxford: Oxford University Press.

Lewis, J. (1992) 'Gender and the development of welfare regimes', *Journal of European Social Policy*, 2: 159–73.

Lieberson, S. (1985) *Making it Count: The Improvement of Social Research and Theory*, Berkeley and London: University of California Press.

Losh-Hesselbart, S. (1987) 'Development of gender roles', in M. B. Sussman and S. K. Steinmetz (eds) *Handbook of Marriage and the Family*, New York: Plenum Press, pp. 535–63.

Loyd, B. (1982) 'Women, home and status', in J. S. Duncan (ed.), *Housing and Identity: Cross-Cultural Perspectives*, New York: Holmes & Meier, pp. 181–97.

Lury, C. (1996) *Consumer Culture*, Cambridge: Polity Press.

McRae, S. (1986) *Cross Class Families*, Oxford: Clarendon Press.

McRae, S. (1991) *Maternity Rights in Britain*, London: Policy Studies Institute.

McRae, S. (2002) *Women's Employment and Family Life in a Changing Britain*, End of Award Report to the ESRC, Oxford: Oxford Brookes University.

Madge, J. and Brown, C. (1981) *First Homes: A Survey of the Housing Circumstances of Young Married Couples*, London: Policy Studies Institute.

Magnusson, D. (1998) 'The logic and implications of a person-oriented approach', in R. B. Cairns, L. R. Bergamn and J. Kagan (eds), *Methods and Models for Studying the Individual*, London and Thousand Oaks, CA: Sage, pp. 33–64.

Magnusson, D. and Bergman, L. R. (1988) 'Individual and variable-based approaches to longitudinal research on early risk factors', in M. Rutter (ed.) *Studies of Psychosocial Risk: The Power of Longitudinal Data*, Cambridge and New York: Cambridge University Press, pp. 45–61.

Marí-Klose, M. and Nos Colom, A. (1999) *Itinerarios Vitales: Educación, Trabajo y Fecundidad de las Mujeres, Opiniones y Actitudes*, No. 27, Madrid: CIS.

Marín, G. and Marín, B. V. (1991) *Research With Hispanic Populations*, Newbury Park, CA: Sage.

Marsden, D. (1999) *A Theory of Employment Systems: Micro-Foundations of Societal Diversity*, Oxford: Oxford University Press.

Martin, J. and Roberts, C. (1984) *Women and Employment: A Lifetime Perspective*, London: HMSO for the Department of Employment.

Martínez Quintana, M. V. (1992) *Mujer, Trabajo y Maternidad: Problemas y Alternativas de las Madres que Trabajan*, Madrid: Instituto de la Mujer, Ministerio de Asuntos Sociales.

Mason, K. O. and Jensen, A.-M. (eds) (1995) *Gender and Family Change in Industrialized Countries*, New York: Oxford University Press/Oxford: Clarendon Press.

Maurice, M., Sellier, F. and Silvestre, J.-J. (1982) *Politique d'Education et Organisation Industrielle en France et en Allemagne*, Paris: Presses Universitaires de France. Reprinted 1986 in translation as *The Social Foundations of Industrial Power: A Comparison of France and Germany*, Cambridge, MA: MIT Press.

Melkas, H. and Anker, R. (1998) *Gender Equality and Occupational Segregation in Nordic Labour Markets*, Geneva: ILO.

Morcillo, A. G. (1999) *True Catholic Womanhood: Gender Ideology in Franco's Spain*, DeKalb: Northern Illinois University Press.

Morcillo-Gómez, A. (1999) 'Shaping true Catholic womanhood: Francoist educational discourse on women', in V. L. Enders and P. B. Radcliff (eds), *Constructing Spanish Womanhood: Female Identity in Modern Spain*, Albany: State University of New York Press, pp. 51–69.

Morgan, P. (2000) *Marriage-Lite: The Rise of Cohabitation and its Consequences*, London: Institute for the Study of Civil Society.

Morgan, P. (2002) *Children as Trophies? Examining the Evidence on Same-sex Parenting*, Newcastle upon Tyne: The Christian Institute.

Morgan, S. P. and Waite, L. J. (1987) 'Parenthood and the attitudes of young adults', *American Sociological Review*, 52: 541–7.

Morrison, D. E. and Henkel, R. E. (1970) *The Significance Test Controversy – A Reader*, Chicago: Aldine.

Morse, N. C. and Weiss, R. S. (1955) 'The function and meaning of work and the job', *American Sociological Review*, 20: 191–8.

Mott, F. L. (ed.) (1978) *Women, Work and Family*, Lexington, MA: D. C. Heath.

Mott, F. L. (ed.) (1982) *The Employment Revolution: Young American Women of the 1970s*, Cambridge, MA: MIT Press.

Murie, A. (1997) 'The housing divide', in R. Jowell *et al.* (eds) *British Social Attitudes – the 14th Report*, Aldershot: Ashgate, pp. 136–50.

Murphy, M. J. and Sullivan, O. (1983) *Housing Tenure and Fertility in Post-War Britain*, Centre for Population Studies Research Paper No. 83–2, London School of Hygiene and Tropical Medicine.

Murphy, M. J. and Sullivan, O. (1985) 'Housing tenure and family formation in contemporary Britain', *European Sociological Review*, 1: 230–43.

Newell, S. (1992) 'The myth and destructiveness of equal opportunities: the continuing dominance of the mothering role', *Personnel Review*, 21, 4: 37–46.

Nikander, T. (1998) *Fertility and Family Surveys in Countries of the ECE Region: Standard Country Report – Finland*, New York and Geneva: United Nations.

OECD and Statistics Canada (1995) *Literacy, Economy and Society: Results of the First International Adult Literacy Survey*, Paris: OECD.

OECD and Statistics Canada (1997) *Literacy Skills for the Knowledge Society: Further Results from the International Adult Literacy Survey*, Paris: OECD.

OECD and Statistics Canada (2000) *Literacy in the Information Age: Final Report of the Adult Literacy Survey*, Paris: OECD.

ONS (1997) *Living in Britain: Results of the 1995 General Household Survey*, London: HMSO.

ONS (2000) *Standard Occupational Classification*, 2 vols, London: HMSO.

OPCS (1990) *Standard Occupational Classification*, 3 vols, London: HMSO.

Oppenheim, A. N. (1992) *Questionnaire Design, Interviewing and Attitude Measurement*, London and New York: Pinter.

Oppenheimer, V. K. (1977) 'The sociology of women's economic role in the family', *American Sociological Review*, 42: 387–406.

Oppenheimer, V. K. (1988) 'A theory of marriage timing', *American Journal of Sociology*, 94: 563–91.

Oppenheimer, V. K. (1994) 'Women's rising employment and the future of the family in industrial societies', *Population and Development Review*, 20: 293–342.

Oppenheimer, V. K. (1997) 'Women's employment and the gain to marriage: the specialization and trading model', *Annual Review of Sociology*, 23: 431–53.

Oppenheimer, V. K. and Lew, V. (1995) 'American marriage formation in the 1980s: how important was women's economic independence?', in K. O. Mason and A.-M. Jensen (eds) *Gender and Family Change in Industrialized Countries*, Oxford: Oxford University Press, pp. 105–38.

Ormerod, P. (1998) *Butterfly Economics: A New General Theory of Social and Economic Behaviour*, London: Faber and Faber.

Owen, D. (1994) *Ethnic Minority Women and the Labour Market: Analysis of the 1991 Census*, Manchester: Equal Opportunities Commission.

Parnes, H. S. (1975) 'The National Longitudinal Surveys: new vistas for labour market research', *American Economic Review*, 65: 244–9.

Parsons, T. and Bales, R. F. (1955) *Family Socialization and Interaction Process*, Glencoe, IL: Free Press.

Peinado López, A. (1988) *La Discriminación de la Mujer en el Mercado de Trabajo Español: Una Aproximación Empírica a la Discriminación Salarial*, Madrid: Ministerio de Trabajo y Seguridad Social.

Peterson, R. A. (1992) 'Understanding audience segmentation: from elite and mass to omnivore and univore', *Poetics*, 21: 243–58.

Pfau-Effinger, B. (1993) 'Modernisation, culture and part-time employment: the example of Finland and West Germany', *Work, Employment and Society*, 7: 383–410.

Pfenning, A. and Bahle, T. (eds) (2000) *Families and Family Policies in Europe: Comparative Perspectives*, Frankfurt: Peter Lang.

Pilling, D. (1990) *Escape from Disadvantage*, London: Falmer.

Polachek, S. (1975) 'Differences in expected post-school investment as a determinant of market wage differentials', *International Economic Review*, 16 (June): 451–70.

Polachek, S. W. (1979) 'Occupational segregation among women: theory, evidence and a prognosis', in C. B. Lloyd, E. S. Andrews and C. L. Gilroy (eds) *Women in the Labor Market*, New York: Columbia University Press, pp. 137–70.

Polachek, S. W. (1981) 'Occupational self-selection: a human capital approach to sex differences in occupational structure', *Review of Economics and Statistics*, 63: 60–69.

Polachek, S. W. (1995) 'Human capital and the gender earnings gap: a response to feminist critiques', in E. Kuiper and J. Sap (eds) *Out of the Margin*, London and New York: Routledge, pp. 61–79.

Pratt, G. (1982) 'The house as an expression of social worlds', in J. S. Duncan (ed.) *Housing and Identity: Cross-Cultural Perspectives*, New York: Holmes & Meier, pp. 135–80.

Prior Ruiz, J. C. (1997) *La Calidad de Vida de la Mujer Trabajadora*, Granada: Universidad de Granada.

Procter, I. and Padfield, M. (1999) 'Work orientations and women's work: a critique of Hakim's theory of the heterogeneity of women', *Gender, Work and Organisations*, 6: 152–62.

Ramos Torres, R. (1990) *Cronos Dividido: Uso del Tiempo y Desilgualdad entre Mujeres y Hombres en España*, Madrid: Ministerio de Asuntos Sociales, Instituto de la Mujer.

Reidy, M. (1994) 'Inequalities in Housing Tenure Attainment in Britain', unpublished D. Phil. thesis, Nuffield College, Oxford.

Reskin, B. F. (2000) 'Getting it right: sex and race inequality in work organizations', *Annual Review of Sociology*, 26: 707–9.

Reskin, B. F. and Roos, P. A. (1990) *Job Queues, Gender Queues: Explaining Women's Inroads into Male Occupations*, Philadelphia: Temple University Press.

Rexroat, C. and Shehan, C. (1984) 'Expected versus actual work roles of women', *American Sociological Review*, 49: 349–58.

Rindfuss, R. R., Cooksey, E. C. and Sutterlin, R. L. (1999) 'Young adult occupational achievement: early expectations versus behavioural reality', *Work and Occupations*, 26: 220–63.

Rogers, B. (1981) *The Domestication of Women: Discrimination in Developing Societies*, London: Tavistock.

Romero Lopez, M. (1990) *La Actividad Empresarial Femenina en España*, Madrid: Ministerio de Asuntos Sociales, Instituto de la Mujer.

Rose, D. and O'Reilly, K. (eds) (1997) *Constructing Classes: Towards a New Social Classification for the UK*, Swindon: ESRC.

Rose, D. and O'Reilly, K. (1998) *The ESRC Review of Government Social Classifications*, Swindon: ESRC/London: ONS.

Rose, D. and Pevalin, D. (eds) (2002) *A Researcher's Guide to the National Statistics Socio-Economic Classification*, London: Sage.

Rose, M. (1994) 'Skill and Samuel Smiles: changing the British work ethic', in R. Penn, M. Rose and J. Rubery (eds) *Skill and Occupational Change*, Oxford: Oxford University Press, pp. 281–335.

Rose, N. (1998) *Inventing Our Selves: Psychology, Power, and Personhood*, Cambridge: Cambridge University Press.

Rose, N. (1999) *Governing the Soul: The Shaping of the Private Self*, London and New York: Free Association Books.

Rubery, J. and Fagan, C. (1993) *Occupational Segregation of Women and Men in the European Community*, *Social Europe* Supplement 3/93, Luxembourg: OOPEC.

Rubery, J., Smith, M., Fagan, C. and Grimshaw, D. (1998) *Women and European Employment*, London and New York: Routledge.

Ruivo, M., Pilar González, M. do and Varejão, J. M. (1998) 'Why is part-time work so low in Portugal and Spain?', in J. O'Reilly and C. Fagan (eds) *Part-Time Prospects*, London and New York: Routledge, pp. 199–213.

Saunders, P. (1990) *A Nation of Homeowners*, London: Routledge.

Savage, M., Barlow, J., Dickens, P. and Fielding, T. (1992) *Property, Bureaucracy and Culture: Middle Class Formation in Contemporary Britain*, London: Routledge.

Scott, J., Alwin, D.F. and Braun, M. (1996) Generational changes in gender-role attitudes: Britain in a cross-rational perspective, *Sociology*, 30: 471–92.

Seccombe, W. (1993) *Weathering the Storm: Working Class Families from the Industrial Revolution to the Fertility Decline*, London: Verso.

Shaw, L. B. (ed.) (1983) *Unplanned Careers: The Working Lives of Middle-Aged Women*, Lexington, MA: D. C. Heath.

Shaw, L. B. and Shapiro, D. (1987) 'Women's work plans: contrasting expectations and actual work experience', *Monthly Labor Review*, 110, 11: 7–13.

Siltanen, J. (1994) *Locating Gender: Occupational Segregation, Wages and Domestic Responsibilities*, London: University College Press.

Slater, D. (1997) *Consumer Culture and Modernity*, Cambridge: Polity Press.

Sly, F, Thair, T. and Risdon, A. (1998) 'Labour market participation of ethnic groups', *Labour Market Trends*, 107: 601–15.

Sly, F, Thair, T. and Risdon, A. (1999) 'Trends in the labour market participation of ethnic groups', *Labour Market Trends*, 107: 631–9.

Smith, T. W. (1984) 'Nonattitudes: a review and evaluation', in C. F. Turner and E. Martin (eds) *Surveying Subjective Phenomena*, vol. 2, New York: Russell Sage, pp. 215–55.

Smock, P. J. (2000) 'Cohabitation in the United States: An appraisal of research themes, findings, and implications', *Annual Review of Sociology*, 26: 1–20.

Sobel, M. E. (1981) *Lifestyle and Social Structure: Concepts, Definitions, Analyses*, New York and London: Academic Press.

Spitze, G. D. and Waite, L. J. (1980) 'Labor force and work attitudes', *Work and Occupations*, 7: 3–32.

Sproat, K. V., Churchill, H. and Sheets, C. (eds) (1985) *The National Longitudinal Surveys of Labor Market Experience – An Annotated Bibliography of Research*, Lexington, MA and Toronto: Lexington Books.

Stolzenberg, R. M. and Waite, L. J. (1977) 'Age, fertility expectations and plans for employment', *American Sociological Review*, 42, 769–83.

Szekelyi, M. and Tardos, R. (1993) 'Attitudes that make a difference: expectancies and economic progress', Discussion papers of the Institute for Research on Poverty, University of Wisconsin.

Tam, M. (1997) *Part-Time Employment: A Bridge or a Trap?*, Aldershot: Avebury.

Tanner, J., Cockerill, R., Barnsley, J. and Williams, A. P. (1999) 'Gender and income in pharmacy: human capital and gender stratification theories revisited', *British Journal of Sociology*, 50: 97–117.

Thomas, R. and Elias, P. (1989) 'Development of the Standard Occupational Classification', *Population Trends*, 55: 16–21.

Thompson, C. (1996) 'Caring consumers: gendered consumption meanings and the juggling lifestyle', *Journal of Consumer Research*, 22: 388–407.

Thomson, K. (1995) 'Working mothers: choice or circumstance?', in R. Jowell *et al.* (eds) *British Social Attitudes – the 12th Report*, Aldershot: Gower, pp. 61–91.

Tobío, C. (2001) 'Family and employment in Spain: working mothers' dilemmas', paper presented to the conference on Progressing Gender Relations in Europe, University of Salford, September 2001.

Torns, T. (2000) 'When exclusion is socially acceptable: the case of Spain', in J. Jenson, J. Laufer and M. Maruani (eds) *The Gendering of Inequalities: Women, Men and Work,* Aldershot: Ashgate, pp. 216–27.

Turner, C. F. and Martin, E. (eds) (1984) *Surveying Subjective Phenomena,* 2 vols, New York: Russell Sage.

Van Doorne-Huiskes, A., van Hoof, J. and Roelofs, E. (1995) *Women and the European Labour Markets,* London: Paul Chapman.

Vecchio, R. P. (1980) 'The function and meaning of work and the job: Morse and Weiss (1955) revisited', *Academy of Management Journal,* 23: 361–7.

Visser, J. and Hemerijck, A. (1997) *A Dutch Miracle – Job Growth, Welfare Reform and Corporatism in the Netherlands,* Amsterdam: Amsterdam University Press.

Vogler, C. (1994) 'Segregation, sexism and labour supply', in A. M. Scott (ed.) *Gender Segregation and Social Change,* Oxford: Oxford University Press, pp. 39–79.

Waite, L. J. and Gallagher, M. (2000) *The Case for Marriage: Why Married People are Happier, Healthier and Better Off Financially,* New York: Doubleday.

Waite, L. J., Haggstrom, G. W. and Kanouse, D. (1986) 'The consequences of parenthood for the marital stability of young adults', *American Sociological Review,* 50: 850–57.

Waite, L. J. and Stolzenberg, R. M. (1976) 'Intended childbearing and labor force participation of young women: insights from nonrecursive models', *American Sociological Review,* 41, 235–52.

Walby, S. (1986) *Patriarchy at Work: Patriarchal and Capitalist Relations in Employment,* Cambridge: Polity Press.

Walby, S. (1990) *Theorising Patriarchy,* Oxford: Blackwell.

Walsh, J. (1999) 'Myths and counter-myths: an analysis of part-time female employees and their orientations to work and working hours', *Work, Employment and Society,* 13: 179–203.

Warr, P. (1982) 'A national study of non-financial employment commitment', *Journal of Occupational Psychology,* 55: 297–312.

Wierink, M. (2001) 'Le travail a temps partiel et la combinaison famille-emploi aux Pays-Bas', *Revue de l'OFCE – Observations et Diagnostics Economiques,* No. 77: 307–20, Paris: OFCE.

Wilk, R. R. (1997) 'A critique of desire: distaste and dislike in consumer behaviour', *Consumption, Markets and Culture,* 1: 175–96.

Index